THE SENATE AND US TROOPS IN EUROPE

THE SENATE
AND US TROOPS
IN EUROPE

Phil Williams

M
MACMILLAN

First published 1985 by
THE MACMILLAN PRESS LTD
London and Basingstoke
Companies and representatives
throughout the world

Filmsetting by Vantage Photosetting Co. Ltd
Eastleigh and London
Printed in Hong Kong

British Library Cataloguing in Publication Data
Williams, Phil. *19— -*
The Senate and US troops in Europe.
1. United States—Military policy
2. United States—Armed Forces—Foreign
countries
I. Title
355.2′0973   UA23

ISBN 0-333-33576-7

To the memory of my dad

Contents

Acknowledgements

During the course of writing this book I have incurred great debts to a large number of friends and colleagues. Special thanks have to go to David Greenwood of the Centre for Defence Studies, the University of Aberdeen, who not only initially prompted me to work on the Mansfield Amendment and to apply for a NATO research fellowship in 1974 but has been a source of encouragement throughout. Special thanks too to Professor Lawrence Freedman of King's College London who was a great source of help and inspiration. I must also express my gratitude to Dr Fernand Welter of the NATO Information Service who administered the NATO fellowship sympathetically and efficiently and who has been extremely patient in waiting for the final version of the study.

During the course of researching and writing on the book I have been fortunate to work in two university departments, both of which provided a congenial atmosphere and considerable stimulation. Professor Frank Bealey of the Department of Politics in Aberdeen and Professors Peter Richards, Raymond Plant and Peter Calvert of the Southampton Politics Department all provided strong support, while colleagues Clive Archer and David Capitanchik at Aberdeen and Karen Dawisha, Dilys Hill, John Simpson and Ronnie Beiner in Southampton were a source of sustenance during the periods when I began to doubt whether the work would ever be finished.

My research in the United States was greatly assisted in the early stages by encouragement from Robert Osgood, Annette Baker Fox, Bruce Russett, Frank Rourke, Edward Kolodziej, Gregory Treverton and John Yochelson. I also benefited from the help of Timothy Ireland, Scott Sagan and Roger George as well as from the hospitality of Steve and Debbie Miller. During a visit to the University of Montana, Missoula in 1980 I not only received considerable assistance but made several good friends. Dale Johnson, the archivist was an unfailing source of help and advice about the Mansfield Papers while Professor Charles Hood of the School of Journalism was extremely generous with his time and his massive knowledge about Senator Mansfield. I am extremely grateful for their hospitality as well as that of Claire and Leo Rhein – together they made the visit not only extremely profitable in terms of research but also immensely enjoyable. Apart from the Mansfield Collection, the library at Senate House in London, the American Embassy Library and the press libraries at the International Institute for Strategic Studies and at Chatham House all proved invaluable at different stages of the research. While I owe a debt to many people in all these libraries, special mention must be made of Susan Boyd, Mary Bone, Sarah Stuffins and Mary Davis and all the other press librarians at Chatham House whose unfailing knowledge, professionalism and efficiency is only matched by their patience and good humour.

In addition I would like to thank the United States Information Service and the University of Southampton for the financial assistance which made possible the visit to Montana. Thanks are also due to Jean Pell, Joanne Fluck and Liz Jones who typed successive versions of the manuscript. Too numerous to name are those students who did my courses in Western European Security and Foreign Policy Analysis at Southampton and provided a stimulating atmosphere which made it possible to try out and to refine some of the interpretations contained in the book. Thank you all!

Senator Mike Mansfield, whose troop withdrawal proposals precipitated this study, gave generously of his time both in Washington and Tokyo, and answered all my questions fully and frankly. He was a considerable source of inspiration and his courtesy and consideration have left me in his debt.

I have also been extremely fortunate in having an understanding editor in Anne-Lucie Norton and an efficient copy editor in Anne Beech.

Last, but most important of all, are my wife Avis and my daughter Rhian without whose love, patience and endurance of many hours of neglect this work would never have been completed.

Whatever merit this study may have owes a great deal to all those mentioned; its shortcomings are solely my own responsibility.

1 Introduction

1 PURPOSE AND SCOPE

American foreign policy since 1945 has been surrounded by controversy and debate. Isolationists, internationalists, realists and idealists, conservatives and liberals, have all propounded their particular philosophies and divergent prescriptions. One issue on which there has been fairly widespread agreement, however, has been the need for a strong vigorous Atlantic Alliance. Continued participation in NATO has been a cardinal tenet of United States foreign policy through successive administrations and until the early 1980s the alliance itself appeared to be a revered institution testifying to the wisdom and foresight of its founders in the late 1940s. There has been far less agreement though on the necessity for a large-scale conventional military presence in Westrn Europe as part of the American contribution to the common security programme. Indeed, President Truman's decision, announced in September 1950, to support and strengthen the Atlantic Pact by sending ground forces to Europe met considerable opposition and led, in the early months of 1951, to what was termed the 'Great Debate' on American foreign policy. During the 1960s and 1970s the troops became controversial once again as demands for a substantial reduction in the military contingent in Western Europe were increasingly articulated by prominent and influential politicians. More recently, there has been a further flurry of suggestions that American troops be reduced: along with the growing acrimony in Atlantic relations in the early 1980s there has been a growing disinclination on the part of many critics to maintain the existing level of US forces in Western Europe. As yet, however, this has not become as salient an issue as it was in the 1960s and 1970s, nor has it aroused the same kind of passion as did the deployment of troops to Europe in 1951.

1

In both 1951 and the 1966 to 1975 period the major threat to the troop presence came from the United States Congress, particularly the Senate. The challenges were ultimately defeated, but they caused considerable embarrassment to the executive branch, and, although not without important and beneficial side-effects, were harmful to the reputation of the United States as a reliable alliance partner. To some extent, of course, this was merely a symptom of a more general and enduring problem: how a democracy in which power is shared in ill-defined ways between the executive and legislative branches of government can conduct a stable and coherent foreign policy. This problem was manifested most dramatically in the Senate's rejection of the Treaty of Versailles after the First World War, but with United States entanglement in world affairs after 1945 it became a matter of perennial, rather than merely episodic, concern. Allies and opponents have often had to adjust not only to the men in the White House and the State Department but also to the preferences and prejudices of the men on Capitol Hill. This was particularly true during the later 1960s and early 1970s when the pressure for troop withdrawals prompted a major burden-sharing exercise in NATO and the formation of the Eurogroup, which subsequently identified areas in which the Europeans could improve and increase their contributions to the alliance. It was hoped by the allies that these demonstrations of seriousness would help to undermine the rationale for troop withdrawals. Simultaneously, the Federal Republic of Germany acquiesced in demands for offset payments to cover the foreign exchange costs incurred by the United States in maintaining its troops in Europe, on the grounds that this too would help to stifle the demands for a much smaller American military contingent on the Continent. In addition, NATO as a whole embarked upon negotiations with the Warsaw Pact about the possibility of *mutual* force reductions. Although this opened up the prospect of stabilising the military confrontation in Europe at a lower level, it was primarily a device to discredit further the idea of unilateral troop withdrawals by the United States. In other words, the international repercussions of the demands for force reductions were at times far reaching.

The main focus of attention here, however, is not the external consequences but rather the Senate debates and actions themselves. During 1951 and the later period, fundamental issues were raised about the future relationship between the United States and its European allies – and particularly about how this might be transformed from an unhealthy and one-sided dependence by the Europeans into a more equal partnership. On each occasion questions were also asked about the nature of the Soviet threat and the most appropriate posture and strategy to counter it; about whether Asia or Europe was to be given priority in United States foreign policy; and about the domestic political, economic and social implications of maintaining a military presence in Western Europe. Furthermore, the challenge to this military presence was also a challenge to executive dominance in foreign policy-making.

The major purpose of the present study, therefore, is to analyse the controversy and the way it developed. It is concerned with the causes, the course and the outcome not only of congressional opposition to the initial deployment of a large garrison of troops to Western Europe, but also of the later demands for a partial withdrawal of these forces. In other words, the analysis seeks to provide an outline legislative history of the proposals which were introduced into the Senate in an endeavour to alter the size and shape of the United States military presence in Western Europe. Although a great deal has been written about specific aspects of, and particular incidents in, the troops *to* Europe debate and the troop withdrawal controversy, far less attention has been given to the historical development of the issue as a whole. Consequently, one of the main purposes of the present book is to identify when the critical votes took place, what the results were, who made the major speeches, and who the opinion leaders in the Senate were during both the 1951 dispute and the later arguments. In short, the primary aim of the study is the internal politics of one of America's most substantial, expensive and enduring international commitments. Even this apparently straight forward task, however, is not without its difficulties.

2 PROBLEMS OF ANALYSIS

The first major set of problems reflects the fact that the American Congress is a highly complex institution. Although it would be an exaggeration to claim that it defies analysis, the difficulties involved in any but the most superficial investigation of its activities are formidable. Some of the difficulties are avoided here, of course, because the study is confined to the Senate. Such a restriction is possible because it was in the Senate that the pressure on the executive branch was most intense. There have occasionally been responsive echoes from the House of Representatives, but its criticisms of Administration policy on the troop issue have been far less vociferous and less sustained than in the upper chamber. This is undoubtedly a considerable advantage since the smaller size of the Senate makes an analysis of its behaviour more manageable. Yet it is important to remember that the Senate consists of 100 highly individualistic politicians, each with his own distinct outlook, needs, ambitions and interests. Furthermore, the Senate is constantly in flux. Although turnover is not usually very rapid, the fact that one-third of the membership comes up for reelection every two years ensures that there are at least marginal changes in its composition. This in turn may have considerable impact on legislative outcomes, particularly on issues where the voting is very close.

The internal operations of the Senate are also significant. Formal procedures are supplemented by what have been described as the 'folkways', norms of behaviour or unwritten rules of conduct of the Senate. The structure of power and the distribution of influence within the upper chamber will also affect voting. Yet this is something on which commentators often disagree. Some observers have claimed that the Senate is run by a small 'inner club' of senators whose most obvious common feature is vigorous adherence to the folkways. Other analysts have emphasised the decisive role of committee chairmen or have seen the actions of the formal party leaders as the key to the Senate's accomplishments. Yet others have argued that power is shared fairly evenly amongst the entire membership of the Senate and that even deviation from the accepted norms of behaviour does not render a senator totally devoid of influence.[1] Such varied interpretations, far from being in conflict, may actually complement each other since the distribution of power and influence within the Senate probably varies considerably, both over time and from one issue to the next.

The formal party leaders, for example, may have a decisive influence at certain times and on particular issues while at other times and on different issues their influence will be negligible.

In attempting to discern the pattern of influence, however, it is essential to avoid equating prominence in debate with the exercise of influence. The two may go hand in hand but there is no necessary or automatic correspondence between them. Indeed, there may be certain key figures whose only apparent contribution is formally to record a position on a roll-call vote. Yet by this very act they may determine the votes of several of their colleagues and thus have a significant, and possibly even a decisive, effect upon the result. The converse may also be true. There are probably some senators it is better not to have on one's side as they succeed only in antagonising their fellows and thereby tend to harden if not actively to arouse opposition.

These subtleties of personal influence within the Senate are not readily visible. Nor is it always possible to establish unequivocally why particular individuals voted the way they did. Such problems are heightened by the second major factor impeding a full analysis: incomplete evidence and inadequate information. One facet of this is that the primary historical sources – the Congressional Record, committee reports and transcripts of committee hearings – are excessively formal and do not convey the full flavour of Senate life. Indeed, it is sometimes suggested that speeches on the Senate floor in particular are little more than public posturing for both dramatic and political effect, and that debates usually consist of haphazardly related speeches delivered to an almost empty chamber. Such a criticism, however, is too extreme and overlooks the positive functions of these debates. As one observer has pointed out, floor debate is

an important means of communication between advocates. Bills that reach the floor are backed by a coalition of senators, congressmen, staff assistants, lobbyists, voters and administrators, and if the bill is at all controversial, are opposed by a similar coalition. Communication between advocates is not always simple and 'signals passing between leaders and followers are by no means always given behind the scenes.

Floor statements are often the quickest and most effective method of passing the word around. . . .' Moreover, the arguments made over and over again in debate tend to reinforce the commitments of supporters, to whip up enthusiasm among the group, and to activate the latent predispositions of those whose overall policy positions are congenial but who remain uncommitted.[2]

Nor is it impossible – although it is probably exceptional – for speeches actually to succeed in changing a few votes.

In other words, Senate speeches cannot be dismissed as trivial and insignificant. There are problems with them, however. Not all speeches can, or should, be taken at face value. Most statements reflect the input of one or more aides who may have more specialist knowledge and stronger views than the senator who delivers the speech. Difficulties also arise when the statements of a particular senator all indicate that he will cast his vote in one direction yet in the event he votes the opposite way. Even more formidable problems occur when debates are confined to a relatively small group of senators on either side. It is virtually impossible to assess the calculations of those who vote but do not explain or elaborate their positions.

Despite the shortcomings, the Congressional Record is an invaluable source providing an enormous amount of information that is not available elsewhere. Yet in relation to certain areas of activity there is a dearth of reliable evidence. The telephone and personal lobbying are indispensable in exercising influence but rarely leave a trace. Furthermore, important committee hearings are sometimes held in executive session, with the result that it is impossible to discern how decisions are reached or recommendations arrived at by the committee. If a complete historical record is unobtainable, however, the insights of skilful and well-informed journalists, supplemented by personal interviews with senators or their staffs, and an examination of the private papers of key senators, make it possible to piece together the major developments.

A third problem is that there is something highly artificial in focusing on one specific issue and seeing it apart from the whole maze of issues with which the Senate was confronted at any one time. Indeed, this can lead to an unnecessary exaggeration of the saliency of the troop withdrawal controversy. To some extent this has already occurred. For most West European governments in the late 1960s and early 1970s congressional attitudes towards the United States military commitment to NATO were a matter of great moment to be monitored and observed with care; for the majority of senators it was merely one matter among many, something which was periodically discussed and then dismissed and forgotten until the next time it was raised. In other words, the troops issue must be kept in proper perspective.

Another aspect of this is that extraneous factors sometimes impinge directly on the issue. An awareness of the context of the major episodes in the continuing controversy is, therefore, essential. The debate of 1951, for example, can only be fully understood when considered against a background of bitter partisanship in which McCarthyism was allowed to flourish. The later period, in turn, was a particularly acrimonious and troublesome one in the relationship between President and Congress. Largely because of the Vietnam War and the excesses of the 'Imperial Presidency', Congress was attempting to set limits to presidential power in foreign policy and to reassert some of the prerogatives that had been allowed to lapse during the Cold War years. The troop controversy was obviously affected by – and, indeed, was part of – the wider hostility between the Executive and the legislature. What all this means in practice, of course, is that throughout the analysis it is necessary to place the dispute about troops in its broader context.

The fourth problem is one of bias. It is beyond the scope of the study to undertake a comprehensive examination of the substantive questions involved or to make an independent and thorough assessment of the likely consequences of substantial US troop withdrawals from Western Europe. The issues themselves are dealt with as they were perceived, understood and discussed by senators as part of the continuing debate. At the same time, allowance must be made for the fact that in a controversy such as this – as in many other political disputes – the realities of a senator's position are all too easily obscured by the rhetoric of both allies and opponents. Misunderstanding and misinterpretations are inevitable, and terms such as isolationism are often used for derogatory rather than analytical purposes. As a result the stance of the participants may be considerably distorted. To some extent this has happened with Senator Mansfield, Democratic Majority leader from 1961 to 1976 and the leading figure in presenting the case for withdrawals. Mansfield's proposals have usually received a hostile reception from the Eastern establishment press and from the West Europeans. He is typically described as a soft-spoken, level-headed, moderate politician who has been fanatical in his opposition to the continued presence of American troops in Europe. He is also portrayed as an old-fashioned isolationist, oblivious both to America's security needs and to its alliance obligations. Such criticisms reflect an all too eager acceptance of what Mansfield's opponents within the Senate and the administration have said about him. An examination of his own statements leads to very different conclusions. The analysis though is not intended as an apologia for the Majority Leader, nor indeed for any other leading figure. Presenting Mansfield's position fairly and factually does not necessarily imply approval. Indeed, it is not the intention here to make gratuitous judgements about the troop reduction proposals one way or the other: there are no 'right' or 'wrong' answers. If the analysis serves only to provide greater insight into the nature and scope of some of the disagreements it will have fulfilled much of its purpose.

3   A PRELIMINARY OVERVIEW

The focus of Chapter 2 is on the events leading up to the decision to station American ground forces in Western Europe. It traces the gradually deepening involvement of the United States in the affairs of Europe, and looks at congressional reactions to the policy innovations of the late 1940s. The assumptions on which the North Atlantic Treaty was accepted by the Senate are highlighted in some detail and it is suggested that the change in Administration policy towards Europe prompted by the Korean War violated these assumptions. The subsequent revolt in the Senate is the main theme of Chapter 3. It becomes clear here that many senators felt that the President had behaved improperly by deciding, without any prior consultation with Congress, to send troops to Western Europe. Ultimately, however, the Senate acquiesced in this decision and the issue did not become controversial again on Capitol Hill until the mid 1960s. Thus Chapter 4 looks at the period from 1952 to 1965. Towards the end of the period there were occasional stirrings of discontent in the Senate which, in 1966, were to grow into a chorus of protest. Beginning in 1966, several senators embarked upon a serious campaign to reduce the size of the American military presence in Western Europe. Chapter 5 examines the first stages of this campaign, during which the Senate confined itself to consideration of a simple resolution lacking the force of law. In 1971 the conflict entered a new phase as the proposed resolution was replaced by amendments which, if passed, would have mandated reductions. This is discussed in Chapter 6, while Chapter 7 focuses on 1973, during which the attempt to alter the *status quo* was particularly forceful. After 1973, however, the demands for troop withdrawals diminished very considerably. The reasons for this are explained in Chapter 8, while the final chapter presents the major conclusions and briefly considers the prospects for the future.

2 The North Atlantic Treaty, Military Assistance and the Troops to Europe Decision

1 INTRODUCTION

Although the American military presence has become a central feature of security arrangements in Europe, the United States in the late 1940s had no intention of making such a deployment. As late as 1948 an 'entangling alliance' with Western Europe was still regarded as 'worse than original sin'.[1] The Truman Administration had committed itself to the economic recovery of Western Europe through Marshall Aid, but this was intended to restore an indigenous balance of power in Erope and thereby ensure that the United States did not become more directly involved.[2] Not only was the aid programme based on the principle of European self-help, it also anticipated that it would promote European self-reliance. The consequences for the United States, however, were very different from its intentions, and what had been regarded as the final stage in America's European policy became merely an interim measure, as it became clear that the economic recovery programme was unlikely to come to fruition without steps to reassure Western Europe that its security would also be underwritten.

The Truman Administration had to move carefully, however, as there was still a powerful group of senators – mainly midwest, conservative Republicans – who were strongly opposed to American entanglement in European affairs. There

11

had been vigorous battles over aid to Greece and Turkey, and without the increase in international tension in the Spring of 1948 the European Recovery Programme would have faced very considerable difficulty in Congress. Assisted by events such as the Czech *coup* and with the support of Arthur Vandenberg, the Chairman of the Senate Committee on Foreign Relations and the leading Republican spokesman on foreign policy, however, the Marshall Plan was approved with relatively minor modifications.[3]   Although Vandenberg is rightly regarded as one of the leading figures in the development of US policy towards Europe in the late 1940s, his role was more ambiguous than is generally assumed. Indeed, when the Administration in April 1948 attempted to obtain his support for a security treaty with Western Europe, he cautioned against going too far too fast. The Senate resolution – recommending American association with regional collective security arrangements based on self-help and mutual aid – which he introduced after close consultation with State Department officials may have paved the way for a security treaty with Western Europe, in 1949, but it was also a substitute for such a treaty in 1948.[4]

Prior to the formulation of the Vandenberg Resolution there had, in fact, been preliminary negotiations between Britain, the United States and Canada on the possibility of a treaty. The existence of these negotiations had not been disclosed, however, because of the political sensitivity of such a step. The passage of the Vandenberg Resolution in June 1948 legitimised the idea of a formal security agreement with Western Europe, and made it possible to broaden the discussions to include France, Belgium and the Netherlands. The negotiations for an Atlantic Pact were officially under way.

2   THE NORTH ATLANTIC TREATY

Formally entitled 'Exploratory Conversations on Security Problems of Common Interest' the discussions which took place from 6 July to 10 September 1948 were given considerable impetus by the Berlin Blockade.[5] Even so, they encountered serious difficulties. One of the most important sources of discord – and an issue which was to remain controversial until the United States Senate finally gave its consent to ratification of the North Atlantic Treaty – was the nature of the pledge or commitment the United States was expected or willing to make.[6] Even in the trilateral negotiations the US delegation had insisted that the appropriate model was not the strong pledge of the Brussels Treaty but the rather looser formula enshrined in the Inter-American Treaty of Reciprocal Assistance signed at Rio de Janeiro in September 1947. While acknowledging that an attack against one American state would be regarded as an attack against them all, the Rio Treaty left room for discretion in determining the scope and type of assistance to be given to the victim. This formulation appealed to the United States negotiators as politically expedient: the further any agreement went beyond a discretionary guarantee the less likely was it to receive Senate approval. This is not to suggest that all the problems were caused by American insistence on retaining freedom of action. The French delegation was equally, if not more, intractable, largely because it was concerned primarily with obtaining military supplies from the United States.[7] A system of guarantees, while desirable, was of only secondary importance to France.

In spite of these problems, a compromise was finally reached, and a document known as the Washington Paper was produced on 9 September.[8] Although the paper was a broad, if still somewhat tentative, analysis of the problems of European security, three of the issues discussed were of particular importance: the role of US troops in Europe, the need for a European–American treaty and the idea of European self-help. Acknowledging the continued insecurities in Western Europe, the paper highlighted both the utility and the limitations of American occupation forces in Germany in alleviating these fears. As it stated: 'The continued presence of United States forces in Western Europe is important since an attack upon them would bring the United States immediately and directly into war. Nevertheless, something more is needed to counteract the fear of the peoples of Western Europe that their countries might be overrun by the Soviet army before effective help could arrive.'[9] Some sort of long-term arrangement binding the parties to meet aggression jointly was vital, therefore, and there was no serious alternative to a treaty. At the same time, the paper was categorical that the 'United States could not constitutionally enter into any treaty which would provide that the United States would be at war without a vote of Congress'.[10] What else was contemplated in addition to a treaty was not entirely clear. There were hints, however, that some form of material assistance might be provided by the United States, although there was no indication as to the scope or scale of this.[11] It was clear though that such aid would only be proffered within the framework of the Vandenberg Resolution with its emphasis on self-help and mutual aid. Indeed, the Washington Paper not only used the language of the resolution but reaffirmed one of the principles which Vandenberg had been so intent on establishing – that United States assistance 'must supplement rather than take the place of the maximum efforts of the other nations on behalf of themselves and each other, and that assistance must be reciprocal'.[12]

It is apparent both from this and from the concern that nothing should be done to infringe the constitutional provision regarding congressional declarations of war, that the American delegation was acutely aware of the need to produce an agreement which would be acceptable to two-thirds of the American Senate. Hickerson, in fact, told the working group of negotiators on 12 August that State Department officials were being particularly cautious because

> it would be disastrous if they were to put forward to the Senate an unacceptable pact or treaty. It would be almost equally disastrous if a pact or treaty were to be ratified with a series of hampering reservations after protracted debate. During negotiations, therefore, it was the intention of the State Department to maintain the closest possible contact with political leaders in both Houses and to take their advice and counsel as to the phraseology and the content of a pact or treaty which would be acceptable to Congress.[13]

This concern over what Woodrow Wilson had once described as the 'treaty-marring powers' of the Senate may have been accentuated as a result of analogies with the Senate's rejection of the Treaty of Versailles. Indeed, the mere presence in the Senate of Henry Cabot Lodge Jr, whose grandfather had been one of the decisive figures in the defeat of Versailles and the abandonment of any idea of US participation in the League of Nations, must have been a sharp reminder that the 'advice and consent' clause of the constitution could not be treated lightly.[14] Yet what is perhaps most striking about the exploratory conversations – and most surprising in view of Hickerson's comments of 12 August – is that senators were *not* kept fully informed. The anticipated reaction of the Senate to any treaty may have had a profound impact on the negotiations, but this was essentially an indirect effect and one stemming from executive branch assessments of what the Senate would accept, rather than from close and continuous consultations with individual senators or with the Foreign Relations Committee.

In fact, Escott Reid has suggested that from mid-June 1948 until the beginning of February 1949 there was little direct consultation: at best it was sporadic and unsystematic; at worst it was non-existent.[15] A large part of the reason for this, of course, was the presidential election. Despite the broad consensus between the parties on foreign policy, the negotiators may have been trying to ensure that the proposal for a treaty did not become caught up in the election campaign. There was also an element of marking time while waiting for the change of Administration which was widely, albeit wrongly, expected. Thus it was not until after the election that copies of the Washington Paper were given to Senator Vandenberg and to Senator Connally of Texas who – as a result of election gains giving the Democrats a 54 to 42 majority in the Senate – was to become the new Chairman of the Foreign Relations Committee in the eighty-first Congress. And even this paper was soon to be superseded by events. With Truman's victory, the way was open for another burst of negotiations. The exploratory conversations resumed on 10 December and by 25 December agreement had been reached on a draft treaty incorporating a pledge which was much stronger and more explicit and precise than had been anticipated in the Washington Paper. As Eayrs has pointed out, 'the Americans under pressure backed away from their insistence that the commitment article explicitly state the right of each signatory to determine for itself if an armed attack had occurred'.[16] It was also agreed that the pledge should include provision for military action in the event of an attack upon any of the signatories. In other words, the sensitivity of American negotiators to congressional preferences for a weak guarantee seems to have been eroded by the desire of the allies to have a strong and unequivocal commitment. This departure from the position of the summer was not immediately controversial, however, largely because congressional leaders were not informed of it. Part of the reason for this may have been the simple fact that Lovett had become acting Secretary of State because of Marshall's illness and was consequently under considerable pressure. Even so, it is odd that such an important matter was not given a higher priority and that Hickerson's injunction of the previous August was so blatantly disregarded.

The result was that the task of 'selling' the draft treaty to the Senate fell to Dean Acheson who was appointed Secretary of State on 20 January 1949. As Reid put it: 'Acheson was not present at the creation of the North Atlantic Treaty. He was present only on the sixth, the last day of the creation, but that was a particularly busy day.'[17] It was also the day most fraught with domestic political difficulties. Indeed, Acheson's appointment itself was part of the cause of these difficulties. It was one of several measures which suggested that the victorious Democrats would be less solicitous of Republican opinion on foreign policy issues than they had been in the eightieth Congress. Acheson was not popular in the Senate and his appointment had not been preceded by consultation with congressional leaders of either party. Furthermore, actions such as the alteration of the ratio of the majority to minority party members on the Senate Foreign Relations Committee from seven to six to eight to five, although relatively minor in themselves, added significantly to Republican antipathies, coming as they did after an election defeat that was all the more bitter for being so unexpected. Inevitably Dewey's defeat caused many Republicans to question the advantages of a bipartisan approach to foreign policy, since this seemed to have done little to advance the party's electoral fortunes.[18] Thus Acheson's problem was a dual one: he had to contend not only with the 'institutional pride' of the Senate as a whole, but also with a disaffected opposition party. His first task, therefore, was to win the support of Connally and Vandenberg. Although this was complicated by the intense rivalry between the two senators, the major obstacle was that their expectations were based primarily on the Washington Paper – the draft treaty contained a far stronger pledge than they had been led to anticipate.[19]

Acheson met with the new chairman of the Foreign Relations Committee and the ranking Republican member on 3 and 5 February to discuss the treaty. Both senators objected strongly to the proposed wording of the draft. Connally, in particular, was worried about 'automatic commitment' in the event of hostilities, and although Vandenberg was more sympathetic in that he accepted the 'concept of making our position clear as a preventive measure' he too expressed serious reservations about the pledge.[20] Over the next two weeks, Acheson found himself in the difficult position of having to mediate between Connally and Vandenberg on the one hand and the negotiators on the other. As he later wrote: 'The negotiation of Article 5 became a contest between our allies seeking to impale the Senate on the specific, and the Senators attempting to wriggle free.'[21] When told of the senators' preferences, the allies in turn objected strenuously to any watering down of the commitment. The controversy burst into the open on 14 February, when a newspaper article discussing the proposal precipitated a tirade on the Senate floor by Forrest Donnell of Missouri against the idea of an open-ended pledge. Connally, in what has been described as a 'probably ill-considered and certainly intemperate' outburst, responded by claiming that the treaty would contain neither a legal nor a moral commitment to go to war.[22] He reiterated this position in further consultations with Acheson, drafting several alternative versions of the pledge which he regarded as less of a challenge to congressional responsibilities. With President Truman's support, Acheson was able to withstand such pressures and an excessive dilution of the guarantee was avoided. Nevertheless, the two congressional leaders were severely criticised for their actions. Hume Wrong, the Canadian Ambassador, informed Ottawa that although Connally and Vandenberg had no real objections to the treaty, they were 'ready to delay proceedings, make difficulties and assert their prerogatives. Connally is woolly and may not like Acheson's incisive style of discussion. Vandenberg is in a sulky mood which started on 3 November and still endures.'[23] More recently David McLellan has suggested that Acheson was much perplexed by the objections of the two senators: 'These were the Senate foreign-policy leaders. Both had knowingly embarked upon alliance diplomacy; both were intimately aware of the serious state of European opinion. Yet now, instead of trying to master the situation they were more concerned about how to evade the burdens of leadership.'[24] Both these judgements are overly critical of Connally and Vandenberg. After all, it would be their role and responsibility to manage the treaty through the Senate, and it is hardly surprising, therefore, that the serious state of European opinion was less salient in their calculations than the equally serious state of senatorial opinion – as displayed in the flare-up on 14 February. In attempting to weaken Article 5 the two senators sought to eliminate a potentially troublesome rallying point for opposition to the treaty. There was also a feeling that the Administration had been too lax in soliciting congressional opinion. Indeed, Connally later claimed that it was only after he told Acheson in early February that he would 'not accept a finished document stuck under our noses' that the Secretary of State decided that it would be unwise to present the Senate with a *fait accompli.*[25]

Whether it was the result of this prompting or of conclusions that he had reached independently, Acheson's recognition that Senate 'advice' on the North Atlantic Pact was a prerequisite for its later 'consent' initiated a period of close consultation and intensive cooperation between the State Department and the Senate's foreign policy leaders. Rather than the treaty being finalised and then handed to the Senate for its approval, it was presented to the Committee on Foreign Relations, meeting in executive session, before completion, thereby providing a virtually unprecedented opportunity for the members to play a part in the drafting process.[26] At the first of these meetings on 18 February, the Committee examined the treaty article by article, identifying areas of possible controversy or misunderstanding and offering suggestions for modification and improvement. Although some attention was devoted to Article 3, it aroused little opposition at this stage, largely because it was understood primarily as a reminder to the Europeans that they had to make maximum efforts to help themselves.[27] Inevitably the main focus of the Committee's discussion was Article 5. Although the words 'such action as it deems necessary' had been included as a result of the pressure from Connally and Vandenberg, senators remained uneasy about its implications. In order to alleviate these concerns it was decided – largely as a result of the promptings of Connally and Senator George – to incorporate a safeguard clause dealing with 'constitutional processes' into the treaty (and not merely the preamble) either as part of Article 5 or as a separate article.[28] At a second meeting of the Committee on 8 March changes made in Articles 1, 2 and 3 as a result of the earlier discussions were approved, as was Article 11 which now covered the consititutional processes point. A slight alteration was made in the word order of Article 5 and then this too was given the Committee's blessing. It was also accepted that the treaty would be for 20 years duration, the members agreeing with Acheson that this was an appropriate compromise between European demands for a 50-year treaty and the State Department preference for a shorter arrangement. Indeed, the session of 8 March was particularly harmonious, the only discordant note arising on the question of the military assistance programme and whether it was to be presented to Congress before or after the treaty had been dealt with. Connally was adamant that it should be witheld until the Senate had acted on the treaty.[29] The wisdom of this delaying tactic was borne out by subsequent events, especially the scale and intensity of the opposition aroused by the military assistance programme.

Thus the executive sessions of the Committee on Foreign Relations had a substantial impact on both the substance of the treaty and the procedure to be followed in its presentation to the Senate. The importance of the meetings is difficult to overestimate. By acting as a dress rehearsal for the debate on the Senate floor, they provided an opportunity for the Administration to identify the major areas of doubt and uncertainty on which it would be necessary to placate the critics. In fact, the conciliation process started in the meetings themselves. On the one hand, the sessions enabled committee members to suggest modifications designed to protect congressional prerogatives; on the other, they allowed the Administration to extend reassurances about the purpose and scope of the treaty without appearing to be acting under duress. Both processes helped to preempt later criticism and defuse opposition.

Another valuable result of the consultations was the conversion of hesitant or uncommitted senators into active supporters, willing to campaign and speak for the treaty on the Senate floor. As Achilles put it: 'by the time the Treaty was signed every member of the Committee knew it by heart and had a vested interest in it'.[30] The consent of the Senate would be much easier to obtain now that its advice had been taken into account.

The next important step in the attempt to build a two-thirds majority was the opening on 27 April of public hearings on the treaty. The purpose of the hearings was not to convert the members of the Foreign Relations Committee – that had already been accomplished so successfully that by 27 April, 'each member of the Committee had publicly expressed his support of the Treaty'.[31] They did provide an opportunity, however, for the members publicly to record their concerns and elicit arguments from Administration spokesmen which could be used in the forthcoming floor debate. The Committee also took the unusual step of allowing two non-members to join in the interrogation of witnesses. This possibility was discussed on 19 April when the Committee considered whether or not Senator Donnell, who was regarded as 'absolutely inexhaustible' should be given a 'license to hunt' on Acheson and other officials.[32] After some hesitation, it was decided that the advantages would probably outweigh the disadvantages and that both Donnell and Senator Watkins of Utah, another likely opponent of the treaty, should be allowed to participate. In the event, their probing and critical questions – while antagonising Chairman Connally, who felt that Watkins in particular was 'warting us to death'[33] – helped to elicit reassurances and allay anxieties.

The open and closed hearings also enabled Administration spokesmen to present an impressive array of arguments for the treaty. Together with the Committee Report they reveal the basis on which it was understood and accepted by a majority in the Senate. Not all the implications of the pact were entirely clear, of course, particularly in light of the impending military assistance programme which was widely regarded in the executive branch as being of at least equal importance as the treaty, and was deemed in Western Europe to be even more vital. Indeed, as early as 20 February, James Reston, writing in the

New York Times, suggested that there were two competing conceptions of the alliance in Washington, one a political conception which saw the pact as something akin to an extended Monroe Doctrine (although with the added advantage that the obligations were mutual rather than unilateral) and the other a more military-oriented venture which contemplated, at least in the long term, a restoration of the military balance of power in Europe.[34] The leading proponents of the treaty in the Senate almost invariably adhered to the first of these conceptions. They understood the Atlantic Pact as essentially a political guarantee intended to stimulate further economic recovery and promote a will to resist Communism in Western Europe. The American contribution was to be strictly limited and the prerogatives of Congress in any subsequent implementation of the treaty were maintained intact.

The first major assumption of its proponents was that the treaty was a natural and necessary concomitant to the Marshall Plan. As Acheson told the Committee on Foreign Relations, one of the chief purposes of the treaty was to 'promote full economic recovery through removing the drag of insecurity'.[35] Although considerable progress had been made in Western Europe, a much higher level of economic investment was essential if this momentum was to be maintained. It was not forthcoming because of a lack of confidence in the future. The treaty was intended to remedy this and provide an atmosphere in which recovery could proceed unimpaired by anxieties over security. Thus the relationship discussed by Vandenberg and implicit in Senate Resolution 239 was now made fully explicit. The belief that 'provision for overall security was a necessary step in the economic, political, and social recovery of Europe' had become a basic theme of executive spokesmen and provided perhaps the most powerful single argument in support of the treaty.[36] But would the treaty alone be sufficient to accomplish this?

The second assumption of Senate proponents of the treaty was that it would go a long way towards meeting this objective. They accepted it as a political guarantee likely to have a far-reaching deterrent effect. What impressed Arthur Vandenberg about the treaty was the 'notification to Mr Stalin which puts him in exactly the contrary position to that which Mr

Hitler was in, because Mr Hitler saw us with a Neutrality Act. Mr Stalin now sees us with a pact of cooperative action.'[37] It was *not* essential, in Vandenberg's thinking, to have substantial forces in being on the front lines in Europe: such a build-up could in fact be harmful since it was liable to precipitate an arms race. The vital thing was that the treaty was unequivocal in linking the massive American war potential to Western Europe and in conveying to the Soviet Union the ultimate futility of aggression against any member of the alliance. An almost identical point was made in the open hearings by General Omar Bradley who argued that the pact, by emphasising the inevitability of United States involvement in East–West hostilities in Europe could be decisive in preventing the outbreak of a Third World War. When asked by Senator McMahon of Connecticut if this was so 'whether or not we have a gun or a man or an airplane on the continent of Europe', the General replied: 'Yes sir, because of the potential of putting it there later if it is desired.'[38]

A third factor in obtaining Senate support was the emphasis placed on the idea of European self-help. This principle was established in the Vandenberg Resolution and enshrined in Article 3 of the treaty. Furthermore, it was repeatedly stated by Acheson and other spokesmen – in language strongly reminiscent of the Washington Paper of the previous September – that US efforts would be merely a supplement to those of the allies and could not act as a substitute for them.[39] In other words, self-help by the Europeans on a collective basis was a prerequisite for 'mutual aid' from the United States. Privately, Acheson was even more forthcoming and assured the committee members that the main purpose of Article 3 was 'to ensure that nobody is getting a meal ticket from anybody else so far as their capacity to resist is concerned'.[40] Thus it was clear that if an attempt was to be made to put teeth into the treaty – and this was the point at which many senators became unhappy anyway – the burden of the effort would fall upon Western Europe.

The fourth, and closely related premise, was that although the United States might assist in the build-up of European forces – the scope and extent of this assistance, of course, being at the discretion of Congress – its efforts would be limited to material aid. Manpower was definitely excluded. In response to the probing of Senator Donnell, several witnesses confirmed that there were no plans to deploy American ground forces in Europe, over and above the two divisions already there carrying out occupation duties. Both Lovett and Bradley made this clear, but it was stated most emphatically of all by Secretary of State Acheson in an exchange with Senator Hickenlooper of Iowa which was to be given an unexpected, and for Acheson somewhat embarrassing, prominence by later events. Because of this it is worth quoting the remarks in full. Hickenlooper made his point at length:

I believe you said earlier in your testimony today that it was contemplated that a great portion of the armament, or the developed armament, of Western Europe, in the actions of this pact, would be carried under their own weight. I presume that that refers also to their manpower in their armies. I am interested in getting the answers as to whether or not we are expected to supply substantial numbers – by that, I do not mean a thousand or two, or 500, or anything of that kind, but very substantial numbers – of troops and troop organizations, of American troops, to implement the land power of Western Europe prior to aggression.

Is that contemplated under Article 3, where we agree to maintain and develop the collective capacity to resist? In other words, are we going to be expected to send substantial numbers of troops over there as a more or less permanent contribution to the development of these countries' capacity to resist?

Acheson's reply was short and decisive. He merely said: 'The answer to that question, Senator, is a clear and absolute "No".'[41] There could be little misunderstanding and the Secretary's statement was sufficient to dispel any fears that the United States was making an open-ended and potentially very expensive commitment.

The fifth premise on which the treaty was accepted – and this was where Connally, Vandenberg and the other members of Foreign Relations had proved so important – was that it in no way infringed upon or impaired the constitutional rights and prerogatives of the Congress. The United States retained some discretion in deciding on an appropriate response in the event of an attack upon one of its allies. And if the President did conclude that the situation required the United States to go to war he could not use the treaty as a pretext for bypassing the Congress and ignoring its constitutional power to declare war. The committee report was categorical on this point, declaring that nothing in the treaty 'increases or decreases the constitutional powers of either President or Congress or changes the relationship between them'.[42] As a result of the efforts of Connally and George, there was a built-in safeguard to ensure that the principle was adhered to. Article 11 which stated that 'The Treaty shall be ratified and its provisions carried out by the Parties in accordance with their respective constitutional processes' was all-inclusive. It applied not only to Article 5 but to all the provisions in the treaty.[43]

On the basis of these assumptions and with the unanimous support of the Foreign Relations Committee, the treaty was finally approved by a vote of 82 to 13, on 21 July, at the end of a debate that had commenced 16 days earlier and been 'exhaustively detailed'.[44] The overwhelming number of votes cast for the treaty probably owed something to a favourable public opinion and to the fact that its rejection would have been a complete repudiation of President Truman's foreign policy. Vandenberg's unwavering support for the pact was also important. His pleas to the Senate to support the treaty were impressive in their sincerity, even though he introduced few new arguments. Emphasising that the treaty was a force for peace, he claimed that it was firmly rooted in United States self-interest: it was 'the most sensible, powerful, practicable, and economical step the United States can now take in the realistic interest of its own security'.[45] He recognised that there were risks involved in adopting the treaty, but argued that even greater risks would be incurred in rejecting it. Indeed, there would be problems and dangers in almost any course of action now that the United States had emerged as leader of the non-Communist bloc. As Vandenberg put it: 'We cannot escape from our prestige nor from its hazard.'[46]

While such arguments were ultimately accepted as compelling by a large majority of senators, several Republicans – most notably Taft, Wherry and Watkins – remained uneasy. Their scepticism, both about the assumptions upon which the treaty proponents had argued their case and the reassurances offered by the Administration, provoked considerable debate over both Article 5 and Article 3 of the treaty. Distrust of the Truman Administration led them to believe that the only acceptable safeguards were legally mandated ones: according-ly, the pact could not be approved without reservation. Senator Watkins's main concern was Article 5 and he submitted two reservations designed to weaken the pledge. The first would have absolved the United States of any obligation to provide armed help to its allies in the event that they were attacked, except by authorisation of Congress through an act or joint resolution. The second reservation claimed that in such cir-cumstances Congress would be under neither moral nor legal compunction to declare war. Both were overwhelmingly de-feated. Their decisive rejection stemmed on the one hand from the possibility that they would undermine the pact as a deter-rent to Soviet aggression and a boost to European morale, and on the other from the fact they appeared to be superfluous. The actions of Connally, Vandenberg and the Foreign Relations Committee had ensured that congressional prerogatives for the future were sufficiently well protected without the reservations. Although Connally's objections had been unpalatable to the European and American diplomats in February, the floor debate over Article 5 in July suggested that his intuition had been right. Without his earlier intervention the two Watkins reservations might have attracted more than 11 and 8 votes respectively.[47]

Perhaps even more interesting than the arguments over Article 5 were those over Article 3. Although Ireland has suggested that the Senate's preoccupation with the 'theoretical obligations' of the commitment article helped to obscure the long-term implication of Article 3, considerable attention was in fact devoted to the question of mutual aid.[48] A small group of senators, led by Robert Taft, were more strongly opposed to this element in the treaty than to anything else. Indeed, Taft was essentially in favour of the pact, but wanted to make explicit that in approving it the Senate did not incur any obligation to implement it with a military assistance programme for Western Europe. The relationship between the two proposals provoked much confusion which bedevilled the Senate debate from the outset. When asked at the Hearings whether a vote for the treaty would carry an obligation to vote for the military assistance programme, Acheson had replied that it would imply acceptance of the principle of mutual aid but would not preclude the exercise of individual judgement about its scope and extent.[49] Not all the proponents of the treaty agreed with this. Connally argued, both publicly and privately, that there would be no obligation to furnish anything.[50] John Foster Dulles, who had just been appointed senator from New York, took a similar position.[51] Senator George, in contrast, argued that approval of the pact would entail a moral obligation to support its implementation.[52] Consequently Senators Taft, Watkins and Wherry proposed a reservation to the resolution of ratification which declared that none of the parties to the treaty were committed to furnish arms to any of the other parties. Partly an exercise in clarification, the reservation was even more significant as an attempt to ensure that the political conception of the alliance prevailed and that there would be no large-scale military involvement in Western Europe. In this respect, the debate had some parallels with that which had taken place within the State Department. Taft argued that in so far as the pact was intended as an extension of the Monroe Doctrine it was both permissible and desirable; but to the extent that it foreshadowed a military alliance resting upon large forces in being it was not.[53] In this he was not far removed from the position that had been taken by George Kennan. He was also remarkably close to that adopted by Vandenberg. As Osgood has noted, Vandenberg and Taft 'shared an aversion to building sufficient forces in being to hold the line against Russia'.[54] The difference was that whereas Vandenberg did not see this as being a necessary consequence of the treaty, Taft did – unless Article 3 was somehow qualified. It is ironic that the emphasis on 'mutual aid and self-help' which had been intended primarily to define European obligations was now seen, with some justification, as compelling the United States to go beyond a political guarantee in ways which could be militarily dangerous and economically expensive.[55]

Although the Taft–Watkins–Wherry reservation was defeated easily, it still received 21 votes – most of them coming from the Senate economy bloc. By and large the names were familiar: Republicans such as Jenner of Indiana, Donnell and Kem of Missouri, Langer and Young of North Dakota, Malone of Nevada, Williams of Delaware, Bricker of Ohio, Cordon of Oregon and Cain of Washington were joined by a few Democrats including Byrd of Virginia and Johnson of Colorado. As one analyst has observed, they came primarily from 'states where large numbers of the businessmen engaged in local rather than international trade. They represented voters who lived in small towns rather than large cities, and who owned small businesses and small firms. They did not see any way their constituents would gain from a tax increase to arm Western Europe.'[56] This is not to suggest that the senators were acting solely out of expediency; conviction too played an important part. Indeed, it was the strength of these convictions which suggested that the forthcoming military assistance programme would encounter even more resistance than the pact. Although the North Atlantic Treaty had been approved, its implementation remained uncertain.

3   THE MILITARY ASSISTANCE PROGRAMME

Both the Truman Administration and the European allies believed that the purposes of the North Atlantic Treaty would only be achieved if accompanied by a programme for military assistance (MAP) to Western Europe. It is all the more surprising, therefore, that nothing like as much effort was devoted to consultation with Congress before the programme was formally presented. It was discussed with the Committee on Foreign Relations prior to the treaty being sent to the Senate floor, but this was primarily to decide upon tactics and timing, rather than to provide an opportunity for substantive discussion and possible modification of the Administration's proposal. Consequently, even senators relatively sympathetic to Truman's foreign policy were disturbed. Vandenberg, in fact, was appalled and angered by a disregard for liaison procedures that had been so essential to the creation of bipartisan support for previous undertakings. As he told a State Department official:

'The thing that astounds me . . . is that this Committee was scrupulously consulted regarding every detail of the Atlantic Pact, and yet I do not recall a single word submitted to us at any stage of the proceedings regarding the military implementation.'[57] These concerns over procedure were accompanied by anxieties over the implications of the programme itself. Chairman Connally, for example, was worried that the Europeans – Acheson's protestations to the contrary notwithstanding – might be getting a meal ticket, or, as he put it in his own inimitable way, be coming 'to tap the till'.[58] During one of the executive sessions Connally expressed his anxieties in full:

> What I have been fearing about this whole program . . . is that most of those countries in Europe are just going to sit down and fold their hands and say 'Well, the United States is going to arm us. The United States is going to protect us. The United States isn't going to let anybody invade us.' On the other hand, they have to be told and made to realize that they have to do all within their power themselves to arm themselves. The American people are not favorable to our just saying 'All right, now, you just go ahead, we will take care of you. We will furnish you food, linament and money and arms, and men if necessary.' The next call we are going to have will be for men. They are going to want men, soldiers.[59]

In order to allay such fears and repair the damage caused by its failure to solicit congressional involvement at an earlier stage the Administration began its attempt to 'sell' MAP during the hearings on the treaty. Indeed, both during these sessions and the hearings on the programme itself, it attempted to establish the conditions on which military assistance would be given to Western Europe.[60] Most of its arguments merely elaborated the principles of the treaty. At the same time, it became clear that there was some ambiguity about the overall objective of the proposal. State Department officials tended to emphasise that it was limited in scope, duration and purpose. Because priority was given to economic recovery, the scope of the programme was restricted to reequipping forces already in existence rather than building new ones.[61] And with economic recovery and an increased productive capacity, the European states would themselves be able to meet their military requirements. Thus the amount of aid from the United States would gradually diminish.[62] Finally, it was argued that the prime purpose of the programme was to boost morale and thereby not only maintain the momentum for economic recovery but encourage Western Europe to make substantial efforts for its own security and protection.[63] As the US Special Representative in Europe under the Economic Cooperation Administration, Averell Harriman testified: 'confidence is contagious'.[64] Confidence would be improved because the military assistance programme would enable the Europeans to cope with border incidents, Communist-inspired rioting, and other fifth column movements. They would cease to be vulnerable to more indirect forms of pressure, thus leaving the Soviet Union only with the option of direct aggression which would require a willingness, in Dean Acheson's words, 'to start World War Three'.[65]

At times, however, Acheson appeared to assume that the Europeans would develop a capacity to cope with direct attack as well as the more limited contingencies. Military witnesses who appeared during the joint hearings held by the Committees on Foreign Relations and Armed Services also seemed to suggest a more ambitious objective for the assistance programme – at least in the long term. Arms aid, according to them, was designed to stimulate European rearmament to the point where the Europeans would be able to hold a conventional attack.[66] Although this placed a greater emphasis on 'forces-in-being' than senators like Vandenberg believed necessary or desirable, it was argued that ultimately it would only benefit the United States. A more powerful and self-sufficient Western Europe would permit not only a reduction in military assistance but also a cut in the overall level of American defence expenditure. In reply to a question from Senator Gurney of South Dakota, General Bradley stated:

> In my opinion when you get the countries of Europe in a position to furnish their own security, that furnishes that much more to us, and thereby I should think that your requirements here at home for ability to do something would

be lessened very critically. That was the situation we had before World War Two. These countries were able to hold for a considerable length of time, which meant that we did not have to keep in being the same expensive forces that we have to maintain today. I would say in answer to your question that when the final results are obtained here, undoubtedly it would lessen the requirement for an immediate defensive force here at home.[67]

Although this did not contemplate West European forces equal in size to those of the Soviet Union, it did demand a large-scale and formidable rearmament effort.

This was underlined by the prevailing strategic concept. It became apparent during the hearings that a division of labour was envisaged in which nations specialised in building the forces necessary to carry out specifically assigned roles and missions. Thus the United States would be 'charged with strategic bombing' while it was intended that 'the hard core of ground power in being will come from Europe aided by other nations as they can be mobilised'.[68] Western Europe was also to provide the tactical air power required for its own defence, leaving the United States to concentrate on its strategic air power as a deterrent. Within Europe the bulk of the ground forces were to be supplied by France, supported as far as possible by the other signatories of the Brussels Treaty.[69] General Lemnitzer expressed the point brutally when he stated that if the Soviets were to be stopped on the ground 'the Europeans are the only ones that can do it'.[70] And it was essential that they were stopped on the ground, as otherwise – and Acheson and the military were in complete agreement about this – the United States would be 'liberating a corpse'.[71]

In the light of this strategic design, the emphasis laid on the limited scope of the military assistance programme by State Department officials rang rather hollow. Yet the planning concept was also reassuring, as it confirmed that there was no rationale for stationing United States land forces on the European continent. The witnesses also attempted to alleviate the fears of Connally and others that America would end up carrying an inordinate share of the burden. Indeed, if there were divergent interpretations of the fundamental purposes of military aid, there was unanimity on the fact that it was only a small part of the total security programme, which was based primarily on European self-help. It was stressed that for every dollar of aid received from the United States, the Europeans themselves would be spending six dollars.[72] The ratio of European–American efforts was a central plank in the Administration's case – so much so, in fact, that it unintentionally set a precedent that would be used during the troops to Europe debate when several participants suggested establishing arithmetical ratios between the number of divisions raised in Europe, and the number to be contributed by the United States.

In spite of all this, several key senators remained unhappy. Vandenberg, in particular, believed that the Administration's initial proposals for aid tended to embrace the military conception. As he put it:

> the pending proposals are only an inadequate downpayment on a stupendous future account if the concept and objective are to build sufficient forces-in-being to hold the Russian line. That is not my concept or objective. I think it presents ruinous corollaries both at home and abroad ... I would have infinitely preferred to rely upon the potential in the North Atlantic Pact as a discouragement to Soviet aggression. My original expectation in connection with Articles 3 and 9 was to highlight this potential by putting existing forces-in-being in mutual gear and on a basis of maximum efficiency chiefly for the practical purpose of assuring adequate defense against internal subversion.[73]

Given such sentiments, it is little surprise that when on 25 July (the same day that he signed the North Atlantic Treaty) President Truman submitted to Congress his request for military assistance to the allies, Vandenberg took the lead in curtailing and modifying it – quickly obtaining the support of other members of the Foreign Relations Committee including Democratic Senators George and Fulbright, and Republicans Lodge and Wiley. As well as being too big and putting too much emphasis on 'forces-in-being' the bill in its original form also granted the President virtually unlimited powers to give aid wherever he deemed it appropriate. And Vandenberg was afraid that this would make the President 'the number one war lord of the earth'.[74] He also felt that the proposal ignored the machinery referred to in Article 9 of the treaty which established a council and a defence committee to recommend measures for the implementation of Articles 3 and 5. Despite such reservations, Vanderberg's opposition was neither total nor indiscriminate. After pressing the Administration into making its own changes in the proposal, Vandenberg played an active part in steering it through – and his influence was crucial in restoring the essentials of the programme after the House of Representatives had cut the original appropriations request in half. Working closely with John Foster Dulles, Vandenberg devised amendments ensuring that the aid would be used by the Atlantic Pact countries in an overall plan for integrated defence.

Acheson has described Vandenberg's actions on the military assistance programme as the Senator merely adopting his 'familiar gambit of opposing and obtaining amendment before he would support it'.[75] In fact Vandenberg's objections to the proposal as initially presented were far more fundamental than the Secretary of State seemed to realise, going as they did to the heart of the conflict between the competing conceptions of the pact. The Senator saw his conception of the treaty as a political device threatened by measures which would transform it into a more costly and expensive military arrangement. As Ireland has commented, Vandenberg

> believed that the chief benefit of the treaty rested in its deterrent value rather than in its implementation through the Military Assistance Programme, but if there was to be an aid programme, it is clear that he did not want the United States to enter into a long-term and indefinite commitment to provide military assistance. Therefore, he favoured the setting up of the North Atlantic Council and the Defence Committee in order to get a better picture of the defence needs of the Europeans and to develop an aid package that would place realistic limits on America's continuing obligation.[76]

It would also encourage the kind of cooperation among the Europeans themselves that Vandenberg and other senators had long desired.

Even with these modifications, some senators remained dissatisfied. Senator George was particularly unhappy and proposed an amendment to cut the one billion dollar aid programme in half. Although Vandenberg was influential in the defeat of this, the two men were in certain respects not that far apart. Indeed, when George complained that while he had voted for the North Atlantic Treaty, its conversion 'into a great armaments program extending over the years would belie all the professions we made when we said the Treaty was intended to preserve peace', he was merely echoing some of the anxieties that had earlier gnawed at Vandenberg.[77] Nevertheless, on 22 September, as a result of Senator Vandenberg's efforts, the bill finally passed on a roll-call vote of 55 to 24 – and with a far smaller cut than in the House. Whether the Senate could have sustained its version of the bill in the House–Senate Conference Committee without the sudden crisis atmosphere generated by the news of a Soviet atomic explosion is uncertain. As it was, however, the House quickly agreed to adopt the Senate's position.

Although the Administration thereby achieved most of what it wanted, the debate over the military implementation of the North Atlantic Treaty was disquieting:

> the animosity which characterized relations between both parties on this issue in the early spring and summer, the truculence with which pro- and anti-Administration groups held to their demands, the bitter and partisan tone of debate in Congress, the widening gap between isolationist- and internationalist-minded members in each party, and the controversy raging concurrently over American foreign policy in the Far East – all of these indicated that if bipartisanship had not altogether vanished, it was rapidly disappearing from American foreign affairs.[78]

In such circumstances, the ability of the Administration to generate sufficient enthusiasm and support in the Senate to sustain the momentum of its foreign policy was highly prob-

lematical. It was made even more so by the fall of China to the
Communists in October 1949, an event which galvanised the
Republican opposition and led to what Dean Acheson has
called 'the attack of the primitives'.[79] From late 1949 and
throughout the early months of 1950 the executive branch had
to face not only criticisms about the substance of its policy, but
also an incessant attack upon the loyalty and integrity of the
policy-makers themselves.

What made all these developments even more disturbing for
the supporters of the President was their emergence at a time
when the American role in underpinning European security
remained ambiguous and uncertain. The debate on the military assistance programme underlined the fact that United
States responsibilities had not been clearly and adequately
defined by the Atlantic Pact: widespread agreement on the
need for the treaty could not hide substantial disagreement
over the nature and scope of the resulting obligations. For the
moment this was tolerable since 'there was no significant fear of
a massive Russian invasion'.[80] The fall of China and the Soviet
atomic explosion, however, provoked a reappraisal of American security problems and even before the outbreak of the
Korean War, an important segment of opinion within the State
Department had concluded not only that the *military* danger
from the Soviet Union was significant but that it would become
more so: as Soviet atomic developments eroded the United
States advantage thereby neutralising or nullifying the deterrent effect of American atomic weapons, Soviet conventional
aggression could be anticipated. Consequently, more vigorous
efforts were required by both the United States *and its allies* to
augment their own capabilities. Indeed, NSC-68, the report of
a joint State and Defence Department Study Group submitted
in April 1950, seemed to contemplate European rearmament
on a scale that had only been hinted at in the hearings on the
military assistance programme. As it stated:

> the armaments increase under the present aid programs will
> not be of any major consequence prior to 1952. Unless the
> military strength of the West European nations is increased
> on a much larger scale than under current programs and at
> an accelerated rate, it is more than likely that these nations

will not be able to oppose even by 1960 the Soviet armed
forces in war with any degree of effectiveness. Considering
the Soviet Union military capability, the long range allied
military objective in Western Europe must envisage an
increased military strength in that area sufficient possibly to
deter the Soviet Union from a major war or, in any event, to
delay materially the overrunning of Western Europe and, if
feasible to hold a bridgehead on the Continent against Soviet
Union offensives.[81]

And if Europe was to be restored to such a position of influence
and military strength then 'deeper participation by the United
States than has been contemplated' would be required.[82]

Although the report was not formally accepted or acted upon
by President Truman, it exposes the trend of thinking of several
key officials, most notably Dean Acheson. It reveals too that the
aims and attitudes of the executive and legislative branches
were becoming increasingly divergent. The Secretary of State
and his department were in favour of further involvement in
European affairs whereas the sentiment in the Senate was that
the limits of participation had already been reached. For the
moment though the issue was not joined directly, as Acheson
still had to convince both Truman and the European allies of
the need for greater efforts. His efforts to impress this upon the
allies at the North Atlantic Council meeting held in London in
May 1950 were not entirely successful, and although agreement was reached upon the desirability of balanced collective
forces, the build-up was to be a progressive one during which
European economic recovery would retain priority. Indeed, the
whole tenor of European rearmament seems to have been quite
leisurely: complacency rather than the urgency embodied in
NSC-68 was the order of the day. As one analyst has commented: 'in early June 1950, the North Atlantic Treaty nations,
including the United States, were engaged in strengthening
their collective defences by stages, which seemed slow, casual
and insufficient a few weeks later'.[83] This abrupt change was
precipitated by the North Korean attack on South Korea on 25
June. Indeed, it was this which, after considerable bureaucratic
wrangling, led to the decision to send American troops to
Western Europe.

4   TROOPS TO EUROPE

The outbreak of hostilities in Korea had a profound impact on
the attitudes of American foreign policy-makers. Not only did it
strengthen the proponents of NSC-68 within the Administration, but it led to decisions going much further than anything
contemplated in the report. The immediate response – motivated partly by analogies with fascist aggression in the 1930s –
was to assist the South Koreans, a decision which led rapidly to
direct American intervention. The repercussions of the war,
however, extended well beyond the Korean peninsula – involving a major reassessment of the Soviet threat to Europe as
well as Asia. Consequently, there was widespread concern in
both the United States and Western Europe that the steps
already taken might prove insufficient to deter Soviet aggression.

> The elaborate NATO framework with its numerous sub-
> sidiary units, now appeared an empty shell incapable of
> repelling a sudden attack of any magnitude. What was
> worse, the allies lost confidence for the moment in NATO's
> ability to prevent such an attack from occurring. What had
> happened in the Far East could happen in Europe.[84]

Thus NATO needed a genuine capacity for collective defence.
Containment, if it was to succeed, would have to be militarised.

Accordingly, the United States initiated a massive rearmament programme, and the Europeans, to the extent possible,
followed suit as the prior constraint of economic recovery was
now significantly relaxed if not wholly abandoned. Congress
too agreed on the need for emergency measures and in August
1950 sanctioned an additional three and a half billion dollars
for European aid. It was impossible, however, to create defence
forces of the scale and effectiveness required without both a
contribution from West Germany and the deployment of
American forces in Europe far in excess of those already there
as a result of the occupation. Yet both these issues involved
highly delicate considerations, domestically and international-
ly. The idea of deploying American troops to Europe under
Article 3 of the North Atlantic Treaty had been specifically

ruled out by Acheson in 1949, while any suggestion of West German rearmament aroused enormous anxieties in Europe, and especially in France. For Acheson, the latter consideration was the dominant one, and although he was prepared to advocate the deployment of American troops to Europe, he remained reluctant to abandon his tentative approach to the question of German rearmament. The Department of Defense, however, had different priorities and was only prepared to contemplate sending additional troops to Europe as part of a single 'package' incorporating the creation of a unified command and the inclusion of German armed forces. 'Therefore, the first two weeks in August 1950 was a period of debate between Acheson and those who followed his gradualist approach to German rearmament and a "united and immovable Pentagon", which insisted that any commitment of US troops to Europe be accompanied by the simultaneous rearmament of West Germany.'[85] Although Acheson found little difficulty in agreeing to German rearmament in principle, he wanted this later in the programme, thereby challenging the Pentagon's insistence on the development of a unified package. The issue remained unresolved in late August 1950. Consequently a meeting was held at theWhite House on 26 August in which the President posed a series of outstanding questions about American policy. Acheson and Secretary of Defense Johnson were charged with providing answers – which they did on 8 September. There was broad agreement that if defence rather than liberation was the goal in Europe the United States should proceed with the earliest possible deployment of US troops to Europe. In addition, Washington would promote the creation of an integrated European army, the appointment of a supreme commander and the formation of West German military forces. In the final analysis, therefore, Acheson had accepted the Pentagon's idea of a unified package. The following day Truman made a major announcement:

> On the basis of recommendations of the Joint Chiefs of Staff, concurred in by the Secretaries of State and Defense, I have today approved substantial increases in the strength of the United States forces to be stationed in Western Europe in the interest of the defense of that area. The extent of these

increases and the timing thereof will be worked out in close
coordination with our North Atlantic Treaty partners. A
basic element in the implementation of this decision is the
degree to which our friends match our actions in this regard.
Firm programs for the development of their forces will be
expected to keep full step with the dispatch of additional
United States forces to Europe. Our plans are based on the
sincere expectations that our efforts will be met with similar
actions on their part.[86]

The significance of this is difficult to overestimate. American
forces already in Europe were to be transformed from occupation forces designed to contain Germany to combat forces
which would help to contain the Soviet Union. The French
government was very happy with this element in the American
plan. It had serious reservations, though, about the German
component of the package deal. Acheson's instincts about the
delicacy of German rearmament had been sound, and the next
few months were spent in attempting to reconcile the divergent
American and French views. Agreement was eventually
reached on the basis of what was known as the Spofford
compromise (after Charles Spofford, the American representative on the Council of Deputies), in which 'the United States
agreed to trade support for a European defense structure and a
decoupling of American troop commitments from immediate
German rearmament while the French accepted the idea that
the commitment of American troops to Europe was part of a
larger plan that included German rearmament in the not-too-
distant future.'[87] The compromise prepared the way for the
announcement that Eisenhower had been appointed as the first
supreme commander and that he would take charge of American troops deployed to Europe. The creation of the Atlantic
security system was virtually complete.

The question remained, however, as to whether the President would be able to obtain congressional support for this
initiative. There were three closely interwoven considerations
relating to the experience since 1947 which suggested that this
might be a difficult task. The first was that American policy
towards Europe had been developed on the basis of certain
assumptions, understandings and principles which now appeared to be compromised, abandoned or violated. The second

was that these earlier policies had themselves been 'oversold' in order to win congressional approval. The third was that, notwithstanding this oversell, bipartisanship and the foreign policy consensus had, at several junctures, looked extremely fragile.

The troops to Europe decision was the culmination of a series of decisions, policies and programmes which had begun with the Truman Doctrine and evolved through the Marshall Plan, the Vandenberg Resolution, the North Atlantic Treaty and what had come to be called the Mutual Defence Assistance Programme. Once the Truman Administration had acknowledged that both containing the Soviet Union and maintaining the prosperity, security and independence of Western Europe were vital to its own security and welfare, then it was merely a case of doing what was necessary to fulfil these objectives. It is in this sense that there was a logical progression from the European Recovery Programme (ERP) to the security guarantee enshrined in the North Atlantic Treaty, and from the security guarantee to the military assistance programme (MAP). And when it became clear that in spite of all these efforts deterrence might still not work, it was only a small step to deploy US troops in Europe and to encourage more rapid and extensive rearmament by the allies. In another sense, however, the troops decision was a radical departure from all these previous steps, implying as it did that the United States was now prepared to restore and maintain the balance of power in Europe through its own *direct* participation. All its previous efforts had been designed essentially to rebuild Western Europe to a point where it could look after itself: temporary involvement to recreate an indigenous balance of power was a price it had been prepared to pay to avoid a deeper, more direct and more enduring entanglement. Indeed the nature of American involvement in Europe from 1947 to 1950 is perhaps best summed up in the phrase 'as much as necessary and as little as possible'. By September 1950, however, the administration's reluctance to contemplate direct participation had diminished as it became apparent that the difficulties of reestablishing a balance of power and thereby containing the Soviet Union had been consistently underestimated, especially in the public presentation of policy.

Whether this was intentional or unintentional is open to

argument. A major consideration in the approach of the executive branch, though, was the need to reconcile a reluctant Congress to its policy. Although there was some overselling of the threat during this period, probably of far greater importance was what has been termed the 'overselling of the remedy'.[88] ERP was initially presented as the solution to Europe's problems. When this alone failed to have the desired effect, the North Atlantic Treaty together with the military assistance programme was sold in the same way. Now it was necessary to send United States troops to Europe – an option that had been categorically excluded just over a year earlier. At some point, however, scepticism sets in and oversell breeds reaction. As Lowi has commented: 'when experiments must be sold as sure things and limited sure things must be sold as cure-alls, frustrations and failure are inevitable'.[89]

Consequently, there was now a possibility that the decision to deploy forces to Europe might arouse opposition, because of the earlier overselling of remedies. From the Administration's point of view, though, this tactic had been essential. Even with its extensive use – and the invaluable support of Senator Vandenberg – bipartisanship had been incomplete. An important group of senators could not be reconciled – for reasons discussed above – even to limited involvement in Europe. Although this group was conducting what appeared to be merely a rearguard action, its continued and intense opposition provided the basis for a more far-reaching assault upon the whole thrust of the Administration's postwar foreign policy.

So long as the Democrats remained loyal, the problem was not too serious. The debate over MAP, however, had revealed that such loyalty was not automatic. Indeed, it suggested that the conservative coalition which had long been evident in opposition to Truman's domestic programme might increasingly form a tacit alliance against important aspects of his foreign policy. The reservations of Senator George about military aid, for example, seem to have been symbolic of Southern dissatisfaction not only with the increasing military emphasis of the commitment to Western Europe, but also with the continuing financial burden. And it is significant that support for his amendment to slash the programme came primarily from the midwest Republicans buttressed by such Southern

Democrats as McClellan of Arkansas, Long of Louisiana, Johnston of South Carolina and Byrd of Virgina – senators who, by and large, were more concerned about the threat to the American economy than the threat to Atlantic security. And if one thing about the decision to send US troops was clear, it was that it would be expensive.

Thus, the experience from 1947 to September 1950 did not augur well for the future course of the Truman Administration's foreign policy. The Senate had acquiesced only reluctantly in the creation of an Atlantic security system in which the United States role was severely circumscribed. Would it now allow a completely unexpected expansion of that role to occur without challenge? The answer to this question provides the theme of the next chapter.

3 The Commitment Challenged: The 'Great Debate' of 1951

1 THE CONTEXT

For a nation which had always been reluctant to support a standing army, and had traditionally relied upon wartime mobilisation rather than peacetime preparedness, the decision to send US troops to Europe was momentous – as great a departure from the past precepts of American military policy as the North Atlantic Treaty had been from the orthodoxies of American diplomacy. Yet the announcement of the decision on 9 September 1950 was met by a mixture of acquiescence and apathy. The challenge to the decision was not to emerge until well over three months later; the issue was then to consume the interest and attention of the Senate – to the exclusion of almost all other business – during January, February and March of 1951.

This hiatus is revealing: the changes in both domestic and international politics during the months subsequent to Truman's initial announcement did much to precipitate the controversy. At the outset, though, the policy was seen merely as part of the new tougher stance adopted by the Administration in the wake of the North Korean invasion of the South. Republicans who had been criticising the President for his weakness, vacillation and ineptitude in combating Communism, could hardly fail to applaud his decision – at leat in the short term. Furthermore, this new militancy in United States foreign policy appeared to be paying dividends in Korea. Although there was already some questioning of Truman's handling of the war, this was stifled by MacArthur's successful

43

landing at Inchon. Coming as it did less than a week after the President's announcement on troops to Europe, the landing and the subsequent advance of United Nations forces strengthened the Administration's position, both by validating its interventionist policy and by diverting attention from the Atlantic area. A frontal assault on Truman's foreign policy could hardly be made at a time when it appeared to be highly successful.

Nor was this the only constraint on the Republicans. The delay in the congressional attack on the new policy can be understood in part as a result of the simple fact that Congress recessed before the end of September and did not reconvene until 27 November. Furthermore, 36 Senate seats were being contested in the mid-term elections. Almost inevitably this meant a preoccupation with domestic, regional and local issues. Despite the later claims of Senator Taft to the contrary, foreign policy played relatively little part in an election dominated by the usual issues such as housing, education and employment, and the more unusual one of Communism in government. The only exception to this was Korea.[1]

If foreign policy had little effect on the election, however, the election had a significant impact on foreign policy. This was partly because the Republicans made substantial – although not overwhelming – gains. In the Senate in particular the Democrats' advantage was reduced from a majority of twelve (54 to 42) to a majority of two (49 to 47). The Administration's influence in the Upper House was thereby attenuated – especially as some of the newly victorious Republicans, such as Dirksen, Nixon and Butler, were extremely partisan critics of the President. The more serious change, however, was one of attitude, not of mathematical majorities. As Caridi put it:

> The election results were proof to many in the GOP that there were no benefits to be gained from 'me-tooism'. These Republicans now felt freer to criticise Administration policy, and the patched-over attempt to retain a bipartisan approach to foreign affairs became even more difficult to sustain. If the liberal and internationalist wing of the party wished to continue to support the Administration, they would definitely be outside of the power centre of the GOP. It

was Taft and Millikin, aided by the 'conspiracy group' – Wherry, Jenner, Malone and McCarthy – and the pro-Formosa group – Knowland, Bridges and Smith (New Jersey) – who were in the ascendancy.[2]

This ascendancy was strengthened by the absence of Senator Vandenberg, who had succeeded in moderating, although not suppressing, the criticisms of the conservative, midwest Republicans. Vandenberg's illness deprived the Administration of an influential supporter. It also meant that the critics were both less constrained and less restrained.

To some extent, of course, the Republican tactics and the revival of partisanship were understandable. The GOP had been out of power for a long time, yet part of the rationale for bipartisanship was that it would ease the transition from one Administration to the next and help preserve a much needed continuity in foreign policy. With Dewey's failure to bring about such a transition in 1948, a reassessment was inevitable. It appeared, after all, as if the Democrats were obtaining all the credit and reaping the political benefits for policies which had depended critically upon Republican support. And if 1948 had shown the dangers of cooperation for the Republicans, 1950 appeared to demonstrate the advantages of non-cooperation.

The results of the elections, however, were not only a boost for the Republican Party but a personal triumph for Senator Taft who was reelected by a resounding majority in Ohio, despite strong opposition from the labour unions. It is significant too that Taft's aspirations paralleled those of his party: the GOP wanted to be the party of the presidency, he wanted to be the incumbent. In order to be a serious candidate for his party's nomination, Taft felt he had to establish a personal imprint on foreign policy to complement his position and prestige as chief Republican spokesman on domestic affairs. Vandenberg's illness provided Taft with the opportunity to do this, as it ended the tacit division of labour which had limited the Ohio Senator's influence on the Republican Party's attitudes to foreign policy.[3] Soon after his reelection, therefore, he made a major statement on foreign affairs in which he asserted that isolationism was moribund but demanded that American policy towards Western Europe be reexamined.

If Taft's speech was intended as a direct challenge to the Executive, the Administration decided to meet it head on. Secretary of State Acheson's rebuke was swift and vitriolic. Acheson argued that Taft's approach threatened the achievements of postwar American foreign policy and suggested that 'a re-examinist might be a farmer that goes out every morning and pulls up all his crops to see how they have done during the night'.[4] While this response was understandable from a Secretary of State simultaneously beleaguered by critics who regarded him as a traitor, and proud of his role in creating the Atlantic security system, it was not the kind of speech likely to establish a harmonious working relationship between the Administration and its opponents. If, on the one hand, important segments of the GOP, fortified by electoral success, were looking for a confrontation with the Democratic Administration over foreign policy, it appears, on the other hand, that the Administration itself was prepared to countenance such a challenge with equanimity. Thus, the breakdown of bipartisanship was the result of suspicion and intransigence on *both* sides. The careful efforts to build a bipartisan coalition that had characterised the discussions over the North Atlantic Treaty had not been paralleled by similarly extensive efforts in the military assistance programme. On the question of deploying US forces to Europe, attempts to obtain Republican support seem to have been virtually non-existent. Yet the Administration could not realistically expect politics to stop at the water's edge and its foreign policy to be excluded from partisan attack if it failed to observe the established procedures of bipartisanship and engage in advance consultation.

It may be, of course, that the emergence of McCarthyism had led the President and the Secretary of State to conclude that any such efforts at consultation and consensus-building were futile. Whatever the case, the Administration's policy of decisiveness – with Congress being relegated to a secondary role of providing support *after* the key decisions were taken – was acceptable only so long as the policies were successful. Once the policies themselves ran into trouble, exclusive executive control of the decision-making process would become controversial, provoking a general indictment of the President's handling of foreign affairs.

It is not surprising, therefore, that the setbacks for American and United Nations forces in Korea in November and December 1950 aroused concerns which went well beyond the specifics of the Asian conflict. In fact the course of the hostilities in Korea was one of the key factors which precipitated the 'Great Debate'. It is perhaps one of the rarely noted ironies of United States foreign policy in 1950 that events in Asia helped to fashion not only the official assessment of security needs in Europe, but also the critics' assessment of the risks and costs of the projected troop deployment to Europe. Similarities between divided Korea and divided Germany, suspicions that the North Korean attack was a feint to divert American attention from Europe, and a belief that the Soviet Union was embarking on a more adventurist course, highlighted the need to augment European defences, and led directly to the troops to Europe decision. Many Republicans also made the connection between US policy in Korea and that towards Europe. Their conclusions though were remarkably different from those expressed by the Executive – and had important implications for both the procedure and the substance of US foreign policy. Truman had committed American forces to Korea without formal congressional approval (let alone a declaration of war). The consequences, it now appeared, were disastrous. He had done the same in Europe – but there was little reason to believe that a land war strategy would fare any better there than in Asia. Certainly Congress should have had an opportunity to discuss the matter prior to the actual despatch of American forces. As events had demonstrated, the Executive, far from having a monopoly of wisdom in foreign affairs, appeared at the very minimum to be inept. And for those who went further than this and suggested that traitors and Communist sympathisers were in charge of United States foreign policy, the setbacks in Korea were seen merely as further confirmation of their suspicions.

Thus by December 1950 the domestic political context was highly charged. The day before Acheson left for a meeting of the North Atlantic Council in Brussels, Truman declared a state of emergency. The day of the Secretary's departure, a substantial group of Republicans demanded his resignation. Thus when further details began to emerge about the troop deployment – that US troops would contribute to an integrated force under centralised command and control and that General Eisenhower would be the first Supreme Allied Commander Europe – it was inevitable that these plans would be subjected to careful and critical examination.[5] And while enough was now known about the proposals to arouse controversy, insufficient detail was released to calm the anxieties of those concerned about the size of the American contribution. As one analyst of the controversy has observed, this was 'crucial to the enlargement of the debate'.[6] It encouraged opposition from those who might have been prepared to sanction a limited deployment of ground forces but disapproved of what in the circumstances could all too easily be construed as an open-ended commitment.

It was in this climate of acrimony and suspicion that former President Hoover made a broadcast on 20 December, setting out not only his opposition to the Truman–Acheson foreign policy but what he regarded as a more viable alternative. The main themes of the speech were not new; Hoover had presented a similar, if slightly more moderate, critique in October with little effect.[7] What was new, however, was the receptiveness of the audience. Hoover evoked a sympathetic chord in a nation frustrated by a foreign policy that appeared increasingly costly, burdensome and inconclusive. His position was, essentially, that attempting to combat the Communists on land was wasteful of American manpower and resources and ultimately doomed to failure. Consequently, 'the foundation of US policy must be to preserve for the world this Western Hemisphere, Gibraltar of Western Civilisation'.[8] This could be accomplished by placing almost exclusive emphasis on air and naval forces which would enable the United States 'to hold the Atlantic and Pacific Oceans with one frontier on Britain . . . and the other on Japan, Formosa and the Philippines'.[9] Although this argument was widely characterised as an example of extreme isolationism, Hoover was neither denying the need to combat Communism nor advocating total non-involvement in the world and a retreat to 'Fortress America'. He *was* arguing that containment could best be accomplished through alliance with the island nations on the perimeter of the Eurasian land mass. The implications were certainly drastic, implying a halt – if not a reversal – in the US policy of assisting

Europe. Acknowledging that he was not blind to the need to preserve Western civilisation on the continent of Europe, Hoover emphasised that

> the prime obligation of the defense of Western Continental Europe rests upon the nations of Europe ... To warrant our further aid they should show they have spiritual strength and unity to avail themselves of their own resources. But it must be far more than pacts, conferences, paper promises and declarations. Today it must express itself in organised and equipped combat divisions of such large numbers as would create a sure dam against the red flood. And that before we land another man or another dollar on their shores.[10]

The logical shortcomings of this analysis were obvious: Europe would only receive American assistance when it had demonstrated that it did not require it. Despite this, the statement received wide acclaim, especially from the Hearst press. Several of Hoover's themes were developed further by former Ambassador to the United Kingdom, Joseph Kennedy, who explicitly advocated US withdrawal from both Korea and Europe.[11]

Nevertheless, support for the former President was far from unanimous, and within his own party both John Foster Dulles and Governor Dewey were critical of his proposals.[12] The Administration too attempted to refute his arguments but succeeded only in intensifying the controversy both by invoking presidential prerogative at a time when this was particularly sensitive, and by a lack of coordination among officials which led to several contradictory statements about the implications of the North Atlantic Council meeting. The first of these tactics has been singled out by Walter Lippmann as the major cause of the controversy which flared up when the first session of the eighty-second Congress convened in January 1951. As he put it a few weeks later: 'Mister Truman's troubles with Congress are self-induced. The whole question of his rights and powers would never have been raised had he exercised his rights and powers with tact, with discretion, and with a broader understanding of what is involved.'[13] The Administration's stance succeeded only in arousing the institutional pride of the Senate.

Even without these basic tactical errors by the President, though, the Senate would still have played a major role in the controversy: the opportunity was too good for the Republicans to ignore. Yet to suggest that the assault on Truman's foreign policy was caused simply by high-handedness and ineptitude on the one side and by partisan and personal ambition on the other is to exaggerate the politics and to ignore the principles involved in the 'Great Debate'. This is what makes the controversy so difficult to characterise. The debate was a struggle between the two major parties in the Senate, yet the splits within the GOP itself were almost equally important. It was a conflict between the Executive and the legislature over the control of foreign policy, yet the fissures *within* the Senate over the respective constitutional prerogatives of the two branches prevented a simple confrontation between Congress and presidency. The conflict not only encompassed both procedural and substantive matters, but at times it was impossible to distinguish the one kind of issue from the other. Nor was the controversy over the substance of policy itself any more straightforward. The question of whether or not United States troops should be sent to Western Europe was, of course, the kernel of the dispute; but the Senate deliberations quickly revealed a more fundamental and far-reaching divergence among several competing philosophies of foreign affairs. Such a divergence was not new but, for the most part, had been subdued through the late 1940s, partly by the attempts to build a bipartisan consensus and, more importantly, by the limited sacrifices apparently required for America to fulfil its new role as guardian of Atlantic security. The fear that the United States would send a vast land army to Western Europe, by challenging the comfortable and somewhat complacent assumptions about the limited costs of American involvement, brought the different perspectives into sharp relief, highlighting a lack of consensus on the purpose, scope and instruments of United States foreign policy. The opposing positions, however, cannot simply be characterised as isolationism or internationalism. Such crude epithets, although useful points of departure, fail to do justice either to the subtlety with which certain senators developed their positions or to the variety of opinions espoused. Nor was it primarily a case of Asia-firsters rebelling against the higher priority given to Atlantic relations; there was an element of this traditional division in the conflict, but it was only one of several strands and was hardly the most important in what was an extremely wide-ranging debate.[14] Past as well as present policies were dragged into the controversy as some of the leading Republicans attempted to establish a comprehensive indictment of the Democratic record in conducting United States diplomacy. More significant than the obsession with the sell-out at Yalta and Potsdam though was the feeling – fairly widespread in the Senate – that the Atlantic Alliance had been established on certain premises which were now being either abandoned or drastically altered. It was on this point, in particular, that the concern with the past was juxtaposed with anxiety over the future. Perhaps more than anything else, in fact, the 'Great Debate' was over the future direction of United States foreign policy. Were the efforts to maintain the security and independence of Western Europe to be continued or abandoned? Was the containment of Soviet expansionism to remain a primary objective of United States policy? If so, what was the most efficient, effective and appropriate means of fulfilling it? And finally, what degree of discretion should the Executive have in determining policy and strategy? The answers to these questions were not entirely clear until the finale of the 'Great Debate' in early April 1951 – and even then they were not all final and conclusive. The main issues, however, emerged during the first few weeks of January, during which the troops to Europe decision was subjected to intense, extensive and often bitter debate in the Senate.

2 THE SENATE FLOOR DEBATE: 5 JANUARY – 23 JANUARY

The first formal challenge to Truman's decision came in the House of Representatives rather than the Senate. The day after the opening of the eighty-second Congress, Frederic Coudert, a Republican Representative from New York, introduced a resolution (H. J. Res. 9) requiring specific congressional approval before appropriations could be used to deploy US troops overseas.[15] This resolution, however, was to die in committee

and it was in the other chamber that the more serious assault on
the Administration's policy was to emerge. It began on 5
January, when Robert Taft delivered a 10 000 word speech on
foreign policy to the Senate which – even more than Hoover's
statement of 20 December – defined the agenda for debate.[16]

Although Taft is often dismissed as an unsophisticated and
indiscriminate critic, he perhaps more than any other Republican had a clear conception of an alternative foreign policy to
that pursued by Truman and Acheson. His views, of course,
were not developed overnight. Indeed, many of the concerns he
voiced and the prescriptions he offered in 1951 reflected long-
held and deeply-cherished principles, central to his political
philosophy. What he did during the 'Great Debate', though,
was to elaborate his ideas about foreign policy more fully, more
substantially and certainly more energetically than ever before.
These ideas stemmed in large part from his preoccupation with
domestic affairs. As one commentator has observed, Taft 'took
his stand against big government, a strong executive, and high
taxes; he stood for a strong legislature and the greatest degree
possible of personal and economic freedom, and he abhorred
government meddling of any kind unless it could be shown
unmistakably to protect freedom'.[17] With such a perspective it
was perhaps inevitable that Taft would assess the President's
initiatives in foreign policy according to their likely impact on
the relationship between the state and the individual. For the
Ohio Republican, foreign policy began and ended at home in a
very real sense: the external consequences of United States
policy were ultimately less important than the internal effects.
Thus, Taft's starting point for thinking about foreign policy
was not the kind of world he would like to see, but the kind of
America he wanted. The Truman Administration, in contrast,
began from the premise that the freedom of the United States
was inseparable from that of its European allies, that security
was indivisible for the members of the Atlantic Pact, and that
the obligations and responsibilities shouldered by the United
States from 1947 onwards had to be fulfilled regardless of how
costly and burdensome this proved. Taft was afraid that such
an attitude could result only in the destruction of liberty at
home and emphasised that if the Administration intended to
create a land army of three million men – as had been rumoured

– then the financial costs would be considerable, with high inflation the short-term result and the creation of a 'garrison state' the inevitable long-term consequence. As he put it in his speech of 5 January:

> The key to all the problems before this Congress lies in the size of our military budget. That determines the taxes to be levied. It determines the number of boys to be drafted. It is likely to determine whether we can maintain a reasonably free system and the value of our dollar, or whether we are to be weakened or choked by Government controls which inevitably tend to become more arbitrary and unreasonable.[18]

Aware that Soviet–American hostility was unlikely to be moderated for some time, Taft was anxious both about the effects of a consistently high level of defence expenditure on the size of the Federal budget, and about the impact of a bloated Federal budget on American society. It is arguable, in fact, that Taft in 1951 was not only protesting about the specific decision to send troops to Western Europe, but was engaged in a campaign to halt the development of what has since been described as the 'national security state' in which military requirements automatically take precedence over all other goals and values.

At the same time Taft made it clear that he was not advocating that the United States abandon the rest of the world; it merely had to fulfil its obligations in ways that did not overextend American power and were, therefore, more consistent with domestic needs. The strategy he advocated reflected this requirement: priority was to be given to the defence and protection of America, the 'Citadel' of the free world. This entailed an American attempt to obtain control of both sea and air. Taft was a strong advocate, therefore, of an expanded air force and argued that the strategic capabilities of the United States had been allowed to deteriorate as a result of the Administration's short-sightedness and its adherence to a 48-group air force in the face of congressional advocacy of a 70-group air force. An enlarged air force would have the capacity to destroy enemy air bases and thereby prevent an

attack on the American homeland; it would also act as a
deterrent in a way that ground forces could not. Indeed, Taft
saw considerable risk in a conventional build-up in Europe,
arguing that this augmentation of Western capabilities might
provoke the Soviet Union into an attack before the NATO force
was completed. The ground force strategy was not only destabilising but also futile, as it opposed the enemy where he had
his greatest strength. Taft did not go so far as to deny the need
for a land army, acknowledging its importance for the defence
of air bases, island protection and 'for such occasional exten-
sions of action into Europe or Asia as promise success in
selected areas. But it need not be anything like as large an army
as would be necessary for a land-war on the Continent of
Europe or the Continent of Asia.'[19] In certain respects then,
Taft's position appeared to be very close to that of Hoover, with
a similar emphasis on island nations as the most valuable and
least burdensome allies of the United States. Some commentators even refer to the Taft–Hoover proposals, treating the
stance of the Senator as indistinguishable from that adopted by
the former President. Such an analysis, however, is far too
indiscriminate, and ignores the nuance and the flexibility in
Taft's thinking which set him apart from the more extreme
views promulgated by Hoover and other Republican critics
such as Wherry of Nebraska.

Senator Taft's opposition to sending US troops to Europe
was based on his belief that such a course contravened the right
principles of United States foreign policy – but he recognised
that in practice compromises had to be made.[20] Because the
deployment of troops had been decided upon in the Executive
and discussed with the allies, expectations had been raised
about American support. For the United States now to reverse
course could only damage European morale and American
credibility. Thus Taft accepted the need for some US troops to
be despatched to Europe, with the proviso that their number be
strictly limited and the deployment merely temporary. He
made clear in his statement of 5 January that under certain
conditions he should not object to committing a limited
number of American divisions to work with the Europeans 'in
the spirit of the Atlantic Pact'.[21] He also emphasised though
that this was to be only a 'token force' and not a key point in the

overall military strategy of the United States – which was already contributing between one-sixth and one-seventh of the total military effort made by the alliance.[22] To contribute in addition 25 per cent of the armed forces was unreasonable. Taft was firm in his belief therefore that the United States should not assume the leadership in the 'formation of a great international army' or appoint an American Commander in Chief as this would only encourage European pressures on Washington to enlarge its presence.[23] Commitments, he felt, could develop a life of their own – and it was essential to prevent this happening. Important though these qualifications were, Taft's hostility to the troops idea was neither absolute nor unremitting. Nevertheless, this did not inhibit his continued criticism of Truman's decision. His challenge was aimed not at the execution of policy – which he recognised had to be pragmatic and expedient – but at the principles which provided the framework for action. And it was at this level of principle that the Senator was most dissatisfied and most critical. As a result, the President and Secretary of State tended to regard the Ohio Republican as far more intransigent and uncompromising than he really was. Their mistake was to focus on only one side of what was a dual analysis, for Taft, from the outset, was conducting his argument on two different levels: the level of what had to be done given the prevailing circumstances and the level of guiding principles for the future. The connections between these two levels were also important in Taft's thinking. He was afraid that actions taken for reasons of expediency might nevertheless endanger long-term principles. Thus it was vital to establish restrictions on the deployment of American ground forces to Western Europe; without such safeguards the commitment could all too easily take on a momentum of its own and the United States military presence prove more enduring and substantial than was either desirable or necessary.

If his concern with principle made Taft appear particularly intransigent, so too did his stance on the congressional role in foreign policy-making. A strong critic of bipartisanship, because of the way in which, he felt, it inhibited debate, the Ohio Senator was simultaneously one of the great champions of congressional prerogatives. He regarded the troops to Europe decision as a particularly blatant disregard of congressional rights and responsibilities. The North Atlantic Treaty had, after all, been approved by the Senate on the basis of certain understandings about its provisions and the obligations entailed therein. A policy was now being adopted which not only changed the basis of the Atlantic relationship but contravened explicit reassurances given by Administration officials during the debate over ratification of the treaty. As Taft put it: 'What is being talked about today is something entirely different from what was being considered when we adopted the Atlantic Pact.'[24] To make matters worse, this new policy was being formulated 'without consulting Congress or the American people'.[25] Not only was the President pursuing an ill-conceived course, therefore, but in doing so he was also acting unconstitutionally. Taft's view was that 'The President has no power to send American troops to fight in Europe in a war between the members of the Atlantic Pact and Soviet Russia. Without authority he involved us in the Korean War. Without authority he apparently is now attempting to adopt a similar policy in Europe.'[26]

In this speech of 5 January, Taft not only initiated the Senate's 'Great Debate', but did much to define the key issues and the agenda for discussion. One of the themes he identified was that of burden-sharing. What kind of military contribution was the United States intending to make to Atlantic defence? How did this compare with European efforts? Was the distribution of effort an equitable one? Indeed, was the United States to play a major or merely supporting role in providing for European security? A second theme concerned the optimum strategy for the United States. How should the American defence budget be allocated among the three services? Should priority be given to ground forces as contemplated in NSC-68 or to air power as the critics demanded? Indeed, were the precepts of NSC-68 – with its implication of a consistently high level of defence spending – to provide the framework for the future evolution of United States security policy? The third key element in the controversy was whether the conduct of American diplomacy and strategy was to be in the hands of the Executive alone or determined by executive–legislative cooperation and consultation. Underlying each of these issues was the vexed question of the relationship between the North

Atlantic Treaty and the troops to Europe decision. As suggested above, part of the difficulty was that the assumptions on which the treaty had been ratified appeared to have been either forgotten or deliberately cast aside. Despite earlier protestations to the contrary, the Administration now appeared willing to undertake defensive military tasks best left to its allies – and might, after all, allow American efforts to become a substitute for European endeavours rather than merely a supplement to them. This, of course, was related to the fact that the idea of a division of labour in which the United States provided the strategic air power and the Europeans the ground forces, had been abandoned in favour of an integrated force structure requiring the presence of American ground forces on the European continent. Furthermore, in spite of assurances that all the provisions of the treaty would be carried out in accordance with constitutional processes, and that nothing in the treaty would augment presidential power at the expense of the legislature, Congress was now being ignored.

Whether or not all this constituted a breach of faith, it certainly provoked suspicions that the Truman Administration was guilty of deceit and duplicity and had obtained Senate ratification of the North Atlantic Treaty under false pretences. Indeed, the burden of Taft's 5 January speech was that the President should adhere to the promises obtained in 1949: some parts of his statement were nothing if not reminiscent of the points made by Acheson and other officials in the treaty debate. In expressing his suspicions and anxieties about the new policy, the Ohio Republican seems to have struck a responsive chord among his party colleagues in the Senate. The debate following his remarks was intense; participation in it was extensive. In part, this may be attributable to the Administration's tardiness in presenting its legislative programme to Congress: with no other business requiring immediate action, the troops to Europe decision became the almost exclusive focus of attention. Shill has suggested, in fact, that this legislative vacuum contributed significantly to the enlargement of the debate by attracting the participation of senators who would normally have directed their energies elsewhere. As he put it: 'The *ad hoc* unregulated entry of Senators not sitting on the Foreign Relations Committee into the debate encouraged serious consideration of the Taft–Hoover criticisms by the entire Senate; in a more normal legislative environment the Senate would have been more inclined to rely on the recommendations of its subject matter experts.'[27] Certainly, the blunder by the Administration which provided such an opportunity for a comprehensive assault on its policies was not insignificant. Nevertheless, its importance should not be exaggerated. The opportunity would have mattered little had the incentives been lacking. The Senate was doing far more than filling a hole in its timetable: it was expressing its concern over the direction of United States policy and what many of its members saw as a lack of integrity by the Executive. It was not merely an unusual legislative situation that prompted the 'Great Debate' but an abnormal political situation in which the President suffered from what, well over a decade later, would become known as a 'credibility gap'. The tension between the two branches and the frustration that was widely felt over United States foreign policy provoked a debate that has rarely been matched either in its bitterness and vindictiveness or in the excessive claims made by the proponents of presidential power on the one side and the advocates of congressional prerogatives on the other. Indeed, the discussions in the Senate reflected the lack of consensus within the nation as a whole. Extensive press coverage was given to the debate and frequent attempts were made to assess the extent of support for Taft's position both within the Senate itself and among the public. In a sense this was appropriate, as the themes identified by Taft can be clearly discerned even through the plethora of contributions to what was a wide-ranging and unstructured debate.

On the strategic issue, it was the rebuttals to Taft's arguments which were perhaps most salient. They came primarily from Senator Douglas of Illinois, Tom Connally, the Chairman of the Foreign Relations Committee, and Wayne Morse of Oregon, a maverick senator whose analyses of foreign policy, although frequently idiosyncratic, were almost invariably perceptive. Douglas argued that Taft's concern about provoking the Russians by a conventional build-up in Europe could only keep the United States in a permanent position of inferiority – a concern also voiced by Connally.[28] Considerable emphasis was placed too on the strategic importance of Western Europe to the United States both because of its industrial potential and the availability of air bases from which it was possible to strike directly at the Soviet Union. Both bases and industry required protection, as their loss would be a severe blow to the United States. According to Connally, if the Soviet Union took over Western Europe then its industrial capacity would exceed that of the United States by an uncomfortable margin.[29] Reliance on atomic weapons and strategic air power might not suffice to prevent such an eventuality. Morse, in particular, emphasised that conventional forces and atomic weapons were complementary to one another rather than alternatives. Acknowledging that Taft's prescription was satisfactory and sensible in the short run, the Oregon Republican stressed that adequate conventional forces had to be provided by the time United States atomic superiority was lost.[30] The argument was essentially the same as that encapsulated in NSC-68. And like the authors of NSC-68, Taft's critics almost invariably accepted the need for a higher defence budget. Connally put the point most succinctly in his comment that internationalism could not be bought at the bargain counter, or a price tag placed on United States security.[31] On the whole, though, these strategic and budgetary arguments were neither novel nor distinctive: they paralleled many of the inter-service and inter-agency disputes which had been endemic in the late 1940s. Their importance should not be depreciated, however. The debate over strategy in 1951 was certainly a more *public* if not more intense controversy over the respective roles of atomic and conventional weapons than any that had taken place hitherto. As such it foreshadowed much of the political debate over American strategic doctrine and capabilities that was to take place throughout the 1950s and 1960s.

The burden-sharing arguments of 1951 were also important as a portent of things to come. Dissatisfaction with European efforts had been a major element in Hoover's statement; suspicion and anxiety about excessive European dependence on the United States was a central theme in Taft's argument. These suggestions that the allies were not playing their part and that America was making a disproportionate contribution to Atlantic security were not allowed to stand unchallenged. Truman in his message on the State of the Union, delivered on 8 January, emphasised the willingness of the allies to defend themselves, highlighted their strict systems of conscription and made clear that collectively their force goals were far higher than those of the United States.[32] The theme was pursued further by Senator Lodge of Massachusetts, who (although lacking the stature and influence of the Michigan senator) was probably the nearest thing to Vandenberg's successor as leader of and spokesman for the more internationalist Republicans. Acknowledging that in principle the United States 'should not commit a single additional soldier to Europe without an iron-clad agreement that the despatch of that soldier means an automatic commitment of a very much larger number of European soldiers', Lodge went on to suggest that in practice this was more or less what was happening.[33] West European reluctance to rearm had been greatly exaggerated. Indeed, his understanding at this stage was that a force of 60 divisions was contemplated for European defence, of which the United States would provide only 10 (i.e. $16\frac{1}{2}$ per cent of the total). This seemed to Lodge to be a reasonable arrangement which not only refuted the accusation against the allies but helped to demonstrate the absurdity of Hoover's argument: 'To say that we should not extend any help to Europe until they are completely strong and do not need our help is like telling a sick man that we will not give him his medicine until he has recovered. The test should not be that they are able to carry the load alone, it should be that they are making the greatest effort which they are capable of making.'[34]

In his 11 January speech Lodge seems merely to have been suggesting that there was a fair distribution of effort in the alliance, and does not seem to have been advocating a precise arithmetical ratio between the European and American contributions. Senator Knowland of California, a prominent figure in the China lobby, did exactly this however. Expressing American disappointment that 90 per cent of UN troops in Korea were American, Knowland went on to suggest that the Europeans must furnish the bulk of the ground forces for NATO, as the American contribution of sea and air power far exceeded that of the allies. At the same time, he recognised that the Europeans might need some encouragement in this task and advocated what he described as an 'incentive plan': 'For every six divisions raised and put into the field by our North

Atlantic allies we will send an additional division to Europe until we have a total of ten divisions there and they have sixty.'[35] There was, of course, a precedent for such a ratio. In 1949 Administration officials had justified the military aid programme on the grounds that the Europeans would spend six dollars on rebuilding their military capabilities for every dollar of aid given by the United States. Whether the ratio of six to one advocated by Knowland was chosen on the basis of this or was merely intended to reflect what seemed to be the position anyway is not clear. Whatever the case, the ratio idea was an important one which was to arouse considerable interest from both sides in the controversy. This was perhaps inevitable. The Hoover speech had evoked considerable sympathy from many senators who disagreed almost completely with the former President's recommendations, but were nevertheless concerned about the security efforts of the Europeans. On 6 January, the Associated Press conducted a poll among members of Congress on whether the Administration's policy of providing military assistance to Western Europe should be continued or Hoover's alternative be adopted.[36] Although the majority of those polled generally leaned towards the Truman policy there was a widespread feeling that the Europeans should be pressured into doing more. On the Republican side, Hickenlooper of Iowa, Martin of Pennsylvania and Flanders of Vermont were prominent among those who emphasised the need for demonstrations of European self-help. Such sentiments were not confined to Republican senators, however, and were expressed equally, if not more vigorously, by a number of Democrats, including Smathers and Holland of Florida, Chavez of New Mexico and Robertson of Virginia. Pastore of Rhode Island demanded a 'more enthusiastic effort on the part of others to help themselves' while Senator John Stennis of Mississippi made brutally explicit the view that the US commitment to Western Europe should be conditional on European self-help. As he put it, 'I favour carrying out the commitments of the Atlantic Pact, but unless European nations show quick and conclusive proof of their economic and military support . . . we would have nothing left to do but withdraw our assistance.'[37]

The ratio idea appeared to be the ideal means to assuage

such anxieties. As a result it was taken up not only by Knowland – who appears to have been genuinely and deeply aggrieved by the lack of European support for the United States in Korea – but also by senators who were relatively satisfied with the Europeans but who saw an arithmetical ratio as a tactical device which could help in building a consensus in favour of the 'troops to Europe' decision. Thus a variant of the proposal was advanced on 15 January by Senator Douglas who suggested somewhere between $3\frac{1}{2}$ and $4\frac{1}{2}$ European divisions for every one contributed by the United States, with the whole build-up linked to a definite timetable. In this scheme American troops would be merely an 'increment' to European forces, or what Douglas described as a 'contingent gift'.[38] The original notion of a six to one ratio also received support and was endorsed by such diverse senators as Flanders of Vermont and Johnston of Colorado.[39] To some extent such support was generated by the feeling that not enough was being done to harness European manpower, especially in states such as Spain and West Germany which were not members of the alliance but which had large and, as yet, untapped military potential. Although not as important as the ratio argument, the question of broadening the base of the European defence effort by enlarging the alliance was to recur throughout the Senate's debate.

So too was the constitutional issue. Indeed, it was this question which, formally at least, became the focus of the controversy when, on 8 January, Kenneth Wherry of Nebraska introduced a resolution which declared it the Sense of the Senate that 'no ground forces of the United States should be assigned to duty in the European area for the purposes of the North Atlantic Treaty pending the adoption of a policy with respect thereto by Congress'.[40] Although Wherry had been consistently hostile to the growing American involvement in Europe, the resolution he introduced was neutral on the substance of the troops to Europe decision itself, merely claiming congressional jurisdiction over that decision. Although Wherry's move was apparently made without prior consultation with Senator Taft, it was nevertheless a shrewd political initiative. Not only did it underline the salience of the troops issue – at a time when several other foreign policy issues were competing with it for attention – and thereby contribute to the 'enlargement and prolongation' of the debate, but by focusing on the congressional role in determining United States policy towards Western Europe rather than on the advantages or dangers of Truman's decision, the anti-troops faction appealed to the 'institutional pride' of the Senate and attracted a broader basis of support than would otherwise have been the case.[41] In particular the resolution, or some variant of it, gained the tacit approval of those senators who agreed with the President's policy but not the manner of its making. This became clear in the debate which followed the introduction of Wherry's proposal.

Much of the argument revolved around the respective rights, powers and authority of the President and Congress. Excessive claims of presidential authority were matched by equally exaggerated claims of congressional prerogative and control, with each side invoking constitutional theory, historical precedent and legal judgement in support of its position. The invocation of the constitution, however, served merely to sharpen and escalate the conflict. Corwin has pointed out that the constitution invites struggle over the conduct of foreign policy.[42] This is partly because power is shared among separate institutions, but also because the grant of powers was itself imprecise, leaving the propriety of certain actions to be inferred or assumed by one branch and accepted, challenged or rejected by the other. An equally important effect of the constitution is that it intensifies political conflict: when constitutional principle is introduced into a controversy, the issue is transformed into a struggle of authority, making compromise all the more difficult. Thus it was perhaps inevitable that as soon as the debate turned to the legitimacy (as opposed to the wisdom) of the President's troops to Europe decision, extreme positions were rapidly formalised by both sides.

It was not merely a case of the President versus Congress though. Although constitutional struggles are often cast in terms of a unified Executive versus a unified legislature, this is a considerable oversimplification. On the congressional side at least, unanimity is rare. The President, far from facing a monolithic opposition, can generally count upon vocal, articulate and enthusiastic supporters on Capitol Hill. So it was in the troops debate. In a press conference on 11 January, Truman devoted considerable time to the constitutional question, and emphasised that in sending troops to Western Europe he was acting well within the scope of the President's authority as Commander in Chief of the Armed Forces. Although he was prepared to consult Congress, through its major foreign policy committees, this was not mandatory but a matter of courtesy.[43] Strong support for the President's stance came from several senators, most notably Tom Connally. In fact, Connally's words on the subject were virtually identical to those used by Truman himself. As he put it: 'The scope of the authority of the President as Commander in Chief to send the armed forces to any place required by the security interests of the United States has often been questioned, but never denied by authoritative opinion.'[44] The abrasive Chairman of the Foreign Relations Committee took considerable pleasure in quoting the judgement of Robert Taft's father, former Chief Justice William Howard Taft, in support of his position.[45] Other senators who upheld the President's right to deploy forces to Western Europe were Senator Lodge, who warned Congress against trying to act as a General Staff, and (particularly noteworthy in view of his different position in the later 1960s) Senator Fulbright, who spoke out strongly against any attempt to circumscribe presidential power.[46]

At the opposite extreme to Connally and his supporters was Senator Kem of Missouri, a bitter opponent of Truman, who claimed that in deciding to send troops to Europe, the President (as with the Korean involvement) had not only arrogated to himself powers that were not constitutionally his, but had moved the United States towards a military dictatorship.[47] Wherry, although somewhat more circumspect in his language, took a very similar position, arguing that there was neither constitutional authority nor precedent to support the President's announcement that he was going to send armed forces to North Atlantic Treaty countries to be integrated into a North Atlantic Treaty army. Nor was there anything in the pact itself which empowered the President to take such action. As the Nebraska Senator went on: 'Plainly the President is seeking to implement the North Atlantic Treaty by indirection, under assumed authority of the Constitution, which he cannot do alone under the North Atlantic Treaty . . . that is sheer usurption of Congressional power by the President.'[48] Yet for Wherry the argument was not strictly, and perhaps not even primarily, a constitutional one. It was also about the assurances that had been given in 1949 about the role of Congress in implementing the treaty, especially Article 3 dealing with self-help and mutual aid. This emerged very clearly during a colloquy on the Senate floor with Leverett Saltonstall following Wherry's speech of 16 January. Saltonstall, in an attempt to clarify the intent of Resolution 8, asked: 'Do I correctly understand that the purpose of the Senator's resolution is simply that before there is an extension of our obligations under Article 3 – in other words, in addition to sending arms, to send troops – Congress should state its decision with reference to that policy under Article 3.'[49] Wherry, after acknowledging the accuracy of this interpretation, suggested that many members of the Senate had voted for the Atlantic Pact 'because of the explanation that it referred to arms and not to men'.[50] The Wherry critique, therefore, was a two-pronged one: it dealt with both the constitutional question *and* the assurances and understanding that had helped to elicit Senate consent to the ratification of the North Atlantic Treaty.

On this latter point, Wherry's position overlapped with that of a third and more conciliatory group which gradually emerged as a major influence on the course of the debate. Although members of this group differed from the Nebraskan senator in that they generally supported the troops to Europe decision and, on balance recognised the President's authority to make it, they nevertheless agreed with the Republican Minority Leader about the need for congressional participation prior to the decision being implemented. Among those who adopted this stance were several Republican senators including Lodge, Ives, Morse and (with more reservations about the President's authority) Millikin and Mundt, all of whom argued that in the interests of national unity the President should bring Congress into the policy-making process. Only then would it be possible to 'move forward as a team'.[51] Perhaps the two most important members of this developing, but loose and tacit, coalition were two Democratic senators, George of Georgia and Douglas of Illinois, the former representing the Southern conservative wing of the party and the latter typifying the more liberal Northern Democrats. Douglas made his position clear in a speech on the Senate floor on 15 January. After acknowledging that in strict constitutional terms the President had the power to send forces abroad, he emphasised that the issue was 'too important and the dangers to our survival too great . . . for the Executive to act without positive approval of Congress'.[52] Such approval was all the more necessary because of Acheson's statement in the hearing before the Foreign Relations Committee on the North Atlantic Treaty in which the Secretary denied any intention of sending US troops to Europe. As Douglas put it:

> The Senate ratified that Treaty after a categorical pledge had been given by the Secretary of State that it was not even expected that we would send a substantial number of troops to Western Europe prior to actual attack. Since that pledge was at least one of the considerations which led many Senators to vote for it, it would not be proper in my judgement, for the Administration now to try to put the argument into effect by purely Executive action upon the narrow grounds of its constitutional powers. It would be the path of honour for the Administration to submit the question of approving the Brussels Agreement to the Senate and possibly the House.[53]

The statement by George was made outside the Senate, but arrived at very similar conclusions. It reflected what seems to have been a deep-rooted ambivalence in the Georgian senator's approach. As Malcolm Jewell has pointed out: 'the compromising stand that George took on collective security issues seemed to reflect another conflict in his mind: that between the foreign responsibilities of the United States and the constitutional responsibilities of Congress.'[54] Yet this independent and cautious approach to foreign policy problems only added to his influence within the Senate. A member of the Upper Chamber since 1922, George was a preeminent figure among the Southern Democrats. Thus when both he and Douglas advocated a congressional role in determining the American military posture in Europe, the Administration was almost bound to take heed. It is often the case in the Senate that a studied unpredictability and moderation go hand in hand with power and influence. Because Wherry's opposition, like that of Taft's, was predictable, it could all the more easily be dismissed as Republican trouble-making. But when key Democratic senators began to beat a variant of the same drum, somewhat more respect had to be accorded to Senate opposition. Indeed, it is little exaggeration to suggest that the separate interventions of George and Douglas transformed the issue from a partisan conflict into a genuine institutional struggle.

It was this change, together with the growing support for the position expounded by members of the middle group, which seems to have prompted the Administration and its allies in the Senate to adopt a slightly more conciliatory position, if not on the Wherry Resolution itself, at least on the general question of congressional participation. .

In his press conference of 18 January President Truman made it clear that he would welcome a positive resolution endorsing his policy.[55] In the meantime Connally had come to accept the expediency of such a resolution and had placed his influence behind Majority Leader McFarland who had announced that he would attempt to have the Wherry Resolution referred to the Foreign Relations Committee.[56] This decision was supported too by the Democratic Policy Committee which provided an ideal forum whereby the President's allies in the Senate could coordinate their legislative tactics.[57]

The Republican Policy Committee seems to have fulfilled a similar function – albeit with much greater difficulty. Indeed, the Committee as such was too divided to take a firm and unequivocal stance on the Wherry Resolution. Taft and Millikin though were successful in persuading Wherry that a straight vote on the resolution would be defeated and that therefore it would be expedient to accept referral to Committee.[58] The danger with this, of course, was that the resolution might be allowed to languish in the Foreign Relations Committee. To prevent this, the Republican leaders tried to hammer out a compromise with their Democratic counterparts. Taft, in particular, demanded assurances that the Wherry Resolution or some variant of it would be voted out of the committee within a reasonable time. Connally remained intransigent though and refused to accept detailed instructions as to what should be done with the resolution. Nevertheless, it was agreed on 22 January that the Committee on Armed Services should combine with Foreign Relations to examine the resolution. On 23 January, Wherry once again attempted to get assurances about committee action on his resolution. Beyond accepting that something would be done fairly promptly, however, Connally remained noncommittal, emphasising that the two committees had total discretion in determining the fate of the proposal. Despite this, Wherry agreed to the unanimous request that an amended version of his resolution be referred – and the vote which many observers had expected was averted.

This outcome was generally interpreted as a major tactical victory for the President. Connally described the events of 22 January as a 'triumph' because he had not 'conceded a thing which could tie the hands of the Committees'.[59] Yet it was not quite so clear-cut. Wherry too claimed that he had obtained at least part of what he wanted: the involvement of the Committee on Armed Services was 'the biggest thing because plans of the Foreign Relations Committee to kill it are now blocked'.[60] And to a degree he was right: his apparent capitulation had helped to ensure that the issue remained a live one. At the same time, the *initiative* had been conceded to the Administration supporters in the Senate. The Democratic leadership was now in a position where it could 'attempt to shift the focus of attention away from the issue of the President's constitutional powers . . . and toward the Congress and its response to the President's request for support of his foreign policy'.[61] Thus, on 24 January, the Democratic Policy Committee formally agreed to urge the two committees to design an 'affirmative' resolution approving the President's plan.[62]

The events of 22 January, therefore, marked the end of the period in which the Administration – partly through circumstances and partly through its own ineptitude – had been on the defensive. The initial attempt to defend its action on strict constitutional grounds had rebounded and, somewhat belatedly, the President had adopted a more conciliatory position regarding congressional sanctioning of his decision. The task now was to convince a substantial majority of senators of the wisdom of sending troops to Europe and thereby generate the support necessary for the approval of an affirmative resolution.

The efforts that were made in this direction provide the main theme for the second phase of the Senate's 'Great Debate'.

3   THE ADMINISTRATION OFFENSIVE: EISENHOWER'S TESTIMONY AND THE OPEN HEARINGS

The Administration's attempt to defuse the troop controversy rested in large part upon General Eisenhower who had been sent to Europe a few weeks earlier on a fact-finding mission. The importance attached to this visit by the Executive and its supporters in the Senate had been underlined early in the debate when Democratic Majority Leader McFarland had appealed to the members to avoid rash statements or action on the troops issue, until Eisenhower returned with the facts. It was further emphasised by the arrangements which were made for the general's report – arrangements which were obviously designed to obtain maximum congressional and public exposure for the general and thereby – it was hoped – strengthen the Administration's case. On the morning of 1 February, Eisenhower addressed a Joint Session of both Houses in the Library of Congress; in the afternoon he appeared before the members of the Senate Armed Services and Foreign Relations Committee. The following day General Eisenhower testified before the House Committees on Foreign Affairs and Armed Services and appeared before the Senate Subcommittee on Preparedness.[63]

In his public statement before the Congress, Eisenhower focused on several key points. As well as refuting the charges that had been made by Taft to the effect that a military build-up in Europe was liable to provoke the Soviet Union, he emphasised the need for the United States to provide the leadership which would both rejuvenate West European morale and inspire Western Europe by example.[64] While acknowledging the existence of 'pessimism bordering on defeatism' in Europe, Eisenhower also claimed to have found in countries like France, Belgium, Holland, Denmark and Norway, evidence of a determination to resist any aggression. In Norway, in fact, the prevailing attitude was that 'resistance to the point of destruction' was preferable to subjugation.[65] Much still depended though upon the United States. The potential could only be exploited if Washington acted decisively. Afraid that the concern over burden-sharing would prevent this, Eisenhower issued a warning: 'We cannot ... afford to look over our shoulders with a suspicious thought that our friend is not doing as much as we are. We must by example inspire and insist and get everybody to do his maximum. The fullness of his performance will be limited by his capacity only.'[66] Soon afterwards, however, he appeared to acknowledge the legitimacy of such suspicions in an apparent recommendation that 'the transfer of certain of our units should be *in direct ratio to what Europe is doing* so that we know that we are all going forward together, and no one is suspicious of the other'.[67] At first sight this appeared to be a tacit endorsement of the demands for an arithmetical ratio between American and European force contentions. The comment, however, was made when Eisenhower was discussing the equipment needs of the Europeans, which suggests that he was referring primarily to the transfer of equipment and not men. This is certainly the impression given in Eisenhower's testimony before the Senate Foreign Relations and Armed Services Committees (testimony which was given in executive session but released in March 1951 with the transcript of the public hearings) when he made a sustained attempt to discredit the idea of an arithmetical ratio as too crude, inflexible and indiscriminate to meet the needs of the situation.[68] At the same time, Eisenhower tried to defuse the issue by reassuring those senators concerned that the United States would end up – as in Korea – carrying 90 per cent of the load, that he saw a major part of his task as being to ensure that the Europeans made the maximum effort possible.

Perhaps even more revealing of Eisenhower's aims was an exchange with Senator Smith of New Jersey during which the general made clear that he regarded the US troop deployment to Europe as, essentially, an interim measure. As Smith put it:

You did contemplate, I think, when I spoke to you before you left, the possibility of starting with a certain level of force, and by degrees that could be reduced so far as we were concerned as they took over their own defence in their own spirit and their own desire to defend themselves, along the line of our Marshall-plan aid, which started rather large and came down to zero. I don't know whether you would get to zero in this.[69]

Eisenhower's reply was brief but to the point: 'I don't know whether you would get to zero but that would be the objective in any planning in which I took part.'[70] This idea was reaffirmed shortly afterwards when the general, in response to the probing of Senator Byrd, made clear once again that he saw the American role as being to build up European confidence and to supply 'the needed mobile active strength *pending the time* that the European nations can build up their own defence forces'.[71] That the objective was to reach a position where Europe could, and would, provide for the major part of its own defence was further emphasised in Eisenhower's response to Wherry, who was sitting on the committees as an *ex officio* member.[72]

Despite such reassurances, the general's testimony had less of an impact than the Administration had either hoped or anticipated. The reaction among senators was very mixed. Democrats such as Humphrey (Minn), Benton (Conn) and Sparkman (Ala) were more positive about the President's programme after Eisenhower's statement than they had been before.[73] Others remained sceptical; some were even scathing. Malone of Nevada, a confirmed anti-Europeanist, dismissed Eisenhower's arguments as 'propaganda for the preconcieved decision of the State Department to send our boys to make up a Maginot Line in Europe'.[74] Other Republican critics such as Capehart (Ind), Cain (Wash) and Kem (Mo) expressed disappointment at what they regarded as presentations determined primarily by political considerations and leaving many questions unanswered.[75] Indeed, it appears that by this time positions had become so entrenched that although Eisenhower's arguments further convinced those who were already leaning in favour of the troop deployment, they failed to convert those who had serious doubts about the project. Furthermore, they did nothing to erode the feeling that for the sake of national unity and political propriety, Congress should play a part in determining American security policy in Europe. And perhaps

most important, they did nothing to reassure Robert Taft that
the United States would not end up carrying an inordinate
share of the common burden.

The Ohio senator in fact emphasised that he had been
unimpressed by Eisenhower's report, complaining that it had
made 'this whole plan more hazy and indefinite and uncertain
in outline than it was before his return'.[76] He remained unclear
– and anxious – as to the scale of the project or the American
contribution to it. Vague reassurances by Eisenhower were no
substitute for a 'binding contract' with or 'definite promises'
from the allies that they would provide most of the soldiers.[77]
After all, Taft argued, 'Western Europe ... has more people in
it than we have in the United States and is completely able to
defend itself if we furnish the armament and it desires to do
so.'[78] Despite this Taft adhered to his earlier position that a
limited American troop deployment was acceptable. He
warned, however, that an initial commitment of ground forces
might be the start of an incremental and irreversible process
which would ultimately lead to a much larger American presence in Europe. It was to prevent this that, in a Senate speech
on 8 February, Taft strongly endorsed the idea of an arithmetical ratio.[79] He had first mooted the idea of some sort of
limitation on 26 January, but had been uncertain as to the form
it should take.[80] This uncertainty or indecision was now dispel-
led as Taft advocated a dual restriction, combining a 1 : 9 ratio
of American to European forces with a proposal that no more
than 20 per cent of America's total land forces and 10 per cent of
the air force be stationed on the European continent.[81]

Taft's initiative was important for several reasons. In the
first place, as Shill has pointed out, it was 'the first concrete
alternative to an absolute Congressional veto offered by the
anti-troops faction'.[82] Secondly, it symbolised in a practical
way what Taft had long been emphasising – that his opposition
to the troop decision was far from absolute. Furthermore, it
raised a possibility of a legislative compromise centred on a
resolution which supported Truman's decision but also contained some sort of restriction along the lines Taft was advocating. As discussed above, both Democrats and Republicans who
supported the Administration's decision had – prior to

Eisenhower's testimony at least – spoken in favour of such a ratio. The chances of an agreement appeared, in some ways, to be enhanced when Taft made another address in which, while maintaining his position on percentages, he moved from a 1 : 9 ratio to a 1 : 6.[83] There were still formidable difficulties in the way of a consensus on this. Taft's explicit adoption of the ratio idea, so soon after Eisenhower had condemned it, suggested continued confrontation rather than conciliation. Taft's enthusiastic endorsement of Hoover's speech of 9 February conveyed the same impression – especially as the former President had recommended not only that his policy of sending American divisions to Europe be replaced by 'watchful waiting' until the Europeans resolved their disunities and created a more formidable military force but also that Congress recapture its constitutional authority over starting wars through the power of the purse.[84] This suggests, in fact, that there were conflicting pressures upon the Ohio senator: militating against his tendency to compromise (about the practice although not the principles of foreign policy) seems to have been the desire not to deviate too far from the position of his more conservative colleagues who remained singularly unimpressed by Eisenhower's arguments.

Indeed , it was because Eisenhower's statements had not had the desired effect, that the Democratic Policy Committee, between 6 and 9 February, decided to hold hearings on the troops issue.[85] This was a tacit admission that the Senate was still unwilling to support a resolution affirming Truman's policy. The announcement of the hearings, however, brought no respite in the debate. Although Republicans outside the Senate such as Dewey and John Sherman Cooper (who had just returned from a fact-finding tour of Europe) publicly supported the troops proposal, the effect of this was offset when on 14 February, 120 or so House Republicans (together with a few disaffected Democrats) led by Representative Laurence Smith of Wisconsin, issued a 'Declaration of Policy' supporting the principles of the Wherry Resolution and highly critical of the Democratic Administration's foreign policy.[86] Thus, as the hearings began, the outcome of the 'Great Debate' remained uncertain. What was clear, however, was that unless the second stage of the Administration's offensive was more successful than the first, the troops to Europe decision might not receive the endorsement of a majority of the Senate.

The joint hearings held before the Foreign Relations and Armed Services Committees were intended by the Chairman, Senator Connally, to provide a platform from which the Truman Administration could explain and justify its troops to Europe decision and thereby, it was hoped, defuse the issue or, at a minimum, mobilise additional support in the Senate. Thus, although Senator Wherry submitted a list of possible witnesses to appear before the committees, Connally was at first reluctant to accept many of the suggestions, arguing that they would prove repetitious and time-consuming.[87] It was only under pressure from the Republican members of the committees that the hearings were broadened to include avowed opponents of the decision to send troops to Europe as well as its proponents.[88] The result was a complex set of hearings stretching over 19 sessions held on 12 separate days and in which 41 individuals testified.[89] Even so, the proceedings were structured in a way designed to maximise the impact of those witnesses arguing in favour of the President's position and against the Wherry Resolution. The initial stages of the hearings were in fact dominated by a parade of Administration spokesmen who outlined at length the underlying rationale for the decision to send United States troops to Europe. The final witness, General Clay, although not formally an Administration spokesman, was certainly in sympathy with the decision and presented a powerful and effective statement in its favour. Although the timing of Clay's appearance may have been fortuitous, it seems more likely that it was a calculated attempt to ensure that the Executive not only had the final word but had an opportunity to refute arguments and discredit suggestions made by its critics in the preceding sessions.[90]

Much of the Administration's case for troops to Europe was familiar from the earlier floor debate. It was, however, presented more fully, more systematically and more energetically than ever before. In some respects, of course, it was merely an extension of the earlier arguments for underwriting European security, and Acheson in particular reiterated the importance of an independent Western Europe to United States security and prosperity. As he put it,

> Outside of our own country, free Europe has the greatest number of scientists, the greatest industrial production and the largest pool of skilled manpower in the world. Its resources in coal, steel and electric power are enormous. It has a tremendous ship-building capacity, essential to control of the seas. Through its overseas connections it has access to a vast supply of raw materials which are absolutely vital to American industry.[91]

It was vital, therefore, to ensure that Western Europe remained friendly to the United States and to deny its resources to the Soviet Union. Whereas in 1949 it was thought that these objectives could be achieved through a combination of political guarantee and military assistance, they now required the deployment of US troops to the European continent. There were several reasons for this. In the first place, European morale had been severely shaken by events in Korea and a substantial American military presence would not only restore confidence but encourage the allies to undertake the large-scale rearmament efforts that were necessary for their own and American security. The situation demanded the kind of generous leadership from the United States in military affairs that it had earlier displayed to such good effect in relation to the economic problems of Western Europe.[92] If the Atlantic Pact nations were going to create a genuine capacity for collective defence, though, it would have to be leadership by example. This did not mean matching the Soviet Union division for division, merely creating and deploying enough forces to slow down, if not halt, any assault and provide an opportunity for American air power to destroy the Soviet capacity to prosecute the war any further. That air power and atomic weapons would ultimately prove decisive in any war was not disputed, it was merely felt that their effect would not be immediate – and that in the meantime it would be necessary to prevent the occupation and subsequent liberation of Western Europe.[93] An additional advantage of more substantial conventional forces was that they would be able to deal with any satellite aggression of the kind that had taken place in Korea: their very existence would do much to forestall such a contingency, thus contributing to deterrence as well as defence. Indeed, deterrence and defence were regarded as complementary and although the emphasis was on conventional forces for defensive war-fighting purposes in the short term, in the long run they were equally important for deterrence. Acheson in particular emphasised this point: reiterating both the logic of NSC-68 and the argument used on the Senate floor by Wayne Morse of Oregon, he suggested that it was essential 'to build the balanced collective forces in Western Europe that will continue to deter aggression long after our atomic advantage has been diminished'.[94] All this, of course, was in the interests of the United States as much as that of Western Europe. In fact, if American air power was to have maximum effect in any future conflict with the Soviet Union, then bases in Western Europe were essential – and these bases had to be protected by ground forces. The military and political arguments were reinforced by an economic one in an attempt to challenge one of the basic premises of fiscal conservatives like Taft: although the deployment of US troops to Europe would involve substantive expense, it would still be less than the costs of defence in Fortress America.

Naturally, not all these arguments were fully accepted by the members of the two committees – and some were flatly contradicted by other witnesses. Nevertheless, the Administration's case was a formidable one, and all the more so for being presented with such apparent unanimity, particularly by the Joint Chiefs of Staff (JCS).[95] Indeed, the testimony of the members of the JCS had an impact beyond the substantive arguments they deployed: with the prestige and popularity of both the President and the Secretary of State at a low ebb, they gave the decision a certain authoritativeness, legitimacy and non-partisan character which would otherwise have been lacking. Furthermore, 'coming in the midst of a long inter-service conflict over strategic roles, their public unity placed Congressional advocates of primary reliance on air and sea power in the disadvantageous position of arguing against the top military experts from all three branches of service on a military issue'.[96] The Administration's position was strengthened further when

General Curtis Le May, head of Strategic Air Command and one of Senator Wherry's witnesses, made it clear that, although he believed higher priority should be given to the development of air power, he concurred in the judgement of the Joint Chiefs and supported unequivocally, albeit not enthusiastically the decision to send US troops to Europe.[97] Thus, although Senator Wherry – who was not a member of either committee but was allowed to participate in the questioning of witnesses – attempted to establish a clear dichotomy between strategic bombing and a land army approach, he did not succeed. The Administration argued that the troop deployment in Europe complemented and strengthened the strategic bombing role rather than detracted from it and although Wherry, together with Herbert Hoover and Major Alexander de Seversky, a noted advocate of air power, continued to stress that the two approaches were mutually exclusive, the former view appeared to be more judicious and therefore more compelling.[98]

A major reason for this was the Administration's disclosure that the number of troops to be sent to Europe was strictly limited and certainly well below the levels suggested by many of the critics. Although Taft had apparently been informed of the figure some time earlier, the debate had not abated. Consequently, on the opening day of the hearings Secretary of Defense Marshall revealed that four United States divisions were to be sent to Europe to join the two already there.[99] In view of the speculation and the wildly exaggerated rumours that were being circulated, the announcement was intended to reassure members of Congress that the Administration's policy was a sober and responsible one. Senator Richard Russell, Chairman of the Committee on Armed Services certainly regarded it as such and claimed that it was fully in accordance with any of the quota, ratio or percentage formulas which had been proposed.[100] Russell also suggested to the Secretary of Defense that had the figure been released earlier 'this whole proposition might have been circumscribed and limited'.[101] The Administration, of course, hoped that even at this stage it would serve to defuse the controversy. Such hopes, however, were doomed to disappointment, partly because the controversy had taken on its own momentum within the legislature, partly because it was a constitutional as well as a policy dispute, and partly because, as the testimony of Taft and Wherry was to reveal, the four divisions figure did not allay fears that this might be merely the first instalment of what could all too easily develop into a much larger contingent.[102]

Thus, the claim that Marshall's disclosure 'took much of the heat out of the great debate' and 'left the conservative Republicans with an empty issue' seems to be somewhat exaggerated.[103] Had it succeeded in doing this, then the question of a ratio between the American and European contributions would have been shelved. As it was (Senator Russell's comment notwithstanding), the ratio issue remained very much alive and surfaced repeatedly during hearings which were often as revealing about the positions of the committee members as about the stance of the witnesses themselves. Senator Knowland was particularly persistent in his probing as to the merits of such a ratio, while executive branch officials and their supporters were at great pains to suggest that any restriction of this kind was undesirable.[104] General Clay, for example, argued that it would demonstrate a lack of faith in the allies and be such a blow to European morale that it would undo much of the good that had already come from the decision to send troops.[105] Other witnesses insisted that a ratio would, on the one hand, give the Soviet Union a firm basis on which to plan, and on the other hand deprive United States planners of the flexibility they required. This insistence that formal limitations were inadvisable, however, rebounded against the Administration as it seemed to confirm the suspicions of those who were worried that the four divisions were not the end of the matter. Consequently, there was considerable sympathy for those witnesses who insisted on the desirability of Congress establishing an arithmetical ratio between the American contingent and the number of allied divisions. Representative John Kennedy, for example, who – unlike his father Joseph Kennedy – acknowledged the need for the United States to send troops to Europe, nevertheless insisted that the United States should not accept complete responsibility for the land defence of Western Europe. As a safeguard against this a ratio of one American division to six European divisions was appropriate.[106] Advocating the deployment of the six divisions the Administration was currently planning on, Kennedy argued that the United States should not go beyond this until the Europeans had placed 36 divisions under Eisenhower's command, and that for every one additional division sent afterwards the Europeans should raise six. Taft too paid considerable attention to the ratio idea and although it has been argued that this was primarily for tactical reasons, in fact it seems to have been central to his approach. Afraid of an open-ended commitment to European defence – with its adverse implications for the economy and society of the United States – Taft saw the establishment of some kind of ratio as an essential safeguard which would serve both to limit the American contribution and to guarantee genuine European efforts to share the defence burden. Although Taft reverted back to the more stringent one to nine formula in his appearance before the committees, the principle was much more important than the precise arithmetic.[107]

The idea that the Europeans should provide by far the greater bulk of the ground forces under Eisenhower's command was, of course, a sentiment widely shared by those senators conducting the investigation. In part, the demand was that the existing pact members devote more of their resources to defence. Equally important was that the Europeans should make more fruitful use of the available manpower and a great deal of interest was shown throughout the hearings in the possibility of bringing Turkey, Greece, Spain and even Yugoslavia into the alliance. There was also considerable resentment and frustration over the problems of West German rearmament and the failure to exploit more fully and rapidly the Federal Republic's military potential. Even senators relatively sympathetic to Administration policy complained that divisions within Europe were hindering the common defence effort.[108] The strongest criticism, however, came from Hoover who repeated his opposition to sending any American forces until the Europeans displayed – as they had not yet done – clear evidence of the will both to resolve their own differences and to resist Soviet aggression.[109] Although Hoover's testimony evoked considerable sympathy, its impact on the committee members seems to have been offset by General Clay's statement with its vivid contrast between conditions in Western Europe in 1947 and the much more favourable conditions currently prevailing. Clay's arguments gained added authority from the acknowledgement

by the Senate panel that he was more experienced in, and
knowledgeable about, European affairs than any other witness.
Nevertheless, distrust of the European allies and scepticism
about their willingness genuinely to share burdens remained
strong – as did the belief that the commitment should be
conditional upon substantial evidence of West European self-
help.

Although Administration spokesmen may have had some
success in alleviating anxieties about the wisdom of the troops
to Europe decision, therefore, they did not manage to dispel
doubts about European reliability. Nor did they do much to
change the minds of those members already convinced that a
congressional role in the decision was essential. Indeed, several
senators distinguished very explicitly between their position on
the substantive issue – where they supported the Administration's policy – and their stance on the constitutional question –
where they approved the intent of the Wherry Resolution.[110]
The Administration's difficulties regarding the congressional
role were intensified by the inevitable exhanges between
Senator Hickenlooper and Secretary Acheson regarding the
assurances given to the Foreign Relations Committee and to
Hickenlooper in particular in 1949. The senator's case rested
on the argument that 'the North Atlantic Pact proposition was
sold to a great many members of Congress on the idea that prior
to aggression we would not be called upon to supplement the
land armies of Western Europe by large numbers of troops'.[111]
Acheson's reply, that his response to Hickenlooper in the
hearings on the treaty had been intended not as a prediction
but merely as a denial that there was any obligation under
Article 3 to provide troops, was less than satisfactory.[112] Equally troublesome was his claim that no commitment had been
made by the United States at the Brussels meeting of the North
Atlantic Council in December 1950. The Secretary's arguments were disingenuous at best and it is all the more difficult,
therefore, to understand some of the criticisms which have been
levelled at the Iowa senator. McLellan in particular has
claimed that 'to a man such as Hickenlooper, accustomed to
viewing international affairs as isolated incidents, each compartmentalised and divorced from the other, Acheson's statement at the time of the North Atlantic Treaty hearings ap-

peared as an irrevocable policy statement governing for all
future time the engagement of American troops in Europe'.[113]
This is to miss the point, however. Hickenlooper did not deny
that changed conditions required modifications in American
policy towards Western Europe. But the treaty commitment
had been accepted by the Senate on the basis of very explicit
assumptions and understandings. Now that the nature and
form of the commitment had been transformed, it was incumbent upon the Executive to seek congressional approval for its
departure. If Hickenlooper was unrealistic, therefore, it was
less in ignoring the requirements of international politics than
in his apparent expectation that consultation procedures akin
to those followed during the halcyon days of bipartisanship
would be initiated by an Administration increasingly subjected
to bitter partisan criticism. Yet even this expectation was not
unreasonable: American policy towards Europe since 1947 had
been based on both a bipartisan consensus (albeit a limited and
incomplete one) and extensive (although sometimes strained)
cooperation between the Executive and Congress. Past practice
as well as past promises placed the Administration under an
obligation to bring Congress into the policy-making process.
Merely to affirm presidential authority to send troops overseas
was not only no substitute for genuine consultation, but suggested that Administration spokesmen had been guilty of a
sleight of hand. This is not to argue that in 1949 the Administration had been planning to send troops to Europe, but had
concealed its intentions from Congress – clearly at the time of
treaty ratification there was *no* intention of making such a troop
commitment. But it is to argue that the reassurances about
maintaining the constitutional balance and assuring a congressional role in implementing the treaty were now revealed as
virtually meaningless. Thus, it is hardly surprising that the
criticisms made by Hickenlooper in the early part of the
proceedings were echoed later in the hearings both by other
members of the committees and by some of the witnesses, most
notably Taft and Wherry. Taft's testimony was particularly
interesting because he did not challenge the President's authority to send troops to Europe *per se*, but focused instead on the
assignment of US troops to an international army. Not only
was this action wholly without precedent, but it involved

agreement with other nations and therefore had the dignity and virtual status of a treaty.[114] This was another reason why congressional approval was mandatory.

Arguments such as those of Taft and Hickenlooper had of course been articulated prior to the hearings. They seem to have been strengthened during the course of the investigation, however, and although the Administration may have gained some support for the substance of its policy, this was probably offset by the increased salience of the constitutional issue which favoured Senator Wherry. This does not mean that the hearings were a major setback for the Administration, but they had certainly not been an unqualified success, in that Wherry had succeeded in keeping the controversy alive. Nevertheless, the President and his supporters must have drawn some comfort from the increasingly pronounced division within the Republican Party. The split, which had been evident in the Senate throughout the later 1940s, was highlighted by the testimony of Taft, Hoover and Wherry on the one hand and the evidence offered by other prominent Republicans such as Harold Stassen, Governor Dewey and John Sherman Cooper on the other. Stassen and Dewey in fact went further than many Democrats in their support for both the President's decision and his authority to make it. It was not surprising, therefore, that some of the most intense and bitter exchanges of the hearings were those between Wherry and Dewey, with Dewey claiming that proponents of the Wherry Resolution represented the last but still powerful bastion of isolationism in the United States. The New York Governor further suggested that passage of the resolution would not only signal that the United States had abandoned its role in Western Europe but would 'invite imperial communism to move into the vacuum thereby created'.[115] Such arguments enraged Wherry who claimed that Dewey was portraying Senate Resolution 8 as a substantive one, when it was in fact only procedural. Indeed, in his own testimony Wherry attempted at some length to refute the arguments of his party colleague. Less obvious than this polarisation of opinion within the Republican Party, but ultimately perhaps of even greater significance, were the subtle differences of emphasis between Republican opponents of the troops to Europe decision. Whereas Hoover wanted firm and visible evidence of

European efforts *before* sending troops, for example, Taft was content merely to know what the allies were committed to doing by way of self-help. Thus the hearings revealed that the Administration faced a Republican Party which was not only deeply divided, but in which even the avowed opponents of the troops decisions did not fully agree.

For all this, the Administration had not succeeded in dispelling the belief that some form of resolution was necessary. Consequently the Foreign Relations and Armed Services Committee undertook the task of producing a positive substitute for the Wherry Resolution which approved the President's decision but nevertheless did something to assuage congressional anxieties. The task was not an easy one, however, and was to preoccupy the two committees during the first two weeks of March. The committees' deliberations, in fact, formed the third phase of the Senate's 'Great Debate'.

4   THE JOINT COMMITTEE AND THE CONNALLY–RUSSELL RESOLUTION

One of the most salient features of the closed sessions of the Committee on Foreign Relations and the Committee on Armed Services was that the members were virtually unanimous in their support for the substance of the troops to Europe decision. Although there were some senators, such as Byrd of Virginia, who remained concerned that the presence of six divisions in Europe would be just the 'entering wedge', remarkably little time was spent considering the merits of Truman's decision as such.[116] After the open hearings the committees held two closed sessions in which they heard testimony about the ability of the United States to resupply its forces in Europe in the face of the threat from Soviet submarines, as well as details about the cost of the deployment of troops in Europe.[117] Nevertheless, the primary focus was on the proposal which was to be reported out as a substitute for the Wherry Resolution. And although there was considerable agreement on the need for something which would explicitly approve the Administration's actions, there were considerable disagreements over both the form this measure should take and its content. Indeed, the positive resolution introduced by Connally and Russell was amended significantly both in the committees and on the Senate floor. Table 3.1 summarises its evolution, identifying its initial content, the changes made by the committees, and the amendments added in the final floor debate.

This process of alteration proved particularly difficult in the committee stage. Part of the problem stemmed from the way in which Chairman Connally handled the meetings. His abrasive style, which in certain circumstances could be advantageous, was wholly inappropriate to the difficult and delicate task of accommodating differing opinions. Indeed, Connally's loyalty to the Administration was so overwhelming, and his partisanship so intense, that he lost much of his credibility with other members of the committees. His approach to both the North Atlantic Treaty and the military assistance programme had been cautious and critical. His attitude to the troops to Europe decision was far less temperate: undeviating loyalty to Truman was combined with a reluctance to countenance anything which appeared to limit the President's power and prerogatives. Far from helping the Administration, however, this may well have been counterproductive. Connally's stance made it difficult for the moderate Republicans on the committees to modify the resolution in ways designed to preempt criticism on the Senate floor. This was all the more unfortunate because Republicans like Lodge and Senator Smith of New Jersey were attempting to establish a *modus vivendi* which would approve Truman's decision but make clear that in the future the Administration would be expected to consult much more fully with Congress on these issues.

This pattern of obstructionism by Connally was evident from the outset. On 25 January there was a closed meeting of the Committee on Foreign Relations in which Senator Lodge informally floated ideas for a possible resolution which would sanction Truman's decision while reasserting the need for a congressional role in the policy-making process.[118] Lodge's proposal had four major elements.

Two of these concerned the Joint Chiefs of Staff who would be assigned the responsibility of declaring that the sending of military units abroad was essential to American security and of certifying that the European allies were 'making a maximum

effort at continuous self-help and mutual aid'.[119] The third
recommendation was 'that the percentage of twenty five per
cent, which is now the percentage of American troops in
proportion to European troops be reduced as rapidly as
possible'.[120] Finally, Lodge wanted his colleagues to consider
establishing a Joint House–Senate Committee with the specific
task of overseeing the implementation of the North Atlantic
Treaty.

Connally's reaction to the proposal was immediate and
hostile. When challenged on the percentage recommendation,
however, Lodge made clear that he regarded this primarily as a
tactical device to placate – and head off – those senators who
otherwise might try to impose much stricter numerical limitations on the American contribution to alliance defence.[121] The
idea of relying on the Joint Chiefs of Staff was equally shrewd:
their non-political status and their professional expertise would
give them a degree of authority with Congress which the
President and the Secretary of State lacked. As had become
apparent during the open hearings, the formal involvement of
the Joint Chiefs could only prove advantageous to the Administration. Despite the potential political benefits of the
Lodge proposal, however, Connally remained opposed to anything which appeared likely to curtail the President's freedom
of action. This put the Chairman of the Foreign Relations
Committee on a collision course not only with Lodge but also
with Senator Smith whose approach was essentially a pragmatic one. In fact Smith's position was very close to that of
Senators Douglas and George. The New Jersey senator argued
that in the interest of national unity and credible government,
Congress must have a clearly defined and visible role in
determining America's alliance responsibilities. To some extent Smith seems to have been responding to public disquiet
about the manner as well as the substance of Truman's decision, and he emphasised that his mail contained considerable
'criticisms' of the policy of sending boys to Europe for permanent service on a five to ten year plan'.[122] If public support was
to be elicited, therefore, and a national consensus created in
favour of sending troops to Europe, congressional participation
was essential. Smith's solution was to advocate a dual approach in which there was both a simple Sense of the Senate

Resolution expressing confidence in Eisenhower and the policy
he represented and a joint resolution which defined the relationship between President and Congress in connection with
the implementation of the North Atlantic Pact.[123]

The initial draft of the Connally–Russell Resolution (see
Table 3.1) which provided the main focus of attention, however, was a much more innocuous measure which began by
approving the President's decision not only to appoint
Eisenhower as Supreme Allied Commander in Europe but also
to place US forces in Europe under his command. The second
paragraph of the resolution recommended that the United
States contribute its 'fair share' of forces to Atlantic defence,
while the third stated that in sending troops to Europe under
Article 3 of the North Atlantic Treaty the President should
consult not only the Secretaries of State and Defense and the
Joint Chiefs but also the Senate Committees on Armed Services
and Foreign Relations and their equivalents in the House. The
President was also to make sure that the allies were making
contributions commensurate with their ability and was to
submit six-monthly reports on the implementation of the
treaty.[124]

It is not surprising that this resolution was regarded as
unsatisfactory by many members of the two committees. In the
first place Connally and Russell had drafted what they regarded as simply a Sense of the Senate Resolution. Most of the
Republicans and one or two key Democrats though wanted
either a concurrent resolution or joint resolution, both of which
would involve the House as well as the Senate. Whereas the
concurrent resolution was merely a recommendation by both
Houses (as opposed simply to the Senate), a joint resolution
would also require the President's signature, after which it
would become law.

The two Georgia senators, George and Russell, played a
major part in resolving this particular issue even though they
were on opposite sides. George was unequivocal that whatever
emerged from the committees had to make clear that Congress
as a whole had a central role in any implementation of the
Atlantic Pact. Although he did not want to challenge the
wisdom of sending troops to Europe, he did want to establish
that Congress and not the President had the authority to decide

TABLE 3.1

The original Comnally–Russell Resolution	The resolution as amended in Committee	The resolution as amended on the Senate Floor
1. the Senate approves the action of the President of the United States in cooperating in the common defensive effort of the North Atlantic Treaty nations by designating, at their unanimous request, General of the Army Dwight D. Eisenhower as Supreme Allied Commander in Europe, and in placing Armed Forces of the United States in Europe under his command;	1. the Senate approves the action of the President of the United States in cooperating in the common defensive effort of the North Atlantic Treaty nations by designating, at their unanimous request, General of the Army Dwight D. Eisenhower as Supreme Allied Commander, Europe, and in placing Armed Forces of the United States in Europe under his command;	1. the Senate approves the action of the President of the United States in cooperating in the common defensive effort of the North Atlantic Treaty nations by designating, at their unanimous request, General of the Army Dwight D. Eisenhower as Supreme Allied Commander, Europe, and in placing Armed Forces of the United States in Europe under his command;
2. it is the belief of the Senate that the threat to the security of the United States and our North Atlantic Treaty partners makes it necessary for the United States to station abroad such units of our Armed Forces as may be necessary and appropriate to contribute our fair share of the forces needed for the joint defense of the North Atlantic area;	2. it is the belief of the Senate that the threat to the security of the United States and our North Atlantic Treaty partners makes it necessary for the United States to station abroad such units of our Armed Forces as may be necessary and appropriate to contribute our fair share of the forces needed for the joint defense of the North Atlantic area;	2. it is the belief of the Senate that the threat to the security of the United States and our North Atlantic Treaty partners makes it necessary for the United States to station abroad such units of our Armed Forces as may be necessary and appropriate to contribute our fair share of the forces needed for the joint defense of the North Atlantic area;
3. it is the sense of the Senate that the President of the United States as Commander in Chief of the Armed Forces, in taking action to send units of ground troops to Europe under article 3 of the North Atlantic Treaty, will consult the Secretary of Defense and the Joint Chiefs of Staff, the	3. it is the sense of the Senate that the President of the United States as Commander in Chief of the Armed Forces, before taking action to send units of ground troops to Europe under article 3 of the North Atlantic Treaty, should consult the Secretary of Defense and the Joint Chiefs of Staff, the	3. it is the sense of the Senate that the President of the United States as Commander in Chief of the Armed Forces, before taking action to send units of ground troops to Europe under article 3 of the North Atlantic Treaty, should consult the Secretary of Defense and the Joint Chiefs of Staff, the

TABLE 3.1 *continued*

The original Connally–Russell Resolution	The resolution as amended in Committee	The resolution as amended on the Senate Floor
Committee on Foreign Relations of the Senate, the Committee on Foreign Affairs of the House of Representatives, and the Armed Services Committees of the Senate and the House of Representatives, and that he will likewise consult the Supreme Allied Commander in Europe;	Committee on Foreign Relations of the Senate, the Committee on Foreign Affairs of the House of Representatives, and the Armed Services Committees of the Senate and the House of Representatives, and that he should likewise consult the Supreme Allied Commander, Europe;	Committee on Foreign Relations of the Senate, the Committee on Foreign Affairs of the House of Representatives, and the Armed Services Committees of the Senate and the House of Representatives, and that he should likewise consult the Supreme Allied Commander, Europe;
4. it is the sense of the Senate that, in sending units of ground troops to Europe under article 3 of the North Atlantic Treaty, the President will make certain that our North Atlantic Treaty partners are making contributions to the joint defense of the North Atlantic Treaty area commensurate with their ability, geographic position, and general economic condition;	4. it is the sense of the Senate that before sending units of ground troops to Europe under article 3 of the North Atlantic Treaty, the Joint Chiefs of Staff shall certify to the Secretary of Defense that in their opinion the parties to the North Atlantic Treaty are giving, and have agreed to give full, realistic force and effect to the requirement of article 3 of said treaty that 'by means of continuous and effective self-help and mutual aid' they will 'maintain and develop their individual and collective capacity to resist armed attack', specifically insofar as the creation of combat units is concerned;[a]	4. it is the sense of the Senate that before sending units of ground troops to Europe under article 3 of the North Atlantic Treaty, the Joint Chiefs of Staff shall certify to the Secretary of Defense that in their opinion the parties to the North Atlantic Treaty are giving, and have agreed to give full realistic force and effect to the requirements of article 3 of said treaty that 'by means of continuous and effective self-help and mutual aid' they will 'maintain and develop their individual and collective capacity to resist armed attack', specifically insofar as the creation of combat units is concerned;
5. it is the sense of the Senate that the President will submit to the Congress at intervals of not more than six months reports on the implementation of the North Atlantic	5. the Senate herewith approves the understanding that the major contribution to the ground forces under General Eisenhower's command should be made by	5. the Senate herewith approves the understanding that the major contribution to the ground forces under General Eisenhower's command should be made by

TABLE 3.1 *continued*

The original Connally–Russell Resolution	The resolution as amended in Committee	The resolution as amended on the Senate Floor
Treaty, including such information as may be made available for this purpose by the Supreme Allied Commander in Europe.	the European members of the North Atlantic Treaty, and that such units of United States ground forces as may be assigned to the above command shall be so assigned only after the Joint Chiefs of Staff certify to the Secretary of Defense that in their opinion such assignment is a necessary step in strengthening the security of the United States; and the certified opinions referred to in paragraphs 4 and 5 shall be transmitted by the Secretary of Defense to the President of the United States, and to the Senate Committees on Foreign Relations and Armed Services, and to the House Committees on Foreign Affairs and Armed Services as soon as they are received;[b]	the European members of the North Atlantic Treaty, and that such units of United States ground forces as may be assigned to the above command shall be so assigned only after the Joint Chiefs of Staff certify to the Secretary of Defense that in their opinion such assignment is a necessary step in strengthening the security of the United States; and the certified opinions referred to in paragraphs 4 and 5 shall be transmitted by the Secretary of Defense to the President of the United States, and to the Senate Committees on Foreign Relations and Armed Services, and to the House Committees on Foreign Affairs and Armed Services as soon as they are received;
	6. it is the sense of the Senate, that in the interests of sound constitutional processes, and of national unity and understanding, congressional approval should be obtained of any policy requiring the assignment of American troops abroad when such assignment is in implementation of article 3 of the North Atlantic Treaty;[c] and the Senate hereby approves the present plans of the President and the Joint Chiefs of	6. it is the sense of the Senate that, in the interests of sound constitutional processes, and of national unity and understanding, congressional approval should be obtained of any policy requiring the assignment of American troops abroad when such assignment is in implementation of article 3 of the North Atlantic Treaty; and the Senate hereby approves the present plans of the President and the Joint Chiefs of Staff to send

TABLE 3.1 *continued*

The original Connally–Russell Resolution	*The resolution as amended in Committee*	*The resolution as amended on the Senate Floor*
Staff to send four additional divisions of ground forces to Western Europe;[d]		four additional divisions of ground forces to Western Europe, but it is the sense of the Senate that no ground troops in addition to such four divisions should be sent to Western Europe in implementation of article 3 of the North Atlantic treaty without further congressional approval;[e]
	7. it is the sense of the Senate that the President should submit to the Congress at intervals of not more than six months reports on the implementation of the North Atlantic Treaty, including such information as may be made available for this purpose by the Supreme Allied Commander, Europe.	7. it is the sense of the Senate that the President should submit to the Congress at intervals of not more than six months reports on the implementation of the North Atlantic Treaty, including such information as may be made available for this purpose by the Supreme Allied Commander, Europe;
		8. it is the sense of the Senate that the United States should seek to eliminate all provisions of the existing treaty with Italy which impose limitations upon the military strength of Italy of her obligations under the North Atlantic Treaty to contribute to the full extent of her capacity to the defense of Western Europe;[f]

TABLE 3.1 *continued*

The original Connally–Russell Resolution	The resolution as amended in Committee	The resolution as amended on the Senate Floor
		9. it is the sense of the Senate that consideration should be given to the revision of plans for the defense of Europe as soon as possible so as to provide for utilization on a voluntary basis of the military and other resources of Western Germany and Spain, but not exclusive of the military and other resources of other nations.[g]

[a] Lodge amendment
[b] Lodge amendment
[c] Smith amendment
[d] Lodge addition to Smith amendment
[e] McClellan amendment
[f] Watkins amendment
[g] McCarthy amendment

whether the troops should be assigned to an international force. While he continued to emphasise the moral obligation for the Administration to seek congressional approval, his arguments in the committees focused at least as much on the legal obligation enshrined in Article 11 of the North Atlantic Treaty stating that the provisions should be carried out in accordance with constitutional processes.[125] And this meant approval of the Congress and not merely the Senate. As he put it during the committees' discussions on 7 March, 'the implementation of the treaty is reserved under the treaty itself to Congress'.[126] In emphasising this, of course, George was reiterating what had been one of his major concerns all along. As discussed in the previous chapter, it was on his insistence that the clause dealing with constitutional processes had been included in the North Atlantic Treaty itself and not merely in the preamble. Now he was concerned to ensure that this provision was not blatantly disregarded. This did not mean that Congress should determine the number of troops to be sent – that was a military decision. It did mean though that Congress should have an opportunity to approve the action. Senator George's approach to this question, therefore, was much closer to the Republicans on the committees than to his fellow Democrats, and he had considerable sympathy for the attempt by some of the Republicans to vote out a joint resolution as well as a simple Senate resolution.

The strongest argument against this course came from the other Georgian senator, Richard Russell. Indeed, Russell's approach was far more persuasive than Connally's objection that bringing in the House of Representatives would be time consuming. The essence of his argument was that a joint resolution would require the President's signature. The difficulty with this was that it would put Truman on the spot and might even provoke a veto.[127] The resulting controversy, he claimed, would have a profoundly debilitating effect on American policy. This argument carried considerable weight with Senator Lodge, who withdrew from his earlier insistence on a joint resolution. The issue came to a head on 8 March. Despite Russell's intervention, Smith proposed that the committees report out a joint resolution. Several senators, including Lodge, moved that this should be changed to a concurrent resolution, a proposal which was upheld by a 13 to 11 vote.[128] Although George and Byrd joined the Republicans in voting against this substitution, their defection was partially offset by Lodge who joined the Democrats, thereby providing the crucial margin of victory. This was immediately followed by a vote on the concurrent resolution itself, which was passed by 16 to 8, with Russell and several other Democrats joining the Republican members in voting for it and Connally, McMahon, Fulbright, Sparkman, Johnson, Kefauver, Hunt and Stennis voting against.

   The significance of this close vote on the question of whether to report a concurrent or a joint resolution is difficult to overestimate. Although the committees, earlier in the day, had displayed what appeared to be a remarkable degree of consensus by voting unanimously on a Senate resolution, with almost identical wording to the concurrent resolution, the 13 to 11 vote was indicative of the divisions which had bedevilled the deliberations from the outset. Nor was this entirely surprising: the spectrum of opinion ranged from Senator Fulbright, who was unhappy about the Senate even expressing an opinion on the troops to Europe decision 'because of the possibility of it setting a precedent that the Congress is to control the deployment of troops' to Senators George, Saltonstall, and Hickenlooper who believed that it was essential for Congress to have a say on the matter.[129] The vote emphasised once again that although there was a reasonable degree of agreement on substantive issues, the question of congressional roles and responsibilities remained as elusive and controversial as it had been from the start. Furthermore, the fact that even the relatively moderate Republicans on the committees were unhappy about the decision not to have a joint resolution, made it almost inevitable that there would be attempts by the GOP to reinstate such a proposal when the resolution came to the floor. If the moderates were dissatisfied at the committees' actions there was little prospect for reconciling the other wing of the party.

   The likelihood of this was further increased by the content of the Connally–Russell Resolution finally reported out (see Table 3.1). Yet Lodge, Smith and Knowland had all made great efforts, especially in the face of Connally's intractibility, to devise a proposal which would command wide appeal in the

Senate by reassuring members both about the Executive and about the European allies.

The lack of faith in the President was evident not only among the Republican members but also among a few of the Democrats. This was reflected in the proposals for modifying the original Connally–Russell draft resolution. Although there was agreement with that part of it approving the President's action in designating Eisenhower as Supreme Allied Commander, some members of the committees were reluctant to approve Truman's action in placing forces under his command. A motion to omit this from the draft was defeated by 12 votes to 11.[130] Discussion then turned to the second and third paragraphs of the resolution acknowledging the need for the United States to contribute its fair share of troops and recommending consultation. Although there had been an earlier change in wording to provide for consultation before the President took action in sending troops to Europe, Senator Lodge introduced an amendment in lieu of both paragraphs. His proposal amalgamated two ideas: one was approving the understanding that the major fraction of the ground forces under Eisenhower should be European while the major American effort should be in air and naval forces; the second was that the assignment of American troops should only take place after the Joint Chiefs of Staff certified that this was necessary for United States security.[131] Although Lodge had moved from his earlier suggestion in which he had proposed reducing the percentage of American to European troops, his proposal did not immediately win approval partly because the emphasis on the naval and air contribution by the United States appeared to be a tacit endorsement of the Hoover–Wherry position. In the meeting of 7 March, the proposal resulted in a 12 to 12 split and as a result failed to carry.[132] Another Lodge amendment, however, specifying that the Joint Chiefs of Staff should certify that the Europeans were giving full, realistic force and effect to Article 3 of the North Atlantic Treaty in the creation of combat units, did receive approval by 13 votes to 10 and was incorporated into the Connally–Russell Resolution as paragraph 4.[133]

In the executive session of 8 March Lodge reintroduced a modified version of his proposal which had failed to carry the previous day. The amendment now stated that 'The Senate hereby approves the understanding that the major contribution to the ground forces under General Eisenhower's command should be made by the European members.' It also specified that the Joint Chiefs should certify to the Secretary of Defense that the assignment of American troops was a necessary step. The rationale for including such a measure, in Lodge's view, was that it might forestall attempts to write a numerical ratio into the bill. Although most of the Democrats were still opposed to the proposal, both George and Stennis voted for it, thereby contributing to a 14 to 10 majority in its favour. Rather than replacing the original language of paragraphs 2 and 3 – as had been Lodge's intention the previous day – the amendment now became paragraph 5 of the resolution.[134]

Even more controversial than the changes proposed by Lodge was an amendment introduced by Senator Smith on 7 March, which stated that in the interest of sound constitutional processes and national unity and understanding the President should act in full collaboration with Congress before adopting any further policies or programmes involving the assignment of US ground forces abroad under Article 3 of the North Atlantic Treaty.[135] Connally's immediate response was that this was like telling the President what time to get up in the morning.[136] Senator George, in contrast, argued the following day that the language was too weak, and that the words 'act in collaboration' with Congress should be replaced by 'with the approval of the Congress'.[137] This suggestion was accepted by Smith and a modified draft recommending that 'Congressional approval should be obtained of any policy requiring the assignment of American troops abroad when such assignment is in implementation of article 3 of the North Atlantic Pact' was adopted by 14 votes to 10, with George, Byrd and Stennis all voting in favour.[138] This then became paragraph 6 of the Connally–Russell Resolution, while the original requirement for reports every six months became the final section. With the language apparently finalised, the committees on 8 March voted out both a Senate resolution and a concurrent resolution.

The reaction to the resolutions was inevitably somewhat mixed. Wherry hailed them as a 'complete victory', while Taft also saw them as a vindication of his stand.[139] Yet the Administration too could take comfort from the fact that the committees had not reported a joint resolution, that there was no mention of ratios (even though Senator Knowland had introduced a resolution on 28 February demanding that six European divisions be provided for any additional US division sent to Europe beyond the four announced) and that the resolutions appeared to give broad approval to the President's actions. Furthermore, it was far from certain that that House would take up the concurrent resolution as the Speaker and the other Democratic leaders in the chamber were reluctant to get involved.[140]

Yet there were problems with the resolutions, especially the Smith amendment which had become section 6. As one columnist observed,

> Almost before the ink was dry, a perturbed Senator Smith was denying that his amendment called for congressional approval of the additional dispatch of four additional divisions to Europe this year. Senator George, however, ... declared he had supported it because it did apply to the four divisions. Senator Smith's counterview caused Senator Byrd to term the resolution a botch ... wholly unsatisfactory.[141]

In the light of this, and the enthusiasm with which Wherry had greeted the resolution, it was not surprising that Lodge and Smith wanted to reconsider. At the request of Smith, a further meeting was held on 13 March to rectify the ambiguities. In what was an immensely confused and confusing meeting, Smith and Lodge emphasised that they wanted to insert into paragraph 2 more definite language approving the four divisions and to remove the ambiguity in paragraph 6 to make clear that this referred only to future actions by the President and not the four divisions. The effect of their action, however, was to open up the constitutional issues all over again and accentuate the differences among the members themselves over the meaning of the existing paragraph 6.

The senators very quickly agreed to Lodge's proposal to approve the four divisions, and this was initially inserted at the end of paragraph 2 of the Connally–Russell Resolution which stated that the United States should contribute its fair share of the forces needed for the defence of the North Atlantic area. The attempt to deal with the Smith amendment, however, was much more difficult, and after considerable discussion the committees settled on a suggestion by Senator George that they merely transfer the Lodge language from paragraph 2 to paragraph 6.[142] Although there was unanimity on this, it was followed by a motion to delete the whole section from the resolution. The difficulty with this alternative, however, was that the previous version had already been made public, and, as Senator Knowland pointed out, to go to the Senate floor without a clause suggesting that congressional approval was necessary, having previously acknowledged that it was, would be to invite trouble.[143] This argument convinced Lodge, and although he was unhappy with section 6 he voted against Senator Fulbright's motion to strike it out of the resolution. With George also voting against its omission, the motion to delete was defeated by 13 votes to 11.[144] At the end of a three-hour discussion, therefore, the committees recessed, having accomplished very little. Indeed, the session of 13 March revealed even more starkly than any of the previous meetings how difficult it was to devise a measure which all the members of the committees could interpret in the same way, let alone support. Although creative ambiguity often has its uses, the committees had not engaged in this; instead they had devised a resolution which was 'so complex, controversial, and self-contradictory' that it invited attack on the Senate floor.[145]

Yet even if the resolution had been less vulnerable to charges of ambiguity and inconsistency it would still have been challenged in the Senate. The drafting sessions had shown the difficulty of obtaining agreement even when the major critics of Truman's decision were not involved. As soon as the Wherry supporters were given an opportunity to launch another attack on the decision, however, they would almost certainly grasp it. Indeed, this was underlined by the continuing, if sporadic, debate in the chamber itself during the period when the Foreign Relations and Armed Services Committees were formulating their resolution. That debate was to become even more intense when the Connally–Russell Resolution was reported to the Senate. Indeed, the 'Great Debate' was as alive during the last two weeks of March 1951 as it had been at any time. And although the open hearings had succeeded in shifting attention from the constitutional to the substantive issues, the drafting of

the resolution had revealed just how salient and how intractable these constitutional issues were.

5   THE FINAL FLOOR DEBATES AND THE VOTING

The Connally–Russell Resolution as amended in the committees was reported to the Senate as Senate Resolution 99 and
Senate Concurrent Resolution 18 on March 14 and debate
formally began two days later. There was little that was new in
the speeches and arguments, however. Indeed, the substantive
issues had already been discussed very fully both on the Senate
floor itself and in the open hearings before the Armed Services
and Foreign Relations Committees. Nevertheless, the final
stage of the Senate's deliberations witnessed an intense attack
on Resolution 99 and the assumptions on which it was based.
This was assisted by the very obvious divisions amongst the
members of the two committees both as to the wisdom and the
meaning of certain of its provisions. Almost as soon as the
debate began Connally emphasised his disapproval of the
concurrent resolution.[146] If the Chairman of the committees
was unhappy about a concurrent resolution because it went too
far, many of the critics argued that it did not go far enough and
that nothing less then a joint resolution would suffice. It was
predictable that Wherry, Taft, Kem and Bricker would adopt
this position. In the event they were joined by Cain and
Hickenlooper, [147] both of whom had been members of the joint
committees. The battle had been lost in the committees but was
being fought once again on the Senate floor.

The concern with the failure of the two committees to report
out a joint resolution was part expediency, part conviction.
Wherry almost certainly realised by this stage that he had no
hope of achieving his substantive objective of prohibiting the
deployment of American troops to Europe. His one remaining
course, therefore, was to attempt to embarrass the Truman
Administration by focusing upon congressional rights and
prerogatives – especially as on this issue he might even obtain
the support of one or two prestigious Democrats such as
Senator George. Yet there was nothing hypocritical about this:

the Republican leader had been concerned from the onset of the 'Great Debate' about what he believed to be Truman's blatant disregard for Congress. The preoccupation with a joint resolution may have been a tactical ploy, but was embarked upon within an overall philosophy that had remained fairly consistent.

The concerns about the role of Congress also had an impact on the reaction of many senators to section 6 of Resolution 99. The paragraph which had caused so much difficulty in the executive sessions of the committees caused even more controversy on the Senate floor. Attempts by members of the committees to interpret it were either inconsistent or contradictory, thereby adding to the general sense of dissatisfaction with the resolution. For some members of the Senate, paragraph 6 was too restrictive; for others it was too permissive. Senator McMahon, for example, berated the fact that it could be interpreted as meaning that authorisation through a concurrent resolution passed by both houses was necessary before the President could send a single man to Europe under Article 3 of the treaty.[148] On the other side, it was suggested by Senator Ferguson that the meaning of 'approval' was far too vague, while Senator Mundt argued that the concern with sound constitutional procedure in the first half of the paragraph was undermined by a second part which referred only to the Senate and not to the Congress as a whole.[149] For Senator McClellan of Arkansas the main concern was that once the policy had been approved there was no imperative for the President to return to Congress if he wanted to despatch more than four divisions to Europe.[150] Senator Smith, the member of the committees primarily responsible for paragraph 6, was in an impossible position: any interpretation which appealed to the advocates of a more restrictive measure inevitably alienated those who preferred a more discretionary approach, while any concession to the latter group antagonised the former. In the light of this it very quickly became obvious that there would be attempts to amend section 6 of the resolution by both supporters and opponents of the Administration. As one commentator has observed, 'The task of the conservative Republicans was to get a strict interpretation of the word "approval" in the Smith amendment, and the task of the moderate Republicans was to keep a loose interpretation. The Democratic leadership's problem was to remove the Smith amendment or to keep it and have it remain ambiguous.'[151]

Each of these groups faced difficulties. The conservative Republicans suffered from the fact – which had become increasingly evident during the open hearings – that Taft was far more willing to compromise than was Wherry. For the moderate Republicans, the problem was that the compromise which they had done so much to create was unsatisfactory. The Democratic leadership too had to contend with the failure of the committees to provide an authoritative substitute to the Wherry Resolution. By producing a measure which actually provoked senators into challenging their authority, the committees had ensured that the last phase of the 'Great Debate' was as bitter as the first phase. Furthermore, during the last two weeks of March and the first few days of April the Senate appeared to be highly fragmented.

If any group did manage to impose its leadership, however, it was the Democrats. Although there were to be important defections – most notably McClellan's amendment to section 6 – the Democrats under Majority Leader McFarland, Russell and Connally managed to keep these to a minimum. Yet there was little evidence of this during the first few days of the debate when the floor was dominated by extreme critics of the troops to Europe decision such as Kem, Homer Ferguson, Watkins, Bricker and Malone. The arguments were as familiar as the names: these were the senators who had consistently opposed US involvement in Europe. That their arguments were allowed to go virtually unchallenged, however, was somewhat surprising. One possibility is that the Democratic leadership was simply giving the opponents of the resolution an opportunity to ventilate their feelings before the votes took place. Another is that by this stage the Democrats were so fed up with the whole controversy that they were content simply to opt out for a few days while considering their strategy for the final floor debates and the votes. There was in fact some argument between Wherry and McFarland as to when limitations should be imposed on debate so that the Senate could proceed to vote.[152] After brief negotiation, it was agreed that the limitation of debate would begin on the morning of 2 April, having allowed a recess for Easter and three days of unlimited debate.

During these three days of unlimited debate, the attacks on the Connally–Russell Resolution continued unabated. The idea of a simple or even a concurrent resolution was variously castigated as an 'expression of pious hope', an 'attempt to fool the people' and 'legislative suicide'.[153] Everett Dirksen of Illinois claimed that the resolution had 'no more kick than has a glass of chocolate milk', while Bricker was even more vitriolic, arguing that attempting to clarify the meaning of the resolution was 'as sensible as 3 men contending for the right to carry milk, or beer, or water when the only thing they have is a sieve'.[154] In Bricker's view the constitution was in danger of being changed by indifference on the part of the Senate. More moderate views were also expressed, with McClellan further elaborating his position that since the constitution gave Congress the power to govern and regulate the armed forces, it was incumbent upon the Senate to establish that the President required congressional approval for sending troops to Europe.[155] McClellan was particularly concerned to find language which approved the four divisions but which simultaneously made it clear that the President did not have a free hand thereafter to increase the contingent in Europe at will. Indeed, he made it clear he intended to offer an amendment to this effect.

By 2 April, a number of other senators had also announced that they intended to offer modifications to the resolution. It was apparent too that there would be an attempt to send the proposal back to the committees with instructions for them to report out a joint resolution. Although the Democrats were fairly confident that they could beat back attempts to recommit the Connally–Russell Resolution, they were reportedly apprehensive about the size of the majority.[156] The resounding vote which they had hoped to obtain in support of the President's policy appeared to be out of reach. There was also concern over the possibility that some of the hostile amendments might carry.

The debate itself began with an attempt by Wherry to substitute a joint resolution for Senate Resolution 99. This was ruled out of order on procedural grounds.[157] After a short

diversion in which a proposal by Francis Case of South Dakota
to prohibit any soldier under 20 years of age being sent to
Europe was defeated by a vote of 62 to 27, the Senate returned
to the major issue, which was what to do about section 6.[158]
Senator McClellan introduced his promised amendment which
simply added to the existing paragraph the proviso that 'no
troops in addition to such 4 divisions should be sent to Western
Europe in implementation of article 3 of the North Atlantic
Treaty without further congressional approval'.[159] This was
immediately attacked by leading Democrats, Connally,
McMahon, McFarland, Lehman, as well as by Lodge and
Smith of New Jersey, and was defeated by two votes in a 44 to
46 split.[160] What was perhaps most surprising about the division was that Walter George voted against the amendment. All
his pronouncements throughout the 'Great Debate' suggested
that he would favour a proposal which explicitly reasserted the
congressional role. Shill has suggested that this was simply a
result of confusion about the vote.[161] An alternative explanation
is that George, who was punctilious about the norms and
folkways of the Senate, felt a certain obligation to support the
wording that had been reported out by the Foreign Relations
and Armed Services Committees. If this was so, then it was not
shared by other members of the committee. Lodge and
McMahon were among those associated with an attempt by
Senator Ives, a Republican from New York, to water down
paragraph 6. The Ives amendment approved the policy of
assigning troops, called for collaboration between the Executive and Congress and stated that if a majority on the military
or foreign policy committees in either chamber thought that a
new policy was being implemented under Article 3 of the North
Atlantic Treaty this was to be brought to the attention of the
House or Senate. The main defect with this proposal was that it
asked senators to put more faith in the Foreign Relations and
Armed Services Committees at the very time when the authority of these committees was being challenged. The final floor
debate in part at least was a revolt against the committees by
rank and file senators.[162] Consequently, the Ives amendment
had little chance of being endorsed. Its prospects were further
weakened by the fact that Connally and a number of other
strong supporters of the Administration also voted against it,

apparently on the grounds that it would exacerbate the divisions in the Senate. It was no surprise, therefore, when the amendment was defeated by 57 votes to 35.[163]

Immediately after this, there was a motion to reconsider the vote on the McClellan amendment. Although it is not clear what manoeuvring had taken place in the lobby, Senator George's criticism of the Ives amendment may have prompted McClellan and others to obtain a second vote. They were successful in this and the defection of George, Case and Allen Frear, a Democrat from Delaware who had played no significant part in the discussions, helped to turn the result around. On the second vote the amendment passed the Senate by 49 votes to 43, with Wiley, who had not participated the first time, adding his support to McClellan.[164] Although eight Republicans – Aiken, Duff, Flanders, Ives, Lodge, Saltonstall, Alexander Smith and Tobey – came down against the proposal, they were more than offset by the 11 southern Democrats who joined 38 Republicans in voting for the addition of the restrictive clause.

The immediate reaction of Connally and his supporters was one of dismay. The amendment was condemned by liberal Democrats such as Herbert Lehman and Hubert Humphrey and an attempt was made to substitute an innocuous measure which had been introduced some days earlier. The amendment – which was now put forward by Lehman – simply called for the 'fullest collaboration' between Congress and the President on the issue. In the circumstances, however, it had little chance of being approved, and was eventually defeated by 55 votes to 35.[165]

With further action on the resolution held over until the next day, Senator Wherry and his supporters could take a certain amount of satisfaction from the events of 2 April. Although the effort to substitute a joint resolution had been thwarted by procedural rules, a restrictive clause had been incorporated into the resolution. Some commentators, however, argued that this had been inadvertently facilitated by poor tactics on the part of the Democrats. William White of the *New York Times*, for example, claimed that 'The Administration Democrats were for part of the day working at cross purposes. The chief Democratic spokesman in foreign affairs, Senator Tom Connally of Texas, and some of his associates had decided not to support efforts to ease the restrictions in the resolutions lest they create additional hostility.'[166] Majority Leader McFarland had been prevailed upon to go along with this strategy, but later in the day claimed that it had been a mistake.[167] Although the conciliatory approach may have backfired, however, it was hardly the decisive factor. McClellan's amendment passed the Senate because many of its members had come to believe not only that institutional pride was at stake but also that a failure to make a firm stand would have serious long-term implications for congressional roles and responsibilities in foreign policy. Support for the McClellan amendment came in part from those who wanted to prohibit the assignment of troops to Western Europe; but it also came from those senators who were unhappy about the Truman Administration's cavalier disregard for Congress. There was widespread concern over the President's failure to pursue a collaborative approach which legally, constitutionally and morally he should have done. If the McClellan amendment was a partial victory for those who opposed the substance of Truman's policy, it was even more of a victory for those who were less worried about the substance of policy than about the process whereby it was made.

For all this the conflict was far from over. When the debate opened on 3 April Senator Lodge immediately introduced an amendment to delete the sentence added to paragraph 6 by McClellan. Despite an impassioned claim that Congress was turning itself into a General Staff, however, he recognised that there was little prospect of the Senate reversing itself a second time, and withdrew his amendment. The anti-troop faction then went on the offensive once again. Kem introduced an additional paragraph to the effect that before any troops, including the four divisions, were sent to Europe the Joint Chiefs should certify to Congress that sufficient air power would be available to control the air over Western Europe and thereby ensure the safety and effectiveness of the ground troops. After a somewhat perfunctory debate, the proposal was defeated by 64 to 24.[168] More serious was a proposal by Bricker that the resolution be recommitted to the committees with instructions to report a joint resolution. This evoked considerable criticism, even from moderates such as McClellan, who argued that the resolution, as it had been strengthened the previous day, was preferable to a joint resolution which was unlikely to obtain the two-thirds majority necessary to override the inevitable presidential veto. Although the conservative Republicans still felt it necessary to make the gesture, this more pragmatic approach, together with concerns about the effect of a further delay, led to the Bricker proposal being defeated by 56 to 31.[169] This did not prevent Senator Mundt from introducing another amendment demanding that the plans to send four divisions to Western Europe should be submitted to Congress for approval in the form of a Senate joint resolution. McClellan, who had emerged as a key figure in the debate, reiterated the practical arguments against this procedure. By this stage it was also becoming apparent that the adoption of the McClellan amendment itself was regarded as sufficient to protect congressional prerogatives. The result was that the Mundt proposal, like that of Bricker, had little appeal beyond the group of Republicans around Wherry and Taft, and was defeated easily with only 29 votes in favour and 52 against.[170] When the debate was recessed until the following day, therefore, the pro-Administration senators appeared to have held on to their positions far better than on the first day.

When the debate began on 4 April attention immediately focused on the question of a West German contribution to the NATO forces in Europe. This reflected the continuing concern that all available sources of manpower in Europe should be mobilised by the alliance. Indeed, this sentiment had already led on 2 April to the passage of an amendment, introduced by Senator Watkins, advocating a loosening of the treaty restrictions imposed on Italy so that she could contribute fully to the defence of Western Europe. Despite criticisms that this proposal was not germane, it received overwhelming approval by 67 votes to 20 and was incorporated into Resolution 99 as paragraph 8.[171] On 3 April, a similar amendment by Joseph McCarthy recommending that plans for the defence of Europe be revised in order to utilise the military resources of Western Germany, Spain, Turkey and Greece, was narrowly beaten. Although there was considerable sympathy for McCarthy's objective, the feeling that the proposal was too wide contributed to its defeat by 45 votes to 44.[172] Nevertheless, on 4 April

Senator Case, a Republican from South Dakota, introduced a similar measure dealing only with Germany. This was withdrawn, however, in favour of another amendment by McCarthy which differed from that of the previous day in that it referred only to Germany and Spain. Given the sentiment in the Senate, and the modifications McCarthy had made in response to criticisms and suggestions from other senators, it was no surprise when the amendment was approved by 48 votes to 41.[173] As well as the original language in the resolution concerning European self-help, there were now recommendations that the resources and manpower of Italy, West Germany and Spain be mobilised for the defence of Western Europe. The rationale for this was that if American troops were going to Europe then at least they should get full support from the European states themselves – including those who had been on the opposite side during the Second World War.

With the burden-sharing issue effectively disposed of, the Senate began to debate the Connally–Russell Resolution as it had been amended on the floor (see Table 3.1). Although this immediately came under attack from Dirksen and Wherry, it was given a considerable boost when Taft announced that he intended to vote for it.[174] Although his intentions had been known for some time, what dismayed the more extreme senators such as Wherry and Cain was that Taft also appealed to other Republicans to give their support to the resolution. Taft emphasised that the most important thing about the existing resolution – especially with the inclusion of the McClellan amendment – was that it reasserted the congressional right to play a role in the decision-making process. With this interpretation also endorsed by Senator George, it became clear that the passage of the resolution itself – which had never seriously been in doubt – would be almost a formality. With two of the most respected champions of congressional rights and prerogatives voting for the resolution, other senators could feel fairly confident about it. Indeed, as it turned out, there were only 21 votes against and 69 in favour. And two of the negative votes were cast not because the resolution was too weak but because it was too strong. Both Senator Fulbright of Arkansas and Ellender of Louisiana voted against Resolution 99 as a protest against what they regarded as an intrusion on presidential prerogatives. Apart from these two, however, the dissenting votes were those of the Wherry faction – senators who had consistently opposed involvement in Europe: Bricker, Cain, Ferguson, Dworshak, Langer, Malone, Cordon, Jenner and Kem had almost all spoken out against the American commitment to Europe on previous occasions. Although their strength was boosted by one or two new recruits from the 1950 election, such as Everett Dirksen of Illinois, the result confirmed that the 'irreconcilables' were isolated from the mainstream of opinion in the Senate.[175]

Wherry did have a partial success, however, in that his motion to substitute the language of Resolution 99 for the existing language of Concurrent Resolution 18 was passed by 59 to 29 and the concurrent resolution itself was approved by 45 votes to 41.[176] Many of the Democrats who had voted for the simple resolution switched sides, partly on the grounds that consideration of the concurrent resolution in the House of Representatives would only delay matters and further embarrass Truman. George, Russell and McClellan, however, remained loyal to the principle that the House should at least have an opportunity to have a say on the troops to Europe decision.

In the event, the House did very little. On 11 April an attempt to include language requiring congressional approval for sending troops to Europe in the draft bill was defeated by 192 to 168. The 'Great Debate' was finally over. And ultimately it was a victory for the Truman Administration. The President's troops to Europe decision had been approved. But the Senate had also displayed considerable sensitivity about its role in the policy-making process and great concern about Western Europe's willingness to make the necessary contributions to the common defence. The controversy had also made clear that the deployment of American troops in Western Europe was not something which many Americans regarded with equanimity. These lessons were to be reinforced by subsequent events.

4 The Interim Period, 1952 to 1965

1 THE AFTERMATH OF THE 'GREAT DEBATE'

By April 1951, the Senate had exhausted both itself and the issue of sending US troops to Europe. It is hardly surprising, therefore, that for the rest of the decade the military presence in Europe was not something which generated much argument. The 'Great Debate' acted almost as a catharsis, allowing senators to ventilate their grievances and anxieties about the direction of United States foreign policy, and then turn to other matters. Nevertheless, the debate had revealed that the US contribution to NATO, and especially the presence of a substantial number of troops in Europe, was an issue with an inherent potential for controversy. Inevitable uncertainties about what constituted fair shares, lingering doubts over the vigour and reliability of the European allies, and a continuing faith in the principle of self-help, all contributed to this potential. Nor was it simply a partisan matter: although the opposition to sending troops had come primarily from one section of the Republican Party, concern over equitable burden-sharing transcended this group and was clearly evident not only among Republicans who were more sympathetic to Truman's decision, but also among loyal Democrats. Furthermore, although the 'Great Debate' had ended with the Senate approving a policy which gave priority to Europe over Asia this was not an issue which was susceptible to permanent settlement. The United States would remain both a Pacific and an Atlantic power, and the question of priorities could certainly not be decided by a Senate resolution. Thus, it was almost inevitable that it would emerge to trouble future Administrations. Perhaps even more important, Resolution 99 had symbolised the Senate's acceptance of the idea of a breathing space for the Europeans, during which they were expected to rebuild their own military establishments to a sufficiently high level that the US presence on the continent could be reduced without any diminution of allied security. The length of the breathing space was indeterminate.[1] But at some point in the future, if the executive branch failed to bring about such a reduction, it was likely that the Senate would take the initiative – especially if it became exercised over its foreign policy prerogatives.

In other words, the mood of acquiescence in presidential policy on the deployment of troops in Europe was not something which could safely be taken for granted or expected to continue indefinitely. It is not altogether surprising, therefore, that by the early 1960s there were growing murmurs of discontent over the continued presence of a very substantial garrison of US troops in Europe. The debate over bringing forces home, however, was to differ in several ways from that over sending them. In particular, the alignment of forces in the Senate on the issue changed very considerably. Although the conservative Republicans had provided the main opposition to the initial deployment of the troops, the demands for withdrawals not only came from elsewhere but found little favour among such senators. The reasons for this transformation must now be examined.

2   THE CHANGING SENATE

Many observers emphasise the innate conservatism and the power of tradition in the United States Senate. Such an emphasis is entirely appropriate. Yet it is equally important not to overlook the forces of change. Indeed, in certain respects the Senate is a chameleon-like institution, with continuity of style and mores disguising profound changes of attitude and outlook. One of the most remarkable changes of the 1950s took place amongst Senate Republicans. A party which had been deeply divided over foreign policy through the later 1940s and into the 'Great Debate', became much more united in its acceptance of internationalist policies, including military entanglement with Western Europe.

There were several important reasons for this, the most important of which was General Eisenhower's victory in the 1952 election. During the 'Great Debate', Eisenhower and Senator Taft had very clearly been on opposite sides. Indeed, Taft's lack of commitment to NATO was a major consideration in Eisenhower's decision to agree to the urgings of Senator Lodge and other East Coast internationalists that he stand for the Republican nomination for President.[2] Nevertheless, the differences between the two men should not be exaggerated. Eisenhower, as the first SACEUR, was naturally much more positive and enthusiastic about US policy towards Western Europe than was Taft. Apart from this, the General's approach to national security issues was based on many of the principles long articulated by the Ohio senator. In particular, the two men shared a fundamental attachment to the notion of fiscal conservatism. Like Taft, Eisenhower believed that the defence budget had to be strictly limited and that the levels of taxation and government intervention in the economy should be minimal. With both men starting from this premise, it is not surprising that their differences were primarily those of emphasis and nuance. They diverged over timing and tactics rather than in their overall appraisal of the most appropriate policies for the United States to follow. Although their differences were intensified by the contest for the Republican nomination, and played up by the press, the famous 'Morningside Heights Agreement' between them may not have been as difficult to obtain as is often assumed. Similarly, although the achievement of John Foster Dulles in devising a foreign policy platform which reconciled both wings of the party was a remarkable one, it was facilitated by the concern, common to almost all Republicans, with minimising the domestic costs of foreign policy. Indeed, many of the anxieties and aspirations expressed by Eisenhower during his campaign for the presidency were reminiscent of arguments that Taft had propounded during the 'Great Debate'. Eisenhower not only emphasised that it was essential to avoid a bankrupt America, but made clear his belief that the United States should not 'station its troops all over the world to protect every area' in which it had vital interests.[3] The essence of collective security, in his view, was 'as rapidly as possible to lodge the defence of these areas upon their own populations'.[4] In other words, while embracing Republican internationalism, Eisenhower did so on principles which had been developed most fully and explicitly by Robert Taft. It was a prudent, discerning internationalism which acknowledged the need to balance the demands of America's foreign commitments against the requirements of the domestic economy. As such, it not only appealed to the electorate but helped to heal the long-standing divisions within the party.

Eisenhower's position, however, owed more to personal conviction than to electoral expediency. In fact, the security policies of his Administration (with the obvious exception of notions of liberation and roll back, which were quickly revealed to be rhetorical flourishes with little practical import) were based to a striking degree on principles he had outlined during the campaign. This was particularly true of the defence policy which evolved during 1953 and was formally enunciated during 1954. The 'new look', with its emphasis on massive retaliation, differed from the policies of the Truman Administration in that it started from the threat to the economy rather than the threat to military security.[5] The appeal of massive retaliation was not that it provided more bang, but that it costs less bucks. This was something, of course, which made it acceptable to the Taft wing of the party. Indeed, both the cuts in the defence budget under Eisenhower, and the strategic doctrine which accompanied them, owed as much to Taft as they did to the President. As Divine has noted, 'massive retaliation was a logical outgrowth of Taft's argument that the United States should rely upon its superior air and naval power to balance off large communist ground forces'.[6] Another – if less explicit – advantage of this strategy, with its lack of intermediate options, was that in all but the most exceptional circumstances, it was a good reason for doing nothing. In other words, Eisenhower combined an internationalist foreign policy with an isolationist strategy. In the words of Townsend Hoopes, massive retaliation 'revealed the strong unilateral, quasi-isolationist strain in the outlook of the new Administration' and displayed a 'yearning to disengage from complexity, while at the same time continuing to exercise a dominant influence'.[7] This yearning was never taken to its logical conclusion, of course, and Eisenhower did not make any substantial reductions in the

United States contingent in Western Europe. The possibility was seriously considered during 1956 as part of a proposal put forward by Admiral Radford, the Chairman of the Joint Chiefs of Staff, to prune the American presence overseas fairly drastically.[8] The plan, which was leaked to the *New York Times*, was severely criticised by Chancellor Adenauer of West Germany, who argued that it implied the United States was about to renege on the commitment made at the London conference of 1954 (which was instrumental in facilitating West Germany's entry into NATO) by Secretary of State Dulles, in which he had pledged that the United States would maintain in Europe such elements of its own forces as were necessary or appropriate to contribute a fair share of what was needed for the common defence of the North Atlantic area.[9] The argument succeeded in convincing Dulles that troop withdrawals would be imprudent. Although the President was probably more sympathetic towards the ideas enshrined in the Radford Memorandum, he too acknowledged the difficulties that would be created by any attempt to implement the plan. Thus, the breathing space for the European allies was extended beyond the period when Eisenhower wanted to bring it to an end. Despite this, the President's policies did much to reconcile the more conservative Republicans to internationalism.

The effect of this was clearly evident in Senate voting patterns on foreign policy and security questions. The number of Republicans who had consistently opposed internationalist policies peaked during 1951 and 1952, but declined sharply during the early years of the Eisenhower presidency. One analyst had identified 27 Republican senators in 1951 and 29 in 1952, whose voting patterns were clearly isolationist. By 1953 the number had declined to 17, and by 1955 was down to 12.[10] During the same period, support for presidential policies rose markedly. 'A majority of Republican Senators supported the Truman Administration on only 37 per cent of roll calls', while 'during the Eisenhower Administration majority support rose to 83 per cent'.[11]

This transformation was not solely the result of Eisenhower's policies. Malcolm Jewell has suggested that partisan loyalty was the crucial consideration.[12] Certainly, the fact that Eisenhower was a Republican President was of immense significance. Having waited since 1932 for another Republican incumbent of the White House, the party in the senate could hardly repudiate his foreign policy. To have done so would have been to undermine completely the President's power and prestige – something that most loyal Republicans were anxious to avoid. The results were remarkable: 'Although the Republicans had a long isolationist tradition, and although many of them deeply distrusted the Democratic authors of the programs inherited by President Eisenhower, and although many of them disliked Eisenhower's internationalist views, Republican Senators reversed their stand on a wide variety of issues to provide strong support for Republican President.'[13] Yet the extent to which Eisenhower's policies contributed to this should not be underestimated. It was not simply that a Democratic Administration had been replaced by a Republican President; perhaps even more significant was the fact that the Democrats had pursued what could easily be construed as a profligate and overzealous internationalism, whereas the new Administration was much more restrained and circumspect in its approach. Although some Republican senators may have occasionally found it necessary to support presidential initiatives of which they disapproved (or indeed, to vote against the President's proposals), for the most part they were spared the necessity of making such choices. It was not only that Eisenhower's party in the Senate kept faith with him; he kept faith with them.

This is not to suggest that Eisenhower was able to convert all the Republicans to internationalism. There remained a small minority who refused to be swayed. This group, though, was declining in both numbers and significance: retirements, defeat at the polls, and illness and death all took their toll. By 1955, Senators Cordon, Kem and Wherry were no longer in the legislature. Those who remained – including Jenner, Malone, Langer, Arthur Watkins and Milton Young – did not relinquish their long-held beliefs, but for the most part were more discriminate in their opposition.[14] Furthermore, after Wherry's departure they lacked a natural leader who could weld them into a cohesive and effective legislative force. The old arguments – that the United States should focus on the American hemisphere and adopt a hands off policy towards Western

Europe – continued to be made, but appeared increasingly irrelevant to mainstream Republican thinking about the conduct of US foreign policy.

The implication of all this is that the Republican Party in the Senate ceased to be the party opposed to an entangling military alliance with Western Europe. This was to have far-reaching consequences. It helps to explain why the 'Great Debate' was followed by a decade or more in which the Senate acquiesed almost completely in the Administration's policy towards NATO. It was also to determine the political alignments during the controversy of the latter 1960s and early 1970s over the level of the American military presence in Western Europe.

The pressure for troop withdrawals, in fact, was to come primarily from the Democrats, with only very limited support from the Republicans. Yet there were only a few signs of this in the 1950s. Many of the Democrats were critical of the Eisenhower Administration for the very reasons that endeared it to Senate Republicans. The President was regarded by the Democrats as too passive in dealing with the Communist bloc and, in particular, as too niggardly in his approach to defence spending. The criticism of the new look was broadly based, encompassing those like Stuart Symington, Henry Jackson, Richard Russell and John Stennis who were most concerned about the effects of the cuts in defence spending on America's air power, and those like Hubert Humphrey and Mansfield who were most disturbed by the neglect of conventional forces.[15] By the late 1950s these two groups had coalesced into a united opposition which demanded greater effort at the strategic level to offset the supposed missile gap, and an upgrading of conventional capabilities to implement a strategy of flexible response. Among the Democrats, liberalism and internationalism seemed to go hand in hand, while the conservative Southern Democrats remained firmly committed to NATO and to greater military preparedness even though they were becoming very disillusioned with what they regarded as extravagant and unnecessary military and economic aid programmes.[16]

One of the most persistent and outspoken critics of aid was Louisiana Democrat, Alan Ellender. Returning from a tour of Europe in late 1951 Ellender was highly critical of the way in

which the military assistance programme was being implemented, charging that it encouraged waste and even graft,
and demanding that the Europeans devote a greater part of
their production to military purposes.[17] Although there were
variations on this theme through the 1950s, the main refrain
was to become a familiar one. Ellender's concern was that the
United States was paying a disproportionate share of the cost of
NATO, a concern he manifested annually in amendments to
reduce the size of the military assistance programme. Underlying his complaints about burden-sharing was a deeply embed-
ded fiscal conservatism coupled with a fear that the United
States was being exploited by allies who regarded Washington
as a 'soft touch'.[18] Although in the 1960s such sentiments would
develop very naturally into support for troop withdrawals,
Ellender's position should not be distorted, nor its significance
exaggerated. One of several senators who regarded themselves
as custodians of America's fiscal integrity, his complaints had a
routine, almost ritualistic quality about them. Furthermore, in
the late 1950s he was clearly within the consensus in favour of
larger conventional forces – a consensus which was
strengthened by the onset of the Berlin Crisis in 1958.[19] Thus, at
the end of the 1950s there was no substantial groundswell of
opinion calling for a reduction of US troops in Europe. There
was, however, a latent dissatisfaction with the European burden-sharing efforts, a dissatisfaction which would be intensified
by changing international conditions, and made explicit by the
conviction of several key senators that a reappraisal of the
American military presence in Europe was essential.

3   THE BALANCE OF PAYMENTS PROBLEM

During the 1950s there were two contradictory trends in
European–American relations. On the one hand, the growth in
United States military power, especially its strategic
capabilities, widened the gap between the allies on each side of
the Atlantic. On the other hand, the disparity in economic
strength between the two parts of the alliance was significantly
reduced by Western Europe's economic recovery.
    The growth in Soviet conventional and nuclear power
throughout the 1950s, in one sense at least, increased the threat

to Western Europe, and made the allies more dependent on the United States guarantee at the end of the decade than they were at the beginning. After the Soviet launching of Sputnik in 1957, however, it became less certain that Washington would use strategic nuclear weapons on behalf of its allies, since to do so could be suicidal. This development further underlined the importance of American conventional forces deployed in Europe – both as a defensive force and as a link to an otherwise incredible nuclear umbrella. At the same time the costs of this deployment were beginning to appear increasingly onerous in the light of the changing economic circumstances. The decline of American predominance must not be exaggerated, of course. In 1960, American economic leadership was still unquestioned. As one analyst has observed: 'The country's GNP by the end of the 1950s topped an estimated $512 billion, compared with a total GNP for six members of the European Economic Community of $188 billion, and of Britain of $72 billion.'[20] Furthermore, the per capita income in the United States was more than twice that in Western Europe.[21] For all this, there were still some disquieting trends for Washington, especially in the balance of payments.

The United States ran a deficit in its balance of payments throughout the 1950s. In the first half of the decade, however, this was regarded as a sign of American strength rather than weakness. The outflow of dollars contributed to economic recovery both in Europe and elsewhere, and facilitated a significant growth in international trade. As one congressional report stated: 'Up to the mid-50s, the great problem for the whole world was the dollar gap, and we were doing our best to close it.'[22] Furthermore, although US troops in Europe contributed to this deficit, part of their cost was offset by the Federal Republic of Germany which, until the mid-1950s was paying occupation costs for the forces stationed on its territory.[23] From then onwards, however, these contributions were reduced to a nominal level. This was a political imperative for Bonn. At the same time, the United States could afford to be magnanimous. By the end of 1958, though, some observers at least were becoming less sanguine.

In 1958 the deficit in the American balance of payments increased. There was also a considerable outflow of gold. American reserves fell from $22 860 million worth in January

1958 (the highest level since the end of 1952) to $20 582 million in December of the same year.[24] The trend was not lost on Senator Ellender, and in a speech in July 1959 he complained bitterly that the European allies were increasing their holdings of dollars and gold at America's expense, while still relying excessively on the United States to provide for their security.[25] Although Ellender's complaints did not evoke a particularly sympathetic response from many of his Senate colleagues, they did provide a foretaste of things to come. Within a few years, the balance of payments problem would play an important part in generating demands for US troop withdrawals from Western Europe. The more immediate challenge, however, came from within the executive branch itself.[26] Not surprisingly, in view of the balance of payments difficulties, it emanated from Secretary of the Treasury, Robert Anderson, and Director of the Bureau of the Budget, Maurice Stans. Stans seems to have been particularly persuasive and apparently convinced Secretary of Defense McElroy that US forces in Western Europe were important primarily as a tripwire. As such, a reduction of three divisions could be made without undermining Western security. Although this suggestion was supported by the air force, it encountered strong opposition from Secretary of State Christian Herter. Indeed, Herter, along with William Draper, head of the Presidential Commission on the military assistance programme, and a former Under-Secretary of the army, convinced Eisenhower of the folly of such a move.

The advocates of reduction, however, continued to press their case during 1960, and were assisted by a further decline in United States gold reserves. The fact that the balance of payments deficit continued despite a surplus of exports over imports also highlighted the importance of overseas troop deployments in contributing to the dollar drain. After much internal discussion, the President judged that the problem could be contained without cutting troops and approved a series of more limited measures, such as reducing the number of dependents overseas and pursuing a more vigorous 'buy American' policy, which it was hoped would alleviate the difficulties. In addition, the Secretary of the Treasury, Anderson, and Under-Secretary of State Dillon led a delegation to the Federal Republic of Germany which, in contrast to the United

States, was running a large surplus in its balance of payments.[27] The demand that Bonn provide $600 million to offset the costs of the US presence, however, smacked of a resumption of occupation payments and ran into the German preference for a multilateral rather than a purely bilateral formula to ease the problem. Not much progress was made, and in a North Atlantic Council meeting on 6 December 1960, Secretary Herter warned the allies that some redeployment of US forces might be necessary if the problem was not satisfactorily dealt with.[28] Yet this did little more than place the issue on the agenda for the incoming Kennedy Administration. Indeed, Eisenhower had done little to change the *status quo* in NATO. Although the President was to claim, a few years later, that he had been in favour of troop reductions, he accepted the arguments of his advisers – especially Dulles and Herter – that it was too sensitive politically for the United States to make such a move. This was an argument which was to be vigorously challenged in the 1960s by Senator Mike Mansfield – and it is therefore to the evolution of Mansfield's thinking that we must turn.

4 SENATOR MANSFIELD AND TROOPS IN EUROPE

At first sight, it is surprising that Senator Mike Mansfield was to become the strongest advocate of American troop reductions in Western Europe. During the 1950s Mansfield was regarded as one of the leading internationalists amongst the Democrats in the Senate. Indeed, he arrived in the chamber with an established reputation as an incisive analyst of United States foreign policy – a reputation which stemmed partly from his position as a Professor of Far Eastern History at the University of Montana, Missoula, and partly from his work on the House Committee of Foreign Affairs. Yet Mansfield's background was not a conventional one for a senator, particularly one who specialised in foreign policy matters. Having served in the army, the navy and the marines, he had worked for several years as a copper miner and then a mining engineer in Montana. With the help of his wife Maureen, he had obtained – somewhat belatedly – a formal education, and after attending the University of Montana, had been offered a position as Assistant Professor of Far Eastern History. From there Mansfield had progressed to the House of Representatives and after a bruising campaign in which he had to contend not only with an intemperate personal attack by incumbent Senator Zales Ecton, but also criticism from Senator Joseph McCarthy, Mansfield was elevated to the Senate. As a freshman senator he obtained a prestigious assignment to the Committee on Foreign Relations and used this as a base from which to consolidate his reputation as a specialist on international affairs.[29]

During both his tenure in the House, and his early years in the Senate, Mansfield appeared to be very orthodox in his thinking on US foreign policy, and although there were some indications of the more innovative and critical stance he was to adopt from the late 1950s onwards, he was clearly within the foreign policy consensus. Although he may have had some fleeting sympathy for Secretary of Commerce Henry Wallace, and the more conciliatory approach towards Moscow which Wallace advocated, Mansfield's thinking on Soviet–American relations quickly fell into the conventional mould.[30] Like other Americans Mansfield attributed the Cold War almost entirely to Soviet efforts to propagate an ideology and an intolerant way of life, both of which were abhorrent to the United States. As he put it in 1951: 'The primary threat to our nation, to peace, and to democratic progress stems from a new totalitarianism which has its core in Soviet imperialism.'[31] And although there were occasional references in his speeches to 'the glacier-like advance of communism' in Asia, he saw the primary area of danger as being in Europe.[32] This view of the Soviet Union and of the geographical focus of the threat seems to have remained consistent for several years and in a report to the Senate Committee on Foreign Relations in 1955 Mansfield made clear his belief that 'Soviet long range objectives, designed to reduce the Continent to totalitarianism, are unchanged'.[33] If Europe was the primary concern, however, Mansfield saw the threat as essentially a global one – and the adversary as tenacious in the pursuit of expansionist objectives. Although in 1956 a new flexibility seemed to enter Mansfield's thinking about the Soviet Union, for the most part he adhered to a view of the rival superpower which had been formed in the 1940s. While he recognised that there had been significant changes in Soviet society and the Soviet state, he suggested there was 'no evidence of a change in the basic aspirations of Communism' which still seeks to 'overturn, by fair means or foul involving the least risk to Soviet security, all the free governments in the world'.[34] Thus it appears that up until at least the mid-1950s Mansfield had a very clear and well-defined picture of Soviet objectives.

Mansfield was more ambivalent, however, about the means the Soviet Union might adopt to achieve these objectives. He regarded the Soviet threat, in its early stages, as essentially non-military in character, and supported the European recovery programme on the grounds that in 1946 and 1947 'international communism was eating its way into Western Europe via the roads of economic misery, social discontent and political instability'.[35] American aid to Western Europe succeeded in halting this process, but did not deal with the military problem – and Mansfield's attitude towards this was particularly interesting. There is little evidence to suggest that he took seriously the more alarmist predictions about the likelihood of a Soviet military assault upon Western Europe. Nevertheless he was not prepared to dismiss the dangers of Soviet preponderance. The military threat was significant but not unmanageable: Stalin could be deterred so long as he confronted a position of strength and a clear display of American intentions. This helps to explain why in 1949 – although he proposed that American civilian and military forces in Austria be cut by half – Mansfield advocated taking American occupation troops in Germany and Austria off the streets and putting them on manoeuvres.[36] It also helps to explain why he supported the North Atlantic Treaty, the military assistance programme, and Truman's decision to send US troops to Europe.[37]

Mansfield's notion of a position of strength, however, went beyond military preparation to include political cohesion. Because he believed that the military threat could be contained, he was extremely sensitive to possible changes in Soviet tactics. Although not indifferent to increasing Soviet military strength in the early 1950s, Mansfield was far more anxious about what he perceived as a two-pronged diplomatic challenge. On the one hand, he feared the Soviet Union might woo the Federal

Republic of Germany away from Western Europe and the United States by holding out the prospect of a unified Germany. On the other hand, he was concerned that the Soviet 'peace offensive' and the 'spirit of Geneva' were designed only to encourage a false sense of security, a relaxation of effort, the neutralisation of Western Europe and the disintegration of NATO.[38] Should the Soviet Union succeed in these efforts and undermine the relationships on which the Atlantic alliance was founded, Mansfield believed the results would be disastrous. It would

> disrupt the complex of Western military and air bases and the so-called infrastructure which stretches through Europe and the Middle East around the Western and Southern rim of the Soviet Empire. If that were to occur, the Soviet Union would have achieved its most important objective because the withdrawal of US defense forces and influence from the European continent would almost inevitably follow.[39]

It was one of the tasks of American leadership to prevent this. Indeed, Mansfield's acceptance of the idea that the United States was the natural leader of the 'Free World' was an inevitable concomitant of his concern over the Soviet danger. Although not enthusiastic about the assumption of this role by the United States, he recognised that since no other state was capable of containing the Soviet Union it was inescapable. The obligations of leadership made a retreat into isolationism both unacceptable and undesirable, leading Mansfield to warn of the fallacy – and also the danger – of regarding the United States as self-sufficient and invulnerable. 'As the leading nation among the free countries of the world we must assume the burdens of leadership if the peoples in the area are to retain any degree of freedom which they now enjoy.'[40] In other words, it was essential for the United States to build positions of strength which would deter Soviet aggression – and nowhere more so than in Western Europe. Prior to 1949, in fact, Mansfield advocated a more vigorous, rather than a more circumscribed, role for the US in Europe. He recognised that American involvement in European security was an inevitable consequence of the occupation of Germany, but argued that Washington had to be less equivocal in its approach. As he stated: 'The only question remaining is: will we be involved for the protection of our own national security, to our own advantage, and in the interest of peace, or will we be involved ineffectively, timidly, and with a vacillating policy which can only lead to calamity?'[41]

The North Atlantic Treaty provided an answer to this question and ended any remaining vacillation. Mansfield justified the entanglement with Western Europe on the grounds that the alliance not only added substantially to America's military, industrial and economic potential, but also denied such resources to the Soviet Union.[42] Thus the American commitment to Europe was based firmly on self-interest: the expenditure of resources and effort on West European economic recovery and military rehabilitation was far less than the cost of competing against a Soviet Union which controlled Western Europe and was able to mobilise European resources against the US. Nor was this the only way in which the Atlantic connection was advantageous to the United States. Western Europe, as the first line of America's defence, was becoming an increasingly strong and reliable ally. Indeed, Mansfield seems to have been considerably impressed by European efforts at self-help which he regarded as being as significant as the Marshall Plan in bringing about economic recovery.[43] Thus, the return on the American investment was substantial and well worth the initial cost.

Perhaps even more important for Mansfield than the evidence of West European self-help, was the willingness of the European nations to move towards integration or unification. Not only would this be highly advantageous in containing the Soviet challenge, but it would also create a greater degree of harmony and stability in Western Europe itself. The traditional divisions among the European states were a major source of international conflict and posed problems which were almost as formidable as the Soviet challenge. Mansfield's immediate prescription was for the removal of trade barriers in Western Europe which he believed were harmful in several ways: 'Aside from being a source of international friction' they 'have curtailed economic development and depressed Europe's standard of living. This along with the international friction has bred discontent and wars.'⁴⁴ Given this outlook, it is hardly surprising that Mansfield welcomed all moves towards greater integration in Western Europe – or that he was alarmed when the impetus towards unity seemed to diminish. The rejection of the European Defence Community by France, for example, led Mansfield to express concern over the possibility of a 'return to age old and probably suicidal rivalries'.⁴⁵ Although the London and Paris agreements and subsequently the formation of the European Economic Community reassured him, Mansfield's hopes for European unity were increasingly frustrated and disappointed. But even if he sometimes expressed his irritation with continued European divisions he recognised that it was the allies themselves who had to take the major steps: the United States, while it could encourage the process, could not coerce the Europeans into moving further and faster than they desired.⁴⁶

Equally disturbing to Mansfield was the fact that the European momentum in rebuilding its economic strength had not been matched in the first half of the 1950s by similar progress in the military sphere. In a report on *Europe After the Geneva Conference* Mansfield expressed his growing concern at some length:

> Perhaps the most striking evidence of the deterioration in Western unity is to be seen in European attitudes towards the defense structure on which the security of Western Community ultimately rests. German rearmament is moving slowly in the face of considerable popular resistance. Throughout the area there is pressure to reduce the number of men under arms and the length of the conscription period. France has deployed at least three divisions committed to NATO from Europe to North Africa. The British Government's present announcement of its intention to reduce its armed forces by 100,000 men is merely the latest development in the general slackening of the defense effort especially since the Geneva Conference.⁴⁷

In these circumstances, continued exhortation by the United States was essential if further backsliding by the allies was to be prevented.

There is little that was novel or exceptional in all this. For the most part Mansfield's approach to foreign policy was highly orthodox. Yet there were elements in his thinking which were not only idiosyncratic and unconventional, but foreshadowed a much more independent, critical and outspoken stance in the 1960s and 1970s.

From the outset Mansfield displayed a cautious and circumspect approach to American power. Sensitive to the need for American leadership, he nevertheless believed that there were certain principles which had to be observed in order to ensure that the United States did not overextend itself and squander its wealth and influence. As he stated:

> The resources which we have available for this international purpose are not unlimited. We can afford to use them only where there is reasonable expectation that they will accomplish the objectives for which they are intended. In general, this will be in situations where the people and governments most directly involved are alive to the meaning and obligations of freedom and will shoulder these obligations if given a helping hand.[48]

This notion of helping only those who were prepared to help themselves rather than unilaterally shouldering the burdens seems to have been influential in determining Mansfield's stance on several specific issues. He argued, for example, that US policy choices regarding the Philippines were not confined to either getting in or getting out, but should be seen rather more in terms of helping out.[49] Similarly, Mansfield approved sending US troops to Western Europe, while applauding the understanding that the majority of forces in NATO were to be provided by the Europeans.[50] He also recognised the inherent instability, strains and tensions in a one-sided relationship whereby the United States invariably acted as donor and the allies were merely recipients of American assistance. As early as 1955 Mansfield was arguing that the Atlantic relationship should be based on partnership not paternalism.[51] There is considerable evidence to suggest, therefore, that although Mansfield was an advocate of an American world role, he saw it as a matter of principle that this should be implemented with care, restraint and economy. Indiscriminate involvement in the affairs of others never had Mansfield's endorsement and in 1957 he was already warning that, while a return to isolationism was impossible, a posture of 'isolated internationalism' was equally unsatisfactory and could lead to the disastrous delusion of omnipotent national power.[52] A much more fervent internationalist than Robert Taft, Mansfield was as sensitive as the Ohio Republican to the need for prudence and restraint in the conduct of American diplomacy.[53]

This was bound up with another crucial element in Mansfield's thinking – his belief that it was essential to subject the precepts of US foreign policy to critical scrutiny and continuous reexamination in order to ensure flexibility and adaptability. Indeed, he saw the task of the Senate as an institution – and the role of individual senators such as himself – as being to provide independent reviews of foreign policy which would help to ensure that new circumstances and changed conditions were not ignored by the Executive. Criticism of, and dissent from, the Administration's position were not only permissible but – so long as they were initiated in a responsible manner and not for narrowly partisan purposes – highly desirable, particularly when they encouraged greater flexibility in foreign policy.[54] It was essential that policies which had outlived their usefulness be abandoned. Such arguments may appear trite and obvious. Yet Mansfield recognised that adaptability was often inhibited by bureaucratic inertia and the personal convictions and preconceptions of key decision-makers such as Secretary of State John Foster Dulles (whom the senator regarded as excessively resistant to change).[55] Mansfield's own thinking accorded fully with this flexibility. By 1956 he was suggesting that the United States should not become preoccupied with military containment to the exclusion of diplomatic threats, and arguing that the changes within Moscow since the death of Stalin revealed the need for a 'healthy attitude of enquiry about the Soviet Union' – particularly as in the longer term there was a distinct possibility that the Soviet Union would mellow and that the revolutionary zeal of Communism would ebb.[56] Although Mansfield was not sanguine about the Soviet threat, he was beginning to believe that it would be possible to develop a more cooperative relationship, and saw the military stalemate between the superpowers as providing 'an opportunity to promote a rationality of dealings' which had hitherto been muted and perhaps even non-existent.[57] Not yet prepared to abandon the Cold War shibboleths, Mansfield was certainly moving away from them and groping towards a new approach to the superpower relationship.

This duality in Mansfield's thinking – emphasising the threat from militant totalitarianism and the military strengths of the Soviet Union on the one hand, and the possibilities for change within the Soviet system and for superpower accommodation on the other – ran through many of his speeches in 1957. Increasingly, though, the emphasis was on the need 'to explore the whole scope of relations with the Soviet Union, with a view to lessening the . . . dangers of nuclear war'.[58] A note of caution was still evident in Mansfield's statements, as he acknowledged the 'basis for a deep concern with Soviet totalitarianism'.[59] But while it was important not to neglect the threat, it was equally important not to exaggerate it nor to overlook the dangers in a policy 'which would inflate this concern beyond actual proportions'.[60] In the light of all this it seems reasonable to suggest that Mansfield's attitudes towards the Soviet Union were undergoing a fairly profound modification which was evident to a limited extent in 1956 but which was much more obvious in 1957 (and which was certainly apparent prior to Sputnik). Mansfield's statements during the years which followed seem to confirm this trend. The phrase 'totalitarian communism' was used much less and Mansfield's major theme became not the threat of deliberate Soviet aggression but the danger of nuclear war arising out of irrationality, accident or miscalculation. Recognising that a 'concept of national security dominated almost exclusively by military equations was plausible and persuasive' but 'seriously shallow and incomplete', Mansfield in the late 1950s and early 1960s became increasingly concerned that the possibility of a *modus vivendi* between East and West should be thoroughly explored.[61]

Mansfield's belief that the major problem was to obtain a 'stable peace' between the superpowers seems to have dictated his advocacy of a 'third way' during the Berlin Crisis of 1958 to 1961. Anxious to avoid the dangers of surrender and of inflexibility in circumstances where standing firm, if coupled with 'subordinate irresponsibility, error or provocation on either side' could precipitate nuclear war, Mansfield suggested the creation of a free city of the whole of Berlin to be held in trust by an international authority.[62] He regarded Berlin as 'the lever which could ease Europe towards a more durable security or push the Western nations and the Soviet Union into a new vortex of irrationality'.[63] His proposals on Berlin were highly controversial and subjected to considerable criticism. Nevertheless, he continued to advocate changes not only in inter-alliance arrangements, but also in the Atlantic relationship itself. Indeed, the two sets of recommendations evolved almost in parallel: along with the changes in his thinking about the Soviet Union, Mansfield began to modify his approach to Western Europe. By July 1956, he was acknowledging that NATO should not be regarded as sacrosanct, since 'military structures' were 'not designed to last unchanged in perpetuity'.[64] The following year, he suggested that 'a concerted effort' was necessary 'to reduce the size of official establishments overseas – both military and civilian'.[65] Not only were these establishments 'costly in a monetary sense', but they were 'building an undercurrent of resentment' towards the United States in many countries.[66] Although Mansfield believed that the penalties for inertia in US foreign policy were severe, these early intimations of his desire for change were not followed up immediately with concrete proposals for troop reductions. Indeed, in 1958 Mansfield came out against some of the ideas for disengagement in Central Europe that were then in vogue. This might seem rather surprising in view of the Senator's position in the 1960s. Any inconsistency, though, is more apparent than real. Even at the height of his campaign for troop reductions, Mansfield admitted the need for a small US force in Europe as a token of the American commitment. He never advocated a complete withdrawal of the US contingent on the continent.

Nevertheless, as early as 1959 there were several indications that he was becoming increasingly disillusioned with European defence efforts – or rather the lack of them. In March, the Legislative Reference Service of the Library of Congress, at the Senator's request, prepared a breakdown of the costs of American participation in NATO.[67] In September, Mansfield, who had become the Assistant Majority Leader in the Senate, suggested that the European allies assume a greater measure of leadership in NATO 'commensurate with their growing stength' – although he added a caveat that this was not intended as advocating American withdrawal from Europe.[68] In December 1959 he came out strongly in support of General Twining, Chairman of the Joint Chiefs of Staff, who had criticised President de Gaulle for not permitting the deployment of American nuclear weapons on French territory. On this last occasion Mansfield was more explicit than ever before, and pointed out that French policy could provoke congressional moves to push the Europeans into doing more for their own defence by reducing US troops on the continent.[69] In an argument that was to become increasingly familiar, Mansfield suggested that two or three American divisions 'would be as symbolic as five'. Although this assessment may have been influenced by Frank Valeo, one of his most trusted advisers and a future Secretary of the Senate, it was also the logical conclusion of Mansfield's own very personal approach to foreign policy with its emphasis on a constant need for reappraisal and adjustment.[70]

In 1959 Mansfield did not belabour the idea of troop reductions; during the early 1960s he was to return to the theme more frequently. By then, of course, as a result of Lyndon Johnson's elevation to the Vice-Presidency, Mansfield was Majority Leader. As such, his words carried more weight. They were given added importance by the fact that he was not alone in his demands for troop reductions. There were growing murmurs of discontent from several senators with the scale of the American contribution to NATO. These grumblings must now be examined, as they provided a prelude to the development of a more concerted effort to bring about troop reductions.

5 MURMURS OF DISCONTENT, 1960–5

'Prior to 1966, Congressional pressure for a reduction of the level of American troops in Europe was neither significant nor formidable.'[71] There was certainly no well-coordinated or frontal challenge to the presence of substantial American forces in

Western Europe. Nevertheless a handful of senators were
becoming increasingly restive about the size of the US contingent. The first half of the 1960s was characterised both by
growing criticism of the NATO allies for their lack of effort and
by individual calls for a reduction in the US presence on the
continent. Furthermore, although both the complaints and the
demands were sporadic, they established themes which would
be elaborated at greater length, and with more force, in the
latter half of the decade.

As suggested above, the leading figure in this embryonic
movement was Senator Mansfield. In 1959 he had hinted that
US troops reductions might result from French intransigence;
but it was in 1961 that he made his first major statement
dealing with this issue. Although Mansfield's remarks were
short and succinct, they were also very revealing. In part, the
argument was a reiteration of the claim that NATO conventional forces did not provide an adequate shield and that
American troops were primarily symbolic. As such, the forces
in Europe 'would be no less a symbol of the US commitment'
were they 'to consist of two or three divisions rather than five'.[72]
Mansfield linked the possibility of such a reduction to reciprocal action by the Soviet Union: 'One would hope that it would be
possible to offer to reduce our total commitment of forces in
Europe by two or three divisions in turn for a Russian willingness to cut their forces in Hungary, Poland and Germany by a
roughly proportionate number – say somewhere in excess of
ten.'[73] The proposal was cautious and circumspect. Heir to the
disengagement proposals of the 1950s, it contemplated a mutual thinning out of forces rather than complete disengagement,
and, as such, was a forerunner of the proposals for mutual force
reductions which, ironically, were to be used in the 1970s to
counter Mansfield's demands for unilateral measures. The
advantage in terms of East–West relations was that it would
ease tensions by lowering the level of military confrontation in
Central Europe, while maintaining the basic structure of the
Soviet and American alliance systems. There were other benefits too, of course, not least, that it would ease the outflow of
dollars and gold from the United States. It would also force the
European allies to face up to their security problems in a way
that they had not hitherto done. If the Europeans believed their

security was jeopardised by a reduction of American forces, they were in 'a financial position ... to strengthen their own military forces and could do so'[74] In other words, a partial withdrawal of US troops could contribute significantly to a redistribution of burdens and responsibilities within NATO that was long overdue.

During the next two years Mansfield was even more explicit about the need for such a redistribution. In a speech in Springfield, Massachusetts, in October 1962, he warned that the United States was in danger of being imprisoned 'in a self-fashioned cage of outworn facts and ritualistic slogans', especially in its relationship with Western Europe.[75] The underlying theme was a familiar one in Mansfield's speeches and centred around the need to adapt to change.

And Mansfield was concerned in particular with identifying the changes which had taken place in Western Europe – and which, he argued, had transformed it beyond all recognition from the continent of the late 1940s and early 1950s, when it had been 'hurt almost beyond help, threatened by revolutionary upheaval from within and aggression from without'.[76] In contrast, Europe was now prosperous and dynamic economically and stable politically; it had also established substantial trading links with Eastern Europe and was far less concerned about the possibility of military aggression by the Soviet Union. American policy, however, was still based on an image of a ravaged, weak and insecure Europe. Thus it had to be modified in ways which would encourage 'a greater sharing of responsibility in line with the diminishing differences between the basic capabilities of the Europeans and ourselves as the effect of World War Two on Europe recedes into history'.[77] There had to be an assumption of burdens by the Europeans commensurate with their economic progress.

The United States also had to take into account that the European concept of its security needs differed from that prevailing in Washington, and that the allies were reluctant to increase their sacrifices for the common defence. In highlighting this difference Mansfield was doing nothing that he had not done before – he had made much the same point in 1955.[78] But whereas he had then been arguing that the Europeans should accept the American assessment of the security needs of

NATO, he now suggested the opposite course: the United States should revise its estimates downwards rather than the allies revising theirs upwards. Mansfield felt able to prescribe such a course of action because his own assessment of the Soviet threat had changed – and his new evaluation was confirmed, consolidated and extended by the European lack of concern. Thus the United States should avoid clinging 'to an excessive responsibility in Western affairs on a mistaken assumption that nothing has changed and the need for us is little different than it ever was and that special sacrifices on our part must continue'[79] Accordingly, Mansfield suggested, it was not unreasonable to consider a future reduction in the expensive commitment of forces to Western Europe. At this time, he still regarded such a reduction as contingent upon reciprocal Soviet action and the resolution of the Berlin question, but within a few years he was to advocate reduction on an unconditional basis.

The themes identified in the Springfield speech were developed further in a report to the Senate Foreign Relations Committee in January 1963. Although the report, entitled *Berlin in a Changing Europe*, was formally the product of a small group of senators, it clearly bore the Majority Leader's imprint, and it is almost certain that he was the dominant figure in its formulation. The main thrust of the report – that a substantial redistribution of burdens and responsibilities between Western Europe and the United States was overdue – reflected conclusions that Mansfield had arrived at after long and careful consideration of the issues. The report also contained recommendations that he was to push increasingly strongly over the next ten years. Indeed, Mansfield argued that it was a matter of principle that such a transition take place: without it, Western Europe would remain dependent on the United States to an unhealthy degree, a condition which would benefit neither party in the long term. Furthermore, it was a dependence which was no longer necessary. One of the concerns of the report, as suggested by its title, was to identify the changes in Western Europe which had made this transition possible. As the report stated:

The economic situation is now strikingly different in Western Europe, and at the same time its overseas military activities have shrunk. These changes clearly suggest the possibility and the desirability of a substantial lightening of the lop-sided burden which we have carried for the common defense.[80]

It is not unreasonable to insist that the continuance of the present costly level of our military commitment in Western Europe be contingent upon a substantial increase in the Western European commitment to NATO. Or conversely, if the Europeans believe that peace can be maintained without the addition of the promised European divisions – as they apparently do – there is no reason to reject the possibility that it can be maintained with fewer American divisions in Europe.[81]

In a sense, Mansfield was merely arguing that there be a return to the original conception of the Atlantic Alliance. The Majority Leader believed (as did Vandenberg in 1949) that the key to European security was the political commitment enshrined in the North Atlantic Treaty. The US military presence in Europe simply underlined this commitment. Consequently, the precise number of troops was secondary: the validity and credibility of the commitment stemmed from the interests the United States had at stake in Western Europe and not from particular force levels. Mansfield wanted a reversion to the concept of the alliance that existed prior to the Korean War. He was also arguing that the Europeans should fulfil their part of the initial 'transatlantic bargain'.[82] The prevailing assumption in 1949 was that Western Europe, through American assistance and its own self-help, would develop into an equal partner of the United States. Mansfield was disappointed that this had not occurred and gradually concluded that it would not do so while the allies relied excessively on the American military presence. A drastic measure, such as troop reductions, was essential. It would propel the Europeans into making the necessary defence efforts and provide a renewed impetus for moves towards greater cooperation and unity.

Although Mansfield, both in his position as Majority Leader and as the senator with the strongest views on the issue, was the key figure in the upsurge of pressure for troop withdrawals, similar sentiments were expressed by several of his Senate colleagues. This is not to suggest a unanimity of outlook amongst the proponents of troop withdrawals. There were differences of approach and emphasis despite agreement on the overall prescription. Senator Ellender, for example, extended his long-standing attacks on foreign aid and his complaints about the 'paper divisions' produced by the European allies into a demand for troop cuts.[83] In February 1961, Ellender advocated a study on the feasibility of reductions.[84] In August 1961, during hearings on the Foreign Assistance Appropriations for fiscal year 1962, he was vitriolic in his criticisms of the allies and argued that 'something ought to be done to make them contribute their fair share. If they don't I would go so far as to get out of Europe.'[85] Ellender's views were not really surprising and consequently had limited importance. The fact that Stuart Symington of Missouri, a former Secretary of the Air Force, and a long-time hawk, arrived at similar conclusions during the first half of the 1960s was more startling and more significant. Symington's position was based on three considerations. The first was the belief that military planning, by continuing to rely excessively on ground forces in an era of air power was outmoded: the forces of tradition should give way to the forces of modernity.[86] The second factor in Symington's thinking was the requirement of the Vietnam War: although he was to undergo a profound transformation in his thinking about Vietnam and (partly under the influence of Mansfield and Fulbright, his colleagues on the Foreign Relations Committee and partly as a result of talking to the men in the field) become one of the Senate's leading doves, through to the late 1960s he advocated the transfer of well-trained units from Western Europe to South East Asia.[87] Perhaps the most important of all, though, was Symington's concern over the balance of payments costs of US troops and their dependents in Europe. His anxieties about the decline in America's economic strength were reflected in a series of Senate speeches during November 1963 dealing with the United States balance of payments problem.[88] Although Symington's analysis identified a variety of causes for the recurring deficits, he concluded that one of the main culprits was American military expenditure overseas. By 1965 he was suggesting that radical steps be taken to reduce offshore military spending and, in a speech on 16 September, was more explicit than ever before in his condemnation of the European allies, alleging that 'the United States would not be faced with this problem if any of our more prosperous West European allies had shown a greater willingness to share in the burden of their defence'.[89] The belief that the NATO allies had exploited American generosity while giving little in return contributed to what by the mid-1960s had become an explicit anti-European stance by Symington.

He was not alone in his anti-Europeanism, however. Nor was he the most strident member of the Senate in his criticism of the allies. That distinction probably belonged to Wayne Morse of Oregon. One of the Senate's most idiosyncratic and independent figures, Morse had supported both the North Atlantic Treaty and Truman's decision to send troops to Europe. Throughout 1963, however, he made a series of speeches suggesting that unless the Europeans paid their share, the United States should withdraw from NATO.[90] The explanation for this may be found partly in the kind of constituency Morse represented. Oregon, after all, was highly dependent on agriculture for its prosperity and was one of the states most likely to be affected by the Common Agricultural Policy of the EEC with its barriers against US farm products, especially poultry, fruit and flour. Indeed, Morse was particularly critical of European, especially French, protectionism on agriculture, and was to emphasise the linkage between the economic and security dimensions of the Atlantic relationship almost a decade before the concept of linkage itself became part of the lexicon of American policy-makers. In a statement that foreshadowed the complaints of Kissinger and Nixon in the early 1970s, Morse argued that it was impossible to separate the economic and military facets of the problem: 'unless these nations want us to be economic allies, we should be through with them'.[91] In addition, he criticised the Europeans for their lack of support for US policy in South East Asia, arguing that the obligations of free nations could not be compartmentalised. Given such sentiments, it was natural that Morse should challenge the assumption of a permanent US presence in Europe which, he argued, had become a 'dogma' of postwar military and diplomatic thinking.[92] Maintenance of this presence, from being regarded as unconditional, should be made contingent upon European support. He was 'emphatically opposed to keeping American forces in Europe if they are not wanted, not needed and not matched. These are coordinate, coequal criteria. Our allies are not matching them.'[93]

Although Morse was probably the most outspoken critic of the allies, he was widely regarded in the Senate as something of a maverick and, as such, was not particularly influential. Richard Russell, in contrast, was one of the Senate 'whales', commanding enormous respect and deference from his colleagues.[94] As Chairman of the Committee on Armed Services he was particularly important on military matters. And in the early 1960s Russell too made clear his dissatisfaction with European defence efforts: during hearings on the defence budget in 1963 he also suggested that troop cuts in Europe would ease the United States balance of payments difficulties very considerably.[95] Indeed, it is one of the ironies of this period that although the Kennedy Administration succeeded in obtaining agreement with the Federal Republic of Germany, whereby Bonn promised to offset a substantial proportion of the foreign exchange costs of the US troops in Germany through purchases of American military equipment, congressional protests against the 'dollar drain' became more vociferous than ever.[96] Without such agreements, of course, the demands for troop reductions would probably have been even more intense. Thus the pressure exerted on Bonn initially by the Eisenhower Administration and then the Kennedy Administration helped to contain congressional pressures even though they did not succeed in defusing the issue completely.

In another way, however, the executive branch may have contributed to the sentiment on Capitol Hill in favour of troop reductions. In 1963, the Department of Defense carried out a highly successful exercise called 'Big Lift' which demonstrated the growing ability of the United States to reinforce its contingent in Western Europe rapidly and effectively.[97] The implication was that there was less need for troops on the spot. This was certainly the conclusion drawn by Senator Talmadge of Georgia, who added his voice to those demanding a reappraisal.[98] There was some evidence that at least a few officials in the Pentagon agreed with this assessment.[99] German sensitivities, however, militated against any marked shift of policy, while Secretary of State Rusk was strongly opposed to the idea that America's NATO commitment should be driven by either financial constraints or technological opportunities – strategic and political considerations had to remain paramount.[100] Rusk, in turn, convinced Kennedy, and at the end of October 1963 both the Secretary of State (during a visit to Germany) and the President himself, pledged that there would be no reduction of US combat troops in Europe, although Kennedy did not preclude the withdrawal of some support troops.[101]

At about this time, however, proponents of troop reductions received an important boost from an unexpected source. Former President Eisenhower, in an article for the *Saturday Evening Post* and a radio and television interview for the American Broadcasting Company, added his weight and prestige to the idea of a smaller American presence in Western Europe.[102] He admitted that during his eight years in the White House he had believed that troop reductions should be made as soon as 'European economies were restored' but that 'the matter was then considered too delicate'.[103] The time for such a move had now come. After all, he argued, in words almost identical to those used by Mansfield, 'One American division in Europe can show the flag as definitely as can several.'[104] The importance of his statement was difficult to overestimate. The argument was not original; nor was it likely to convince uncommitted senators. Furthermore, it was condemned by former Secretary of State Dean Acheson – both in a lecture at the University of Connecticut and in an article for the *New York Times Magazine* – who was concerned that the security system he had done so much to create would be unravelled if the former President's advice was followed.[105] Nevertheless, Eisenhower's endorsement helped to support, legitimise and justify a stance which could all too easily be represented as a premature, dangerous and ill-advised recommendation, liable to disrupt or even destroy a major cornerstone of United States foreign policy. The fact that one of the foremost military authorities in the United States regarded a reduction of American military forces in Western Europe as both feasible and desirable, probably encouraged the critics to continue propounding their views, and provided ammunition that would be used to challenge the orthodoxy of successive Administrations.

Even so, it was not until 1966 that a concrete proposal for troop cuts in Europe was introduced into the Senate. The major lines of attack, however, were established well before this. By 1965 there was a clearly discernible movement for troop withdrawals, although it still remained in an embryonic state. The following year it was to develop into a far more explicit and broadly-based attempt to pressure the Executive into action. The reasons for this transformation and the nature of the pressure during the period from 1966 to 1970 are examined in the next chapter.

5 The Period Of Gentle Pressure: The Mansfield Resolutions, 1966–70

1 FROM INDIVIDUAL PROTEST TO COLLECTIVE ACTION

In 1966 the congressional pressure for troop withdrawals from Western Europe changed significantly. What had hitherto been the isolated murmurings of a small, albeit growing, number of individuals became a much more focused and institutionalised – if still rather modest – protest movement against the *status quo* in NATO. From 1966 through to 1970, Majority Leader Mansfield introduced a series of Senate resolutions recommending that the number of American troops in Europe be considerably reduced. Although these resolutions were never pushed to the vote, Mansfield gathered an increasing number of co-sponsors, thereby displaying the growing sentiment in the Chamber in favour of a smaller American presence in Western Europe.

While this tactic might have artificially inflated the strength of the withdrawal movement – in that a number of senators almost certainly agreed to co-sponsor the resolution as a token gesture, on the tacit understanding that it would not be pushed to the vote – the challenge to Administration policy could not be ignored. Mansfield's commitment to the issue was strong and although he pursued it sporadically rather than systematically, the very fact that he was Majority Leader endowed the initiative with added significance. Yet, as was discussed in the previous chapter, Mansfield had believed in the need to reduce US troops in Europe since at least as early as 1961. Why then did the issue come to a head in 1966?

To some extent, of course, the introduction of a Senate resolution can be understood as the natural development of the concerns that existed prior to 1966. In so far as the presence of a substantial number of American troops was regarded as a breathing space, the passage of time almost inevitably brought with it a growing willingness to challenge the *status quo*. Furthermore, the idea of troop reductions had been legitimised not only by Eisenhower's statement in 1963 but also by the persistent rumours in the first half of the 1960s that the Kennedy and Johnson Administrations intended to initiate a drastic cut in the American military presence in Western Europe. The Pentagon's increasing air-lift capability and the emphasis on mobility and rapid reinforcement in a crisis gave credence to these rumours and in 1966 there was frequent press commentary suggesting that Secretary of Defense Robert McNamara was privately in favour of such a shift.[1] Despite official denials that this was so, the speculation was intensified by McNamara's comments before Senator Henry Jackson's Subcommittee on Government Operations in which the Secretary indicated that the United States might withdraw some of its forces if the Soviet Union agreed to reciprocate in Eastern Europe, a suggestion which won the explicit disapproval of former Supreme Allied Commander Europe, Lauris Norstad.[2] Even more important in fuelling the discussion – and in creating considerable anxiety in Bonn – was the announcement by the Department of Defense in April 1966 that it was withdrawing 15 000 specialists from Europe in order to augment American forces in Vietnam.[3] Despite promises that the garrison in Europe would be restored to full strength by the end of the year, the move not only provoked criticism from West Germany but added to the impression that the size and strength of the American contingent in Western Europe were of only secondary importance. Even so, it is doubtful if the troop issue would have taken on quite the salience it did had it not been for General de Gaulle's decision to take NATO out of France and France out of NATO.

Although it would be exaggerating to suggest that de Gaulle's policy – announced in a press conference on 21 February 1966 and confirmed in a note to President Johnson the following month – caused the Mansfield Resolution, it almost certainly provided the occasion for a congressional reappraisal of the

American presence in Europe.[4] Indeed, what many Administration officials regarded as a threat to the viability of NATO was welcomed by Mansfield as an opportunity to undertake the review of American policy in NATO that he had long been advocating. For Mansfield, de Gaulle's letter was not 'a shocking impertinence' but 'a helpful initiative which could lead to adjustments in NATO' which were as much in the interests of the United States as of France.[5] The Majority Leader regarded the French initiative as a symbol of the changed conditions in Europe which, in his view, made possible a substantial reduction in the American presence. De Gaulle's action was a recognition of the progress of *détente* in Europe. Changing conditions had increased the French President's freedom of action; there was no reason why they should not do the same thing for the United States. After all, why should Washington take the Soviet threat to Western Europe any more seriously than did the governments of the region themselves? In connection with this, Mansfield was increasingly critical of what he regarded as a double standard on the part of the Europeans: an unwillingness to contribute more to their own defence in a period of relaxation combined with a reluctance to contemplate any weakening in the American effort in Europe. It appeared that the Soviet threat was taken seriously only when questions were raised about the size and scale of the American presence.[6] Furthermore, for Mansfield, as for other senators, de Gaulle's move symbolised the desire of the Europeans to take a free ride and highlighted their reticence when it came to sharing the burdens of Western European security. As Senator McIntyre expressed it, the allies were becoming 'fat and lazy' at America's expense.[7] In other words, de Gaulle's actions added considerably to congressional disaffection with Western Europe. Not only had the French President sabotaged Kennedy's 'grand design' for an Atlantic partnership, but his withdrawal from NATO also undermined the strategy of flexible response and conventional resistance promulgated by McNamara. And although the French President could be regarded as idiosyncratic, and his policies dismissed as an aberration, he also seemed to symbolise what many of the congressional critics were increasingly inclined to regard as European ingratitude and antipathy.

These congressional sentiments were neither novel nor unprecedented. Yet they were given greater intensity and respectability by the growing belief that the United States was becoming increasingly overcommitted in the world. The American involvement in Vietnam eroded the margin of tolerance for European ingratitude. Indeed, United States efforts in South East Asia elicited European reactions ranging from indifference to outright hostility. As such they added a further twist both to the burden-sharing argument and to the claim that the allies adopted double standards. The 1966 debates in Congress had echoes of the criticisms levelled at the Europeans by Senator Knowland during the Korean War, when he had complained that the bulk of both the effort and the casualties were American. The point was expressed most forcefully by Senator Pastore of Rhode Island in his comment that while the Europeans were criticising the American involvement in Vietnam they took the position 'that we should be heavily involved where the Red Peril threatens them'.[8]

The growing strain on America's resources also had important domestic consequences. Indeed, the need to reorder American priorities to give more attention to domestic concerns was to become a major theme amongst the proponents of troop withdrawals in the years ahead. In 1966, it was summed up simply but effectively by Senator Symington in his statement that the United States should give less attention to the problems of the world and more attention to the problems of the United States.[9] If the remarks of Pastore contained echoes from Senator Knowland in 1951, this comment by Symington was nothing if not reminiscent of the arguments propounded by Robert Taft against the deployment of US troops to Europe in 1951. It also suggests that the Cold War consensus which had dominated American thinking on foreign policy was beginning to break up. Symington had long been concerned about the debilitating effects of American military policy overseas on the US balance of payments and its internal ecomomic health; that concern was now resulting in a much more assertive approach to foreign policy issues by the senator.

Indeed, the Mansfield Resolution itself can be understood in a similar light. It represented the beginnings of the Congressional revolt against the predominance of Cold War policies, and the dominance of what would later be called the 'Imperial Presidency'. Concerns over the substance of policy and its domestic consequences coincided with a growing realisation that although the executive branch did not have a monopoly of wisdom in foreign policy, Congress had allowed the President to acquire what was virtually a monopoly of power. As Mansfield expressed it during the subsequent debate, 'the time is long past due when this body should exercise the responsibilities which are its own in this matter'.[10] This is not to suggest that the revolt was full-blooded or that, initially at least, it was a conscious effort by congressional leaders to restore traditional rights and prerogatives. On the contrary, the Mansfield Resolution was a cautious step which did not pose a direct and immediate challenge to presidential power. Yet it symbolised, as few other initiatives at this time did, that the Senate could not only play an independent role in foreign policy and national security matters, but that it could do so even in the face of presidential disapproval. This becomes clear in examining the circumstances attendant upon the birth of the Mansfield Resolution.

2   THE MANSFIELD RESOLUTION

The Mansfield Resolution arrived in the Senate by an odd route. Most legislative proposals emerge from one or other of the Senate's standing committees. In contrast, the Mansfield Resolution developed out of discussions in the Democratic Policy Committee (DPC). According to Mansfield, the discussion of the issue at a meeting of this committee on 13 July 1966 was wholly spontaneous.[11] Furthermore, it appears that despite his long-standing advocacy of a reappraisal of the American military presence in Western Europe, Mansfield was not the driving force behind the move. Symington was apparently the key figure in a discussion which arose 'on the spur of the moment'.[12] He had visited Europe in April 1966 and had become very disillusioned with the attitudes and policies of the allies, filing an extremely critical report on his return. In the light of this, it is not entirely surprising that discussions about the involvement in Vietnam led on to a wider analysis of

American commitments in which the military presence in Europe became the main focus of attention. And although Mansfield was not the main instigator of Senate action, he almost certainly welcomed such a move. Indeed, the virtual unanimity of the Democratic Policy Committee must have been a source of considerable gratification to the senator, who had been concerned about the issue for at least the past five years. Furthermore, the endorsement of a committee which contained not only Mansfield himself but other senior and influential senators such as Richard Russell, Warren Magnuson of Washington, Long of Louisiana and Pastore gave the demands for change an immediacy and an impact that had hitherto been absent. Although there were differing emphases and concerns among the members, there were the beginnings of a powerful coalition which the Administration could not afford to ignore. Different senators had different concerns: for some, like Symington, the key issue was the fiscal dimension and especially the balance of payments problem; for others it was the need to encourage greater burden-sharing by the Europeans; for yet others it was a way of expressing resentment against either European trade and agricultural practices or a lack of support in Vietnam. The point about a troop withdrawals resolution, however, was that it promised to satisfy these very diverse concerns.

At the same time, the Democratic Policy Committee had certain loyalties to President Johnson, both as party leader and as a former colleague. Consequently, it is hardly surprising that rather than face Johnson with a *fait accompli*, Mansfield informed him of the deliberations. As a result there were several meetings between the Policy Committee and high-ranking officials including Secretary of State Rusk, Secretary of Defense McNamara, Secretary of the Treasury Fowler, and George McGee, American Ambassador to West Germany.[13] The purpose of these meetings was to reassure the members of the Policy Committee that there was no need for precipitate action. In the event, however, the Administration failed to do this. Indeed, it has been argued that the meetings may even have been counter-productive. According to one commentator, 'at least some of the Senators felt they had been fobbed off with outdated arguments and an unwillingness to be frank. So they wrapped themselves in secrecy from the administration and concocted their own proposal.'[14] As a result of meetings on 10, 25 and 30 August, the committee decided to introduce a Senate resolution which would not be binding on the President but which nevertheless allowed the Senate to make its views known in a formal way. Further discussions of the proposal on 25 and 30 August resulted in the text of what became Senate Resolution 300 which was introduced on 31 August. Senate Resolution 300 acknowledged the importance of Western Europe to the United States, but emphasised that the changes in European economic and military capability which had taken place since 1949 had not been accompanied by equitable military contributions. When set against the relaxation of tension in Europe, the fiscal and monetary problems of the United States, and the development of American airlift capability, the conclusion was clear: 'a substantial reduction of United States forces permanently stationed in Europe' could be made 'without adversely affecting' American 'resolve or ability' to meet its commitment under the North Atlantic Treaty. It was further resolved that Senate Resolution 99 adopted in April 1951 was to be amended to contain the provisions of Senate Resolution 300.[15]

The introduction of the resolution immediately sparked off considerable speculation that Mansfield was acting on behalf of the Administration and that his move was designed to put pressure on the Federal Republic of Germany, and especially Chancellor Erhard who was to visit Washington in September to discuss the problem of offset payments with President Johnson. In fact such speculation was incorrect. Although differences between Washington and Bonn 'over the adequacy of Germany's purchases and Germany's unwillingness to make future commitments provided just that much more fuel to the debate on maintaining the current American troop levels in Europe',[16] the offset issue does not seem to have been a major concern of the Democratic Policy Committee. Another consideration which dispels the idea of collusion between Johnson and the committee is that the President was not aware of the impending initiative until just before the resolution was introduced. Furthermore, when he did discover what was happening he telephoned Mansfield to say that 'he disapproved in strong terms'.[17]

Nor was the President the only one to do so. The resolution encountered a storm of protest in the Senate itself, partly because of the unusual circumstances of its birth. Even some of those Senators who supported the spirit of the proposal were unhappy about the way it had been put on the agenda. Senator Fulbright, Chairman of the Foreign Relations Committee, wrote to Mansfield on 1 September to say that he had added his name as a co-sponsor of the resolution but cautioned that he was not entirely happy with the procedure that had been followed. As he put it: 'While I have some reservations about the implications of the Policy Committee in reporting a resolution of this kind and asking that it be placed directly on the calendar, I have waived these reservations in my own mind in view of the larger implications involved in forthright action at this time on this subject.'[18] Not surprisingly, he also requested that if Mansfield felt it desirable to refer the resolution to a committee it should be sent to Foreign Relations or at the very minimum be referred jointly to the Committees on Foreign Relations and Armed Services.[19] Other senators, especially those who opposed the substance of the resolution, also seized upon what they regarded as a procedural irregularity in an attempt to discredit the committee's proposal. Senator Henry Jackson was particularly critical of the leadership and accused the proponents of the resolution of attempting to 'ram' it through the Senate without giving members an opportunity to explore the issues in formal hearings.[20] Although, strictly speaking, Jackson was correct in his claim that the Senate had not held hearings on the subject, the possibility of reductions had been raised in several different committees including Jackson's own Committee on Government Operations. Indeed, on 2 September, the day after Jackson's comments, Symington telephoned Mansfield to make precisely this point, and reiterated it on the Senate floor a few days later.[21] The opponents of the resolution, however, remained both unconvinced and unrepentant, and the Policy Committee was subjected to uncharacteristically sharp criticism. Although this came from both sides of the aisle, there was inevitably an element of partisanship. Apart from Senator Jackson, the most vociferous critics of the proposal were Republican. Although the Senate Minority Leader, Everett Dirksen, was opposed to it from the outset, after discussions with the President, he came out far more strongly against troop cuts. Even more outspoken were Senator Kuchel, the Republican Whip, Senator Javits of New York, a strong NATO supporter, and Senator Lausche who accused the DPC of 'an arrogant exercise of power'.[22]

In addition to these procedural arguments, it was also suggested, somewhat deferentially, that the matter should best be left for the Executive. Much of the criticism was considerably overstated, since the proposal was no more than a recommendation which, in the final analysis, did not compel the President to take any action that he deemed unwise or undesirable. Nevertheless, the belief that the troop level in Europe was essentially an Administration responsibility seems to have deterred at least a handful of senators from adding their names to the list of co-sponsors of Senate Resolution 300. The idea of executive supremacy still had considerable sway. It was strengthened by the notion that if adjustments were to be made in the American presence, this should be done through consultations with allies – a task that could only be undertaken by the Executive. This was a theme that was adopted by the Administration as well as by its allies in the Senate.[23]

This is not to deny that the resolution had considerable support. Mansfield did not solicit signatories but, drawing heavily upon analyses provided by the Legislative Reference Service of the Library of Congress, made several forceful statements on the proposal.[24] By 22 September there were over 30 co-sponsors. Even earlier than this an Associated Press report of 4 September had claimed that a canvass of Senators had revealed 48 in favour of early and positive action on the resolution and only 17 against.[25] At the same time, Mansfield was obviously taken aback at the intensity of the opposition. There was considerable wrangling over procedure and the Majority Leader was at pains to reassure the opponents of the resolution that he was not attempting to short-circuit Senate procedures and push his resolution to the vote regardless of the concerns that had been expressed. Mansfield's own style of consensus leadership was almost certainly one of the main factors prompting a reassessment of the situation by the Democratic Policy Committee, and a decision to defer further consideration of the issue to the ninetieth Congress which would convene in January 1967. Another consideration which contributed to this postponement was President Johnson's conciliatory speech on East–West relations of 7 October in which he held out the prospect of peaceful engagement and referred to the possibility of 'a gradual and balanced revision in force levels on both sides' in Europe.[26] The Erhard–Johnson summit at the end of September also raised the possibility of a new set of arrangements on both troop levels and offset costs, and resulted in the inception of the trilateral negotiations involving Britain, West Germany and the United States in October.[27] In these circumstances the postponement of action by the Senate was a reasonable response, especially as the proponents of troop withdrawals had already had a victory of sorts merely by putting the issue on the agenda. As Symington noted on 6 September, 'In one sense, much of the purpose of this resolution has already been accomplished.'[28] A signal had been sent to the allies that they could not expect the United States to continue indefinitely to finance their security. Furthermore, by making clear that the deferral decision was only a postponement and not an abandonment of the issue this signal was endowed with even greater weight. And as Mansfield made clear, postponement was not to bury the issue but to sharpen it ready for its reintroduction in the new Senate.[29] The warning had been posted.

3   THE PRESSURE MAINTAINED: SENATE RESOLUTION 49 AND THE COMBINED SUBCOMMITTEE

Although Mansfield had recognised the difficulties of pushing his troop reduction resolution any further in the last few months of 1966, he was anxious that the pressure on the executive branch should be maintained. For the Majority Leader and his colleagues on the Democratic Policy Committee the resolution was essentially a tactical device to force the Administration to initiate what Mansfield believed to be a long

overdue reappraisal of the American military presence in
Western Europe. The inception of the tripartite negotiations
appeared to be a step in the right direction, but far from
placating the congressional critics of the existing troop level, it
probably encouraged them to maintain the pressure. There
was also a concern that unless this was done the negotiations
would have no more than a marginal impact. Indeed, one of the
early results of the negotiations was that the United States
agreed to purchase an additional 35 million dollars worth of
equipment from the United Kingdom in an attempt to offset
the foreign exchange costs of the British Army on the Rhine and
thereby encourage the Wilson Government to maintain the
presence.[30] What the proponents of the Mansfield Resolution
had hoped would be a device for easing the American burden
seemed to be working the opposite way. These concerns were
reflected in a strategy meeting of the DPC in early January
1967, at which it was agreed to reintroduce Senate Resolution
300. Although Senator Carl Hayden of Arizona was not prepared to endorse the proposal, the other members of the
committee gave it their full support.[31] Mansfield sent a letter to
his Senate colleagues on 10 January informing them that he
intended to reintroduce the resolution on the grounds that
nothing had happened during the intervening months to diminish the wisdom of such a measure. His initial intention, as
set out in the letter, was to ask that the measure lie on the table
for one week to allow for additional co-sponsors before it was
taken up.[32]

The following day the proposal was discussed in the Foreign
Relations Committee, as a result of which Fulbright wrote to
Mansfield informing him that 'The unanimous belief of those
present was that the resolution should be referred to committee, especially on procedural grounds. In particular, there was
a feeling that policy committee consideration followed immediately by floor action in effect would preclude expression of
minority party views in the normal framework.'[33] He added
that the sentiment in the committee was that creation of an *ad
hoc* subcommittee would be 'the most efficient and appropriate
way of proceeding', and that he had been charged with discussing this possibility with Senators Russell and Dirksen as well
as Mansfield himself.[34] In a handwritten postscript Fulbright

added a further suggestion on the basis of his conversation with the powerful Georgian Senator, Richard Russell: 'Russell suggests it be a joint subcommittee of 11 members – 7 Democrats and 4 Republicans. He insists that he will not be chairman – that I have to do it. If you are willing I suggest that you take the chair and hold the hearings since it is your Resolution and I am sure the Administration would be much happier with you.'[35]

Almost certainly Mansfield agreed to this procedure before reintroducing the DPC's proposal as Senate Resolution 49 on 19 January. Indeed, from the outset it was made clear to the Senate that the resolution would not be acted upon until it had been examined in committee. Even so, Senate Resolution 49 aroused opposition which was as strong – if more restrained – as that which had greeted Resolution 300. Once again the leading critics included Henry Jackson amongst the Democrats and Jacob Javits amongst the Republicans. Nevertheless, there was also considerable support for the resolution, which on the day of its introduction had 41 co-sponsors, and by 16 February had 44 signatories including 12 Republicans. Although it was still predominantly Democrats who supported the Majority Leader against a Democratic President, there were the beginnings of what its proponents hoped would be more extensive bipartisan support.

Realising this, and aware of the extent of dissatisfaction with the existing situation, the opponents of troop reductions attempted to find a compromise formula which would acknowledge the legitimate grievances of the Mansfield forces but do so in a way which was less of a challenge to the Administration and less of a threat to the allies. Two Democrats, Joseph Clark of Pennsylvania and Thomas Dodd of Connecticut, proposed amendments to Senate Resolution 49. Clark's proposal recommended that the Administration should seek mutual reductions, an idea that Mansfield had put forward in 1961, whereas Dodd's advocated comprehensive hearings on NATO in an effort to establish 'whether, how, and when' a significant reduction in the American military presence in Europe could be implemented without adverse consequences for alliance security.[36] Although these measures were not unimportant, more significant was the alternative proposed by Senator Javits working closely with Senator Thruston Morton of Kentucky.

Senate Resolution 83, or the Javits–Morton Resolution as it became known, acknowledged the need to maintain substantial American combat forces in Europe but also urged the Europeans to do more and advocated consultations with the allies on the possible redeployment of some American forces from Europe back to the United States.[37] This resolution, which was cosponsored by Senators Brook, Griffin, Scott, Tower and Jordan of Idaho took on added significance because it had the tacit support of the State Department. 'Administration officials were understood to have made clear that they favoured the approach embodied in the Javits amendment [*sic*], although they could not commit themselves publicly because to do so would have them favouring a Republican resolution over one sponsored by Democrats.'[38] At the same time it appears that senior Republicans were not entirely happy with the Javits initiative and there was considerable press speculation that Morton was using the issue to undercut the leadership of Dirksen and other conservative Republicans who were backing Richard Nixon for the Republican nomination for the 1968 presidential campaign.[39] In addition, it appeared that Javits himself was attempting to use the troop debate to establish a more flexible Republican policy. Whatever the internal party machinations, however, it was indisputable that Resolution 83, as a Javits aide pointed out, was 'aimed pretty directly against the Mansfield resolution'.[40]

Nor was this the only opposition Mansfield had to face. Although the State Department was reticent about its support for Javits, the Administration was unequivocal in stating that the Mansfield proposal was not helpful. Indeed, Johnson invited Mansfield and other leading senators and representatives to a breakfast meeting at the White House on 27 February. 'The meeting was carefully orchestrated to let Mansfield have his say but to surround his view with opposing positions.'[41] At the same time the President made clear that consideration was being given to the possibility of 'dual-basing', whereby two of the three brigades in a division would be returned to the United States while the third brigade would remain in Germany on a rotational basis.[42] The extent of the redeployment was in fact a source of considerable controversy within the executive branch, with McNamara favouring a more extensive redeployment, the Joint Chiefs of Staff opposing any move in this direction, and Secretray of State Rusk in favour of a limited reduction.[43] John McCloy, who had been appointed by Johnson as the American representative in the trilateral negotiations, was also against any change, and it has been suggested that Johnson used the 27 February meeting to impress upon him that domestic political considerations demanded that he be tougher with the Germans.[44] In so far as it was also an attempt either to isolate or placate Mansfield, however, the meeting seems to have been less successful.

This was partly because the issue had now taken on its own momentum. Arrangements for the *ad hoc* subcommittee had been worked out, and on 1 March it was announced that Fulbright, Church, Aiken and Hickenlooper from Foreign Relations would serve on the subcommittee along with Symington, Jackson, Miller and Pearson from Armed Services. The membership also included Sparkman of Alabama and John Stennis of Mississippi. The composition of the subcommittee was important: Hickenlooper was opposed to the resolution, while the presence of Jackson and Stennis meant that Mansfield, even if he had wanted to – and it is not clear he did – would have been unable to bend the subcommittee to his will. The involvement of two such stalwart defence conservatives also ensured that the subcommittee would find it virtually impossible to obtain a consensus on anything other than broad declarations about the need for greater burden-sharing. Nevertheless, the subcommittee began its hearings on 26 April, just as the trilateral negotiations were reaching completion, and heard further testimony on 3 May. Much of the urgency was taken out of the issue, however, by the announcement of the Trilateral Agreement on 2 May, and the hearings themselves were somewhat perfunctory despite the appearance of McNamara, Rusk and Under-Secretary of State, Nicholas deB. Katzenbach.[45] Indeed, most attention was focused on the package deal which emerged from the discussions and combined the redeployment scheme with new offset arrangements. The United States, as Johnson had intimated in the meeting of 27 February, would 'rotate' one division and one air-wing, an arrangement which in practice meant a reduction of 35 000 men – and not merely the 12 000 that had been feared in early

April. The Federal Republic also agreed to purchase 500 million dollars worth of medium-term Treasury bonds and to make public its commitment not to convert its dollar reserves to gold.[46]

For the most part, the agreement received a positive response in the Senate. Mansfield himself stated that he was delighted at the outcome and clearly regarded it as an overdue but none the less welcome first step in the adjustment he had long been advocating.[47] One slightly sour note was struck by Frank Church in the subcommittee's discussions with Rusk on 3 May when the Idaho senator suggested that the implication of the new offset agreement was that the United States was borrowing from Germany in order to maintain troop levels in Europe, and that the Administration should have insisted upon more direct compensation for the 'gold drain'.[48] Apart from this, though, there was general agreement that the redeployment went a long way towards meeting the objectives that Mansfield and the other members of the DPC had set themselves when introducing the resolution. Consequently there was no need to continue further with the subcommittee's activities, at least for the moment.

Yet there were several indications that the issue had been temporarily defused rather than permanently settled. In response to written questions from Mansfield, Assistant Secretary for Congressional Relations William Macomber emphasised that in the Administration's view no further redeployments of US forces in Europe were warranted and that the adoption of Senate Resolution 49 would be unhelpful.[49] Mansfield, in contrast, almost certainly regarded the redeployment as merely the first of several steps required to bring about the much more fundamental adjustment he desired.

Nevertheless, Mansfield realised that there was little to be gained by exerting further pressure in the immediate aftermath of the Trilateral Agreement. As a result he did not embark on any of the available options. It would, for example, have been possible to extend the subcommittee hearings by asking additional witnesses to testify. Indeed, Senator Clark wrote to Mansfield on 28 April to say that he would like to testify in support of his amendment to Senate Resolution 49.[50] Even before this, Senator Miller had suggested to the Majority

Leader that the subcommittee receive testimony from General Lemnitzer and General Maxwell Taylor.[51] Carl Marcy, Chief of Staff of the Committee on Foreign Relations, had also pointed out that pressure could be kept on the Administration by calling witnesses from the academic world who were in favour of troop reductions as well as former President Eisenhower, George Kennan and General James Gavin – all of whom had also come out in support of a reduction in the American presence in Europe.[52] Another option highlighted by Marcy was for the subcommittee to go to Europe to talk to government leaders. His argument was that such tactics would help to keep pressure on the Administration, whereas if the proposal was passed this might 'take the steam out of the Administration's review of troop policy and hence not be so good'.[53]

In the event Mansfield did none of these things. Part of the reason for this was his realisation that the Johnson Administration would find it immensely difficult, for the moment at least, to make further concessions beyond the planned redeployment. Another factor was that Mansfield himself had many other concerns and responsibilities. 'The field of vision of Senators, and especially of the leadership, is as wide as the President's. Hence Mansfield could concentrate on the question only sporadically.'[54] If the Majority Leader did not push the issue as hard as he could have done throughout the last six months of 1967, however, he did not neglect it completely. One incident in particular demonstrated that both the Administration and the NATO allies could not afford to ignore the concern in the Senate. In July, the West German government announced reductions in defence spending which, it was estimated, would lead to a cut of between 40 000 and 60 000 men in the German armed forces. Mansfield's reaction was prompt if not particularly forceful. He argued that Bonn's action made some of the assurances about West European force levels and the allied contributions to NATO, which had been given by Rusk and McNamara, ring rather hollow. If there was scope for further reductions, then these should be in the American presence. Certainly, the United States should not be more militant about the defence of Germany than were the Germans themselves.[55] Although the Bonn government backtracked a little on its decision as a result of the urgings of the Johnson Administration, the incident demonstrated that the issue was temporarily in abeyance but that it had the potential to reemerge at any time.[56] Indeed, Mansfield used the episode to serve notice that although the redeployment scheme had been a temporary palliative, it was far from a permanent solution. In 1968, however, it was Symington rather than Mansfield who made most of the running on the issue.

4 TROOP WITHDRAWALS AND THE SOVIET INVASION OF CZECHOSLOVAKIA

'1968 was a year of mixed influences on the question of US force deployments in Europe. The underlying pressures continued – demand for troops in Vietnam, balance of payments drain, lag in West European defense programs, and West European opinion in favor of detente.'[57] Yet there were also several considerations which militated against any further erosion in the American military presence in Europe. The Soviet invasion of Czechoslovakia in particular made it appear inopportune to contemplate any reduction in the American troop level. This was reinforced by several other developments in NATO which strengthened the Administration's hand in responding to the congressional critics.

The connection between the calls for a reduction in the American military contingent in Western Europe and the Vietnam War had been apparent in 1966, but was much more explicit in 1968. The Tet offensive, launched by the Viet Cong at the end of January, forced the Johnson Administration to extend the draft. This announcement in turn provoked Senator Symington into suggestions that it would be far better for the Administration to call on its pool of highly-trained manpower in Europe 'rather than hastily trained youth from this country'.[58] Although Symington had made similar demands in the past, these lacked the stridency and urgency that was evident in his speeches of February and March of 1968. His concerns over the Administration's actions in Vietnam were reinforced by his anxieties about the continued deficits in the balance of payments. The 1967 deficit had amounted to 3.5

billion dollars – the largest since 1960 – while there was further pressure on the dollar in the early months of 1968.[59] European injunctions to the United States to reduce both the size of the Federal budget and the balance of payments deficit only added to the resentment felt on Capitol Hill towards the NATO allies. Although Symington was perhaps the leading critic of Western Europe in the Senate, he was far from being the only one. His arguments were reinforced by those of Senator James Pearson of Kansas who, during this period, appeared to be one of the staunchest Republican supporters of proposals to reduce troops in Europe and by Frank Church who complained that proposals he had made in 1966 to 'Europeanise NATO' through the appointment of a European to the position of SACEUR had come to naught.[60] It was Symington himself though who took the lead in reviving the issue in the Senate, and on 19 April introduced an amendment to the defence procurement bill, S.3293, to prohibit the use of funds after 31 December 1968 to support more than 50 000 members of the United States armed forces on the continent of Europe.[61]

The Symington Amendment was more far-reaching than the Mansfield Resolution in both form and content. The resolution was merely advisory; the amendment, if passed and not subjected to a presidential veto, would have been mandatory. Furthermore, the scale and speed of the reductions were far more drastic than anything Mansfield had contemplated. Yet this very fact suggests that the episode was stage-managed as a quick and easy way of renewing pressure on the Administration. It is possible, of course, that Symington's action reflected a degree of impatience with the inaction of the joint subcommittee and with Mansfield's apparent reluctance to press the issue further. Although Mansfield had indicated in an interview in January that he planned to revive this troop withdrawals campaign and hold further hearings early in the session, he had not followed through with this.[62] Nevertheless, it seems probable that the introduction of the Symington Amendment and its subsequent withdrawal was discussed with Mansfield beforehand and the two senators had decided that it would be a useful tactical ploy. The fact that there was virtual unanimity amongst those who contributed to the relatively brief debate on the subject gives further credence to this interpretation. Indeed, Mansfield emphasised that the Administration should take this to heart – a warning which was given greater force by Symington's promise to reintroduce the proposal when the defence appropriations bill came before the Senate later in the year.[63]

In the event, the Soviet intervention in Czechoslovakia made such a move inopportune. Before this, though, there were several indications that the Administration was taking the possibility of a direct confrontation on the issue quite seriously. There were several distinct elements in their response. One was to initiate a low-key lobbying campaign in the Senate in which George McGee, the former Ambassador to Germany and now ambassador-at-large, played probably the central role.[64] Although McGee's activities may have had some effect, however, they were not sufficient to dissuade Symington from going ahead. Nor were Mansfield and Symington impressed by the increasing emphasis on the idea of mutual force reductions. This notion had been floated by Mansfield in 1961, with no result, and he had expressed his scepticism about it when Senator Clark used it as an argument against unilateral measures during 1966 and 1967. He was no less sceptical about the Reykjavik Declaration of June 1968 in which NATO governments outlined their readiness to explore the possibility of mutual force reductions with the Soviet Union and the countries of Eastern Europe. Both Mansfield and Symington were acutely aware that this move was in large part an attempt to undermine the case they were presenting for unilateral American adjustments. Nor was Mansfield happy with the new offset agreement between Washington and Bonn which was also signed in June 1968. Once again, as part of the arrangements the Bundesbank had agreed to purchase 500 million dollars worth of medium-term Treasury bonds from the United States.[65] And as Mansfield and Symington pointed out – in comments which echoed those of Frank Church the previous year – the overall result was that the United States ended up paying interest in order to maintain its own troops in Europe.[66]

Despite his continuing dissatisfaction, however, Mansfield does not seem to have been prepared to devote a great deal of time and attention to the issue throughout most of 1968. In May, Jim Lowenstein, the Foreign Relations Committee staffer who was doing much of the staff work for the joint subcommittee, wrote to Mansfield proposing a further two or three days of hearings and suggesting a number of witnesses who could be called.[67] In the event no hearings were held and it appeared that Mansfield had decided that Symington's amendment offered a better approach. This alternative, however, was derailed by the Soviet invasion of Czechoslovakia on 20 August.

In the aftermath of the invasion Mansfield was aware that the prospects for any adjustment in the American presence in Europe had receded dramatically. One analyst has even suggested that the invasion led Mansfield to abandon his earlier position. This is something of an overstatement, however, as in a number of speeches and reports the Majority Leader emphasised that his convictions had not changed but that the time was not opportune for any further action. As early as 13 September he made clear that his views on 'the anachronistic size of the deployment of American forces and dependents' remained intact.[68] Furthermore, it was imperative that gradual reductions be initiated as soon as it was clear that developments in Eastern Europe would not spill over into Western Europe.[69] The point was reiterated, albeit in a more oblique way in a postscript to an earlier report on Czechoslovakia which Mansfield sent to the Committee on Foreign Relations in December 1968. In his final paragraph Mansfield wrote that 'The relationships of the Western nations' require 'refinement, redefinition, and restatement at this time. There remains in them, at this late date, too much that is drawn from the one-sided dependency on the United States which was the reality twenty years ago but is no longer the case ... The key is a greater contribution of and a more active leadership in European affairs by the Europeans themselves.'[70] The implicit corollary of a greater contribution by the Europeans, of course, was that the United States could then do less.

Indeed, for Mansfield the question of troops in Europe was not simply a matter of equitable burden-sharing. While obviously not averse to this, he wanted a much more far-reaching readjustment of roles and responsibilities in which the American contribution to the defence of Western Europe was minimal. Yet the report of the *ad hoc* subcommittee which appeared on 15 October 1968, placed main emphasis on the fact that the defence efforts of the allies were disproportionately low in comparison to those of the United States. The reason for this was what the report frankly acknowledged as 'a division of opinion in the subcommittee on the question of the level of US forces in Europe'.[71] It is possible that without Czechoslovakia the subcommittee report might have been more far-reaching in its conclusions and gone beyond encouraging the reduction of US administrative personnel in Europe. However, Mansfield's concern with the rights and prerogatives of all senators, irrespective of whether or not they agreed with him, militated against this. If the opinion of the subcommittee was divided, then the report had to reflect the limited consensus that did exist. For all this, the report was not insignificant, and almost certainly added to the pressure on the Europeans to take their own defence more seriously.

Indeed, the Europeans in 1968 faced increasingly compelling demands to shoulder a greater share of the defence burden in NATO. At the Defence Ministers' meeting in Brussels in May, Clark Clifford, who had replaced McNamara as Secretary of Defense apparently made a strong statement to the allies demanding that they make better use of their resources, thereby making it possible for the United States to spend less in Europe.[72] In addition, Secretary of State Rusk made clear that Washington was not averse to the emergence of a European 'caucus' with the alliance.[73] The European response, initiated largely by Dennis Healey, the British Minister of Defence, was to form the Eurogroup, an informal grouping of European NATO members (without France, Iceland and Portugal).[74] From the outset, the Eurogroup had two objectives in mind: one was the coordination of defence efforts in order to maximise effectiveness; the other to demonstrate to both the Administration and the congressional critics in the United States that Western Europe did take its defence obligations seriously. This latter objective was in many ways the more difficult – especially in relation to the Congress. Because Mansfield wanted a much more fundamental reordering of the Atlantic relationship – away from what he regarded as paternalism by the United States and excessive dependence by the Europeans – it was almost inevitable that he would be dissatisfied with the efforts of the Eurogroup. Nevertheless, its activities would form an increasingly important element of the troop debate over the next two years.

5   THE MANSFIELD RESOLUTION AND THE NIXON ADMINISTRATION, 1969–70

Although the formation of the Eurogroup reflected European concerns over congressional pressures for American troop withdrawals from Western Europe, these pressures temporarily eased in the months following the Soviet invasion of Czechoslovakia. The presidential election campaign extended the period of grace, while the election of a new President also meant that Mansfield and Symington had to give the incoming Administration an opportunity to establish its own priorities and policies. If these were not responsive to their concerns, however, then it was almost certain that the battle between the Senate and the Executive over the troop issue would become even more intense than during the last two years of the Johnson Presidency. Furthermore, Nixon would find the Congress, especially the Senate, particularly difficult to handle. Not only did the new President lack the manipulative skills of his predecessor, but he arrived in office at a time when Congress was becoming far less deferential towards the presidency than it had been throughout the Cold War years. Furthermore, the fact that the President was a conservative Republican could hardly fail to have considerable impact. As one analyst observed, 'Nixon's election provided a real tonic to congressional Democrats, for it reduced their internal tensions and integrated the party – and thereby the institution – against a Republican administration. The Senate liberals, in particular, were able to immerse themselves in the occupational therapy of unembarrassed opposition to the White House, a task made easier by their increased seniority in the chamber.'[75] This opposition was manifested in much more vigorous reassertions of congressional rights than in previous years and in arguments over national priorities. The issue of troops to Europe was connected with both these things.

There was no immediate confrontation over troops, however, partly because the new Administration was engaged in a reappraisal of its own. The Johnson Administration had bequeathed it a plan to make a reduction of 30 000 support and administrative personnel in Europe in order to minimise budgetary and foreign exchange costs of the presence in

Europe.[76] This option was incorporated into a much wider review of American commitments, strategy and force levels. It rapidly became clear, though, that Nixon regarded Western Europe as a priority area in American foreign policy. In February 1969 he visited Europe for discussions with allied leaders, and the Johnson plan was quietly set aside.

While the importance of Western Europe was not seriously disputed by the Mansfield supporters in the Senate, the belief had been growing that American interests there could be upheld with a far smaller military presence. Nevertheless, this was not the immediate focus of attention in 1969. The concern over troop levels in Europe was subsumed in a broader reappraisal of American commitments overseas undertaken by a subcommittee of the Foreign Relations Committee chaired by Symington, and in an attempt to pass a National Commitments Resolution which stated that such commitments required some form of affirmative legislative action to give them affect.

The Nixon Administration's response to these pressures was a mixture of accommodation and intransigence. The conciliatory elements were evident in Nixon's statement in Guam in July when the President declared that America's Asian allies would have to take prime responsibility for their own security. The intransigence was reflected in statements characterising the critics as isolationists or neo-isolationists.[77] These comments by the President ended what, despite the activities of the Symington subcommittee, and the manoeuvrings on the National Commitments Resolution, had been almost a six-month 'honeymoon' for the new Administration. Even Mansfield had initially given Nixon the benefit of the doubt and although the Majority Leader had reacted to a Canadian announcement that it was reducing its forces in Europe with further suggestions that the United States do the same, he was not prepared to take any precipitate action at that stage.

By the middle of the year, however, the appearance of consensus had disappeared, and for a brief period during July 1969, it appears that Mansfield did contemplate reintroducing his troop withdrawal resolution.[78] This was almost certainly a response to the announcement on 9 July of a new two-year agreement between Bonn and Washington on offset payments.[79] In the event, he decided to wait until later in the year, primarily because of the impending German elections.[80] On 19 October, however, he made clear in an interview that while he would not take immediate action until the new coalition government in Germany had 'its feet on the ground', he now felt that conditions in Czechoslovakia had settled down sufficiently to permit a reintroduction of the resolution without this being misinterpreted either by the Warsaw Pact countries or by the NATO allies.[81]

On 1 December, Mansfield introduced Senate Resolution 292 which was identical to the two earlier proposals on troop reductions. In discussing the resolution he pointed to an interview with the new German Chancellor, Willy Brandt, which had appeared in *Time* magazine in November, and in which Brandt had suggested that there was an understanding between Bonn and Washington that there would be no substantial changes in the American presence during the period of the new offset agreement. Prompted by Jim Lowenstein, Mansfield had written to Secretary of State William Rogers, requesting details of any commitment that had been made.[82] Although the senator's statement of 1 December gave no indication that he had received a response to this query it revealed that the Administration and the Senate were set on an inexorable collision course on the troops issue. Nixon had demonstrated considerable flexibility in relation to Asia, but there were no plans for Vietnamisation of the Vietnam War to be accompanied by Europeanisation of the defence of Europe. And in Mansfield's view this had become intolerable at a time when the United States was overburdened both internally and externally. The presence in Europe was 'a voracious consumer of US resources' at a time when they were being drained by Vietnam. The result was that 'in terms of surplus for necessary national purposes at home and abroad' the United States was 'beginning to scrape the bottom of the barrel'.[83] This concern over the internal consequences of the American military presence in Europe was not new, of course, but was given greater prominence by the fact that the Republican Administration and the Democratic-controlled Senate had very different priorities. Although Nixon recognised the need for reductions in military expenditure, he was not prepared to go either as far or as fast as his critics desired. Many of the Democrats who supported

Mansfield, however, had been closely associated with Johnson's Great Society programmes and were intent on preserving, if not consolidating, the gains in social welfare provision that had been made in the mid-1960s, and to which Nixon was so hostile. Furthermore, the Senate liberals had developed a degree of independence and expertise in this field that made them unwilling to defer to the Administration. 'They had become experienced in supervising and refining social welfare policies in 1967 and 1968, when President Johnson's interest in the field had been replaced by the imperatives of war management. Now that they were confronted by a Republican president, congressional Democrats felt no obligation to defer to White House priorities to restrict the scope of their reform proposals.'[84] In other words, the Mansfield challenge over troops was potentially a much more fundamental challenge to the Nixon Administration's foreign and domestic policies. Like the dispute over the anti-ballistic missile, which also surfaced in 1969, it raised questions about the direction of American society as well as questions about the respective roles of Congress and the President in establishing that direction.

Whether this was understood by the Administration is not entirely clear. That it took the Mansfield threat seriously though is indisputable. Mansfield's statement of 1 December evoked immediate criticism from Senator Scott, the Minority Leader, and Senator Griffin, the Republican Whip, both of whom were apparently acting at the behest of the Administration. Indeed, it was reported that Senator Scott's speech had been prepared either by the White House or the State Department.[85] Further evidence of an Administration attempt to seize the initiative and discredit the Mansfield Resolution was provided on 20 January 1970, when Under-Secretary of State Elliot Richardson made a widely reported speech to the Chicago Council on Foreign Relations elaborating the dangers of a unilateral American troop reduction in Western Europe.[86] Mansfield's response to the statement, which apparently had been approved by Nixon, was to produce the fiftieth and fifty-first co-sponsors of Resolution 292.[87] The Majority Leader also expressed astonishment at the fact that 'the 250 million people of Western Europe, with tremendous industrial resources and long military experience, are unable to organise an effective military coalition to defend themselves against 200 million Russians who are contending at the same time with 800 million Chinese, but must continue after 20 years to depend upon 200 million Americans for their defence'.[88] In the battle of rhetoric Mansfield was at least holding his own with the Administration, while the number of co-sponsors – although inflating the degree of support Mansfield would have obtained had the resolution come to the vote – was nevertheless significant in conveying to the Administration the extent of its problem.

The Europeans too were becoming acutely aware that the pressure in the Senate to reduce the American contingent was not going to disappear. The message had been brought home to them by Senator John Sherman Cooper at the North Atlantic Assembly meeting in October 1969, and perhaps more importantly, by Secretary of Defense Laird at the NATO Defence Ministerial meeting in December. The growing intensity of the Washington debate in early 1970 underlined these earlier warnings and provoked a realisation by the Europeans that they would have to take positive and concerted measures if the pressures were to be contained. The Nixon Administration itself added to European concerns: despite positive measures such as Nixon's 1969 visit to Europe and Richardson's powerful critique of troop cut proposals, there was some ambiguity in the White House position. The Nixon Doctrine, unveiled in February, emphasised the need for partnership with allies, and although the commitment to retain the existing level of troops until mid-1971 was reiterated, it was also revealed that the United States would increasingly look to the nations directly threatened to assume the primary responsibility for their own defence. The imlication was that there might well be troop cuts after mid-1971. To some extent, this ambivalence may have been a deliberate ploy to prod the European allies into shouldering a greater share of the defence burden. The Mansfield pressure was also useful in this connection as it added an extra dimension which was all the more effective because it was not entirely under the Administration's control. As one study observed, 'Troop reductions were discussed with an air of certainty and inevitability, if also one of reluctance. There was a sense in which the government supported its allies against the burden-sharing criticism but, perhaps equally, there was a sense in which Congress was used to force certain actions on the Europeans by instilling a fear of what might otherwise happen.'[89]

If this was the strategy, there were indications in the summer of 1970 that it was beginning to succeed. Discussions amongst the Europeans about what could be done to forestall such moves and ease the congressional pressure took on an increased urgency. The formation of the Eurogroup had provided the framework for a burden-sharing initiative, but it was far from clear what course to adopt. The German preference was for some form of direct subsidy to the United States, while Britain – largely because the withdrawal from East of Suez made available additional capabilities for NATO – pressed for an increase in force levels. Although Bonn's proposals reflected an understandable concern that the Bundeswehr not be enlarged, other Europeans had reservations about the German scheme, partly on the grounds that it would turn American forces in Europe into mercenaries. Nixon too was aware of this possibility and during a trip to Europe in late September and early October made clear to NATO Secretary-General, Manilo Brosio, that he preferred greater European efforts rather than direct subsidies for the American contingent.[90] The American President also made a speech in Ireland in which he ruled out unilateral American reductions.[91] The ambivalent American stance had already produced results in that the Europeans were seriously considering ways of augmenting their contribution. Consequently Nixon felt able to replace it with a far less equivocal approach. Although this presidential decision hid continuing bureaucratic disputes over the wisdom of troop reductions, it effectively meant that the internal review being carried out by the National Security Council (NSC) had been decided in favour of the *status quo*.[92]

Despite this, the last two months of 1970 were periods of considerable activity on the troop issue in both Europe and the United States. In Washington there was a meeting of the NSC on 18 November at which more formal consideration was given to National Security Study Memo (NSSM) 84 which laid out the range of options available. Although Melvin Laird argued for a cut of between 20 000 and 40 000 support troops – a move which would have yielded savings of between 200 million and 400 million dollars and might have acted as another temporary sop to the Mansfield forces in the Senate – objections from the State Department and the Joint Chiefs of Staff, together with the President's own predispositions, ensured that this option was rejected.[93]

Meanwhile the differences amongst the Europeans continued. There was also an early indication that the level of effort being contemplated would not satisfy the congressional critics when, in early October, Senator Percy, one of the most vigorous proponents of greater burden-sharing, suggested that the amount of extra effort being considered by the allies was totally inadequate, especially when set alongside the 14 billion dollars which the United States was devoting to NATO.[94] Such warnings provided an additional incentive for the Europeans to reach an agreement, the final details of which were hammered out at the Defence Ministers meeting in early December. The package which resulted from these deliberations, and which became known as the European Defence Improvement Programme (EDIP), envisaged additional European defence spending over the next five years of around a billion dollars with $420 million to be voted to improving NATO infrastructure, especially aircraft shelters and communications.[95] It was presented along with a NATO study entitled Allied Defence 70 (AD70) as evidence of a new seriousness of purpose in Europe's approach to its own security. Yet its primary significance was political not military. This became evident when the Eurogroup announced that the programme had been initiated on the basis that the United States would, for its part, maintain its presence in Europe at the existing level.[96] In other words, there was what one analyst has described as a *quid pro quo* linkage between European efforts and American pledges not to reduce unilaterally.[97]

The linkage had been underlined by Secretary Laird on 30 November when he announced that the United States was going to maintain its existing capability in Europe for another eighteen months. Laird's political instincts regarding the need for token reductions, however, were sound. As he almost certainly realised, his announcement put the Nixon Administration and Senator Mansfield on a collision course. Whether the fairly modest cuts the Secretary of Defense had advocated would have been sufficient to placate Mansfield is far from certain. Yet a tactic which in certain respects resembled Johnson's approach in 1967 might have postponed the issue. As it was, the Administration merely provoked Mansfield into announcing that he intended to go beyond a resolution and introduce troop withdrawal legislation.[98] Nor was the senator impressed by the arguments that the United States should reward greater European efforts by maintaining its own position. Although other senators might find this persuasive, if the Administration had ever believed that the linkage would influence Mansfield then they had failed almost completely to understand his position. Although the Majority Leader had at various junctures emphasised the European lack of effort, his concern was not more equitable burden-sharing but a smaller American presence. More extensive European defence efforts were welcome as measures which would facilitate American troop withdrawals, but as a device for legitimising the *status quo* they were not persuasive. Consequently, for Mansfield the period of postponement and flexibility was coming to an end. The implications of this were to become apparent in May 1971.

6 The Mansfield Amendment of 1971

1 INTRODUCTION

In May 1971 the debate over the United States military presence in Europe changed dramatically as Senator Mansfield introduced an amendment to the Selective Service Bill (HR 6531) which required that the American troop deployment be reduced by 50 per cent (i.e. 150 000 men) by the end of 1971. Unlike the earlier resolutions, which were merely non-binding recommendations that could legitimately be ignored by the President, an amendment – potentially at least – would have the force of law. If the Mansfield Amendment managed to obtain the approval of the Senate *and* survived the House–Senate Conference Committee, the President would be faced with the dilemma of either accepting it or vetoing the draft extension bill as a whole. Thus the challenge was much more serious than in previous years and the Majority Leader's actions raised the stakes very considerably. By not bringing his earlier resolutions to the vote, Mansfield had succeeded in keeping the issue alive and maintaining pressure on the Executive, while avoiding a frontal assault on the President's policy; with the introduction of a troop withdrawal amendment, a direct confrontation became unavoidable. This was hardly surprising, as the proposal threatened not only the existing US policy towards Europe, but also the Executive's monopoly of control over that policy.

This change of approach is explicable partly in terms of Mansfield's growing frustration and impatience with the Nixon Administration's stance *vis-à-vis* both Europe and Asia. After a promising start in which he had appeared strongly committed to military retrenchment overseas, President Nixon had reaffirmed his support of the existing troop levels in Europe. The hopes of the troop withdrawal advocates that the Nixon Doctrine would be applied to Europe as well as Asia were disappointed as it became clear that Vietnamisation was *not* the prelude to Europeanisation. Indeed, Mansfield's actions in May 1971 can be understood as a direct response to decisions taken towards the end of 1970 by the President. The Administration's well-publicised review of the troop issue in the Autumn resulted in public pledges by both the President and Secretary of Defense Laird to support the *status quo* – a decision which prompted Mansfield on 1 December to announce his intention to go beyond a resolution and 'introduce an appropriate type of legislation . . . at the appropriate time'.[1] After some success with the Johnson Administration in 1967, the gentle pressure had failed to have much impact on the Nixon Administration – and a reappraisal was therefore necessary. It was not merely that Nixon was less responsive than Johnson had been, however. The reappraisal was also facilitated by the fact that the Democratic Majority Leader was less inhibited in dealing with a Republican President than he had been with one of his own party. This had already been made apparent in Mansfield's support for the National Commitments Resolution which was much more vigorous after Nixon's inauguration had 'removed party loyalty as a restraint'.[2] Nor was the effect of the presidential transition confined to Mansfield. For a Democratic-controlled Congress which had become restive and alarmed over the direction and control of United States foreign policy under Johnson, the election of a Republican President provided a major opportunity for a reassertion of rights and prerogatives. This was obvious as early as 1969 with the passage of the National Commitments Resolution. By the end of 1970, however, the dissatisfaction was much more pronounced and extensive as a result of Nixon's actions in Vietnam and Cambodia and his blatant disregard for congressional opinion. It was not surprising therefore that 1971 saw what was probably the most vigorous attempt since the 'Great Debate' of 1951 to restore the balance between Congress and the President. The efforts to end the hostilities in Vietnam and to impose restrictions on presidential power to make war were two manifestations of this mood. The attempt to legislate US troop withdrawals from Western Europe was undertaken in the same spirit of defiance.[3]

Despite this, it is not certain that Mansfield wanted the amendment to pass the Senate. In so far as the measure was highly symbolic, its introduction may have been more significant than its ultimate fate. Indeed, the drastic nature of the proposal – in terms of both the size of the cut and the time within which it was to be made – militated against its passage. Yet this seems to have been a deliberate ploy by Mansfield and his staff, albeit one which seems to have caused some disagreement amongst the advisers. It has been suggested that of the three assistants who drafted the amendment, Charles Ferris, the Counsellor to the Democratic Policy Committee, and James Lowenstein, consultant to the Committee on Foreign Relations, preferred a 50 per cent cut, whereas Edward L. King, a former staff member of the Joint Chiefs of Staff, advocated a more moderate cut of about 30 per cent.[4] Mansfield, seeing the episode primarily as an 'educational exercise', may have opted for the higher figure in order to dramatise and publicise the issue.[5] Carl Marcy, Chief of Staff of the Foreign Relations Committee, hinted at this when he argued that the only way to shake the bureaucracy was to prepare something quite radical, 'that it was necessary to go at reduction with a meat-axe because the Administration could handle a scalpel'.[6] Charles Ferris, who was one of Mansfield's most trusted advisers, made the same point even more graphically when he described the amendment as an attempt to 'get the Donkey's attention'.[7]

If this was Mansfield's intention then he almost certainly succeeded: his proposal not only caused widespread consternation, but created almost total panic in the Administration. Part of the reason for this was that Mansfield's initiative seems to have taken the President and his advisers by surprise. There was considerable comment both in the press and on Capitol Hill to this effect, and Kissinger has stated that the Administration, 'without any warning', learned of the amendment on 11 May, the day it was introduced into the Senate.[8] If this was the case, however, it stemmed from a failure on the part of the Administration – and especially those officials with responsibil-

ity for congressional liaison – rather than from any attempt by
Senator Mansfield to conceal his intentions and catch the
Administration unawares. On the contrary, Mansfield gave
considerable advance warning to anyone who was listening to
his statements, and when he did finally introduce his amendment, one commentator described it appropriately as a 'long
promised bill'.[9] In December 1970, as discussed above, Mansfield had put the Administration on notice that he was going to
go beyond a Sense of the Senate Resolution, so that the
initiative itself, as opposed to its timing, should not have come
as a surprise. Furthermore, even the timing of Mansfield's
proposal was not entirely unheralded. On 5 May, six days
before the amendment was introduced, Mansfield engaged in a
revealing colloquy on the Senate floor with Stuart Symington.
During the exchanges the Majority Leader suggested that they
had 'laid the foundation for an amendment, not a resolution,
but an amendment – to bring about a reduction of U.S. troops
and dependents in Europe'.[10] The following day the Majority
Leader announced at a news conference not only that he was
considering an amendment to the draft-extension bill which
would make troop reductions from Western Europe mandatory
but also that the troop contingent could be cut in half without
any adverse effect on Western European or United States
security.[11] Correctly interpreted by the press as a renewal of the
campaign to cut forces in Europe, the news conference was a
clear signal for the Administration. There was a further indication on 10 May, when Mansfield announced that he was now
definitely going to propose a troop withdrawal amendment to
the draft-extension bill.[12] The failure of the Executive to pick up
these unequivocal signals is difficult to explain. Part of the
reason may have been a preoccupation with other events and
issues. Kissinger has noted that 'the Amendment came forward
in a week in which we concluded the negotiations for a breakthrough on SALT, set up the trip to Peking, were engaged in
delicate talks on Berlin, and arranged for another round of
private talks with the North Vietnamese'.[13] If the previous week
was equally full and fraught, then it is perhaps slightly less
puzzling that the Administration was caught so unawares: after
all negotiations with adversaries could have left little time,
energy or inclination for negotiating with Congress. Neverthe-

less, it is hard to believe that officials in the White House or the State Department specifically charged with congressional liaison had not been sensitive to at least some intimations of Mansfield's intentions. If this is so, then the problem may have been in alerting their superiors.

Whatever the cause, the failure to anticipate Mansfield's actions put the Administration at an immediate disadvantage. It was not only the unexpected nature of the challenge which was discomforting however. Equally significant was that Mansfield had displayed once again – as he had earlier done with his troop withdrawal resolutions – a shrewd sense of timing. The amendment was introduced at a time when the dollar was undergoing one of its periodic crises. During the first three months of 1971, the United States had suffered a shortfall of over 5 billion dollars in its balance of payments – a figure which represented the highest quarterly deficit it had ever incurred.[14] Concern about this further deterioration in America's financial position went hand in hand with resentment towards the Europeans. This was reflected in Senator Symington's remarks of 5 May, during which he reiterated his familiar argument that US balance of payments difficulties were brought about in large part by American military spending overseas – a large chunk of which was on Europe's behalf.[15] Set against this, European complaints about the American deficit and demands that Washington put its house in order were deemed gratuitous and offensive, to say the least. And the decision of the Federal Republic on 9 May to float the deutschmark not only deepened the crisis by precipitating a *de facto* devaluation of the dollar (which in turn would increase the cost of the American presence in Europe) but also intensified the anti-European sentiment on Capitol Hill.[16] For senators already irritated by what appeared as the gross ingratitude of Western Europe, such action invited retaliation, and even for those who were less antagonistic Bonn's decisions was unpalatable. This is not to suggest that the increasing crisis was the cause of the proposal, merely that it provided an opportune moment for Mansfield to introduce a proposal which had probably been drafted some weeks earlier. Nevertheless, the Administration was worried that the dollar crisis might provoke a groundswell of support for the Majority Leader's amendment. In order to prevent this the

White House embarked on a lobbying campaign which, although belated, was so intensive that one analyst has suggested that it would be necessary to 'go back to the Marshall Plan to find a similar effort'.[17]

2 ADMINISTRATION LOBBYING

The immediate response of the Administration was one of outright condemnation. A series of statements from the White House and the State Department suggested that the proposal was irresponsible and that its proponents were oblivious to the damage it might cause.[18] The profound and far-reaching nature of the amendment was emphasised and it was argued that its passage could do irreparable harm both to the structure of the Atlantic Alliance and to United States security: consequently, the President was completely opposed to it. Significantly, spokesmen for both the White House and the State Department cautioned against rapid or decisive action. Ronald Ziegler, the White House Press Secretary, announced that because of the probable effect of the amendment, it was inconceivable that the question could be addressed by the Senate before full and complete hearings had taken place.[19] In a similar vein, Robert J. McCloskey, for the State Department, commented that the Senate should act only after comprehensive hearings.[20] Such statements were partly a stalling tactic, as the Administration realised that if the amendment did come to a vote quickly the likelihood was that it would pass. This pessimistic forecast was reflected in the warning by Senator Gordon Allot after a meeting of the Republican Policy Committee, that if the amendment was attached to the draft interim bill, the President would veto the whole thing.[21] Even if the amendment did not become law, however, its passage through the Senate would almost certainly have provoked a crisis of confidence among the European allies. To avoid this, the Administration began to consider ways in which Senate approval of the proposal might somehow be forestalled.

The first priority was to obtain sufficient time for officials to bring pressure to bear and to rally the opposition to the amendment. This task was made more difficult by Mansfield's

desire to bring the issue promptly to a conclusion on 12 May.
To prevent this the White House, according to some reports,
instructed sympathetic Republicans in the Senate to delay a
roll-call vote by any means possible.[22] This became clear in a
series of speeches on 12 May in which senators reiterated the
theme that no action should be taken until extensive hearings
had been held – a claim rejected by Mansfield who argued that
hearings had taken place and the issue been debated exhaustively in previous years. After negotiation with Senator Stennis,
Chairman of the Committee on Armed Services and floor
manager of HR6531, Mansfield, although making clear publicly that he deplored the delay, reluctantly agreed that the vote
would not take place until a week later on 19 May. Henry
Kissinger, the President's National Security Adviser, and the
key figure in coordinating the lobbying campaign against
Mansfield, has acknowledged that this delay was crucial: 'We
obtained an extension of 5 days which, while niggardly and
almost preposterous in the light of the issues involved, probably
made the difference.'[23] Although Kissinger seems to have been
mistaken regarding the number of days by which the vote was
put back, the thrust of his appraisal is a convincing one, not
least because the period from 12 to 19 May was an eventful one
in which the Administration, in a variety of different ways, was
able to chip away at Mansfield's support.

At first, however, the Administration seems to have been in
some disarray about the best course to adopt. The main
argument seems to have been whether or not to opt for a
compromise proposal which accepted the principle of troop
reductions in Europe but gave the President far more discretion
in implementing such reductions than did the Mansfield
Amendment. Kissinger's account is somewhat ambiguous
about precisely when this disagreement was resolved. Although not explicit, it gives the impression that the matter was
more or less decided on the morning of 12 May.[24] Other reports,
though, suggest that it was on the night of 12 May that it was
finally agreed to adopt a stance of no compromise.[25] This latter
interpretation is more plausible, not least because the early
part of 12 May seems to have been taken up by consultations
betwen the White House and its allies in the Senate. Kissinger
had an early morning meeting with Senator Hugh Scott of

Pennsylvania, the Republican Minority Leader, and Robert
Griffin of Michigan, the Minority Whip, while Kenneth Belieu
of the Congressional Relations staff discussed the problem with
John Stennis.[26] Although these sessions were partly to decide
upon strategy, they also provided the Administration with
assessments of the likely support for the Mansfield Amendment. It appears that from the perspective of the White House,
forecasts were dismal, with Stennis in particular feeling that
Mansfield probably had a majority in favour – and that therefore the appropriate tactic was to accept, if not encourage, a
more moderate measure such as a Sense of the Senate Resolution urging the Administration to negotiate reductions with
both the allies and the Soviet Union.[27] Kissinger's account
suggests that he spent most of the day telephoning Stennis and
other key senators trying to convince them that a compromise
was not only foolish but against the wishes of the President.[28]

Yet it seems that at this stage the Administration itself had
not decided upon its response to Mansfield's challenge and that
Kissinger, in promulgating the need for a tough line, was
merely following his own instincts. According to his account
there was a strong divergence of opinion among the President's
advisers, with Secretary of State Rogers and the congressional
liaison people in both the White House and the State Department arguing for compromise, and Secretary of Defense Laird
and himself advocating a much firmer stance.[29] Laird's opposition to compromise was tactical rather than a matter of principle: 'He wanted a straight vote on the Mansfield amendment
without modification; he thought that the "worse" the Amendment the better our chances of prevailing in the end.'[30] Kissinger's own thinking was rather different. He believed even a
compromise measure could undermine European confidence,
impede negotiations with the Soviet Union and begin the
process of 'Vietnamising Europe'.[31] The President came down
on the side of his Secretary of Defense and his National Security
Adviser. This was not surprising. For a President acutely aware
of the prerogatives of his office, not only the Mansfield Amendment, but even rather more moderate substitutes could hardly
fail to be seen as a major challenge. As John Yochelson has
observed, the Mansfield initiative of May 1971 transformed the
conflict from a policy dispute into an institutional struggle for

the control of United States foreign policy. 'The troops in Europe issue became a test of executive responsiveness over problems ranging from weapons procurement to military commitments in South East Asia. The costs to the White House of yielding to its legislative critics mounted accordingly.'[32] In other words, high stakes combined with Nixon's determination not to be pushed around by the liberals in Congress to militate against compromise.

This became much clearer on 13 May when Senator Scott announced that the Administration was unwilling to accept 'any alternative that would have the effect of Congress determining the foreign policy of the United States towards NATO'.[33] Ziegler's statements reflected the same spirit. When asked whether the White House was prepared to accept a compromise he replied 'absolutely not'. Pressed about the possibility of a presidential veto, he dismissed this as 'hypothetical' and stated 'We are going to do everything we can to prevent a bill like that coming down.'[34] Some Senate Republicans, however, regarded this as a major mistake and were unhappy about the White Houses's refusal to back what they regarded as a harmless substitute for the Mansfield Amendment.[35] Indeed, in accordance with such sentiment, several senators had already taken steps of their own to defuse the issue. On 11 May, almost immediately after Mansfield introduced his amendment, Charles Mathias of Maryland, a liberal Republican, offered a substitute resolution which supported negotiations aimed at relaxing tensions in Europe, endorsed the President's declared intention to maintain the necessary level of United States armed forces in Europe and requested that significant changes in these force levels should not be undertaken without full consultation with Congress.[36] Other GOP senators felt that this proposal did not go far enough towards meeting Mansfield's demands to command the support of the middle ground in the Senate. Consequently Dominick introduced another possible substitute – again in the shape of a resolution rather than a formal amendment – advocating that the President take immediate action to withdraw troops and dependants from Europe at the earliest practicable date without it in any way denigrating the US commitment to the alliance.[37] Another possible substitute formu-

lated by Senator Javits was apparently discussed at some
length by Scott and Kissinger.[38] Although there were some
press reports that Kissinger was involved in attempting to work
out a compromise measure acceptable to the Administration,
his own account suggests that he was strongly opposed to this
idea and that he regarded the Javits proposal (which Kissinger
attributes solely to Mathias) as highly dangerous.[39] Whether
Kissinger was as firm and unyielding at the time as he suggests
in retrospect is not certain. It does seem clear though that the
Administration was fairly hostile to the Javits proposal partly
on the grounds that it would commit the President to report to
Congress at six-monthly intervals on the progress of negotiations with both the allies and the Soviet Union to bring about
reductions. As well as making the President accountable to
Congress this had the other disadvantage, from the point of
view of the Administration, that it would keep the troops issue
alive and almost invite further congressional action. Despite
this lack of support from the White House, the Javits proposal
was introduced into the Senate on 17 May. Co-sponsored by
Javits, Mathias, Humphrey and Stevenson as a more realistic
alternative to the initial Mathias substitute, it was formally
known as the Mathias Amendment even though the initial
conception came primarily from Javits and his staff.

Although these four senators remained wedded to the notion
of a compromise, Stennis seems to have been won over to the
'no-compromise' school much more readily. As Chairman of
the Armed Services Committee and manager of the pending
bill, he was a key figure in the floor debate, where he led the
assault on the Mansfield Amendment with considerable vigour, and proved particularly effective in challenging the
economic arguments for troop withdrawals from Western
Europe. While Stennis was obviously well versed in these
matters, merely by dint of his position and experience on
Armed Services, he may have received assistance in preparing
speeches from the Pentagon or the State Department, both of
which were highly active in producing briefs and speeches
critical of the Mansfield Amendment and in favour of retaining
the existing level of forces in Europe.[40] Although not unimportant, however, floor debate rarely succeeds in changing votes.
Thus the Administration recognised that its activities had to

extend far beyond the preparation of statements for delivery by sympathetic spokesmen in the Senate. The key to the outcome was a substantial group of uncommitted or wavering senators who could still be influenced in one direction or the other. By 13 May a major attempt was under way to win over this group with a lobbying campaign which was to develop considerable momentum during the next few days.

During the early stages of this campaign, Secretary of State Rogers seems to have had a pivotal role, although one which was to be subordinated to Kissinger's as the lobbying progressed. A popular and well-respected figure on Capitol Hill, Rogers attempted on 13 May to persuade Mansfield either to drop or to modify his proposal. Although Mansfield may have acknowledged that the amendment had been introduced without the usual preparatory measures, he was unwilling to accede to the Secretary's request, probably arguing that it was necessary to go ahead as planned in order to focus attention on the issue and provoke an executive reappraisal. Consequently, Rogers turned his attention to the defeat of the proposal and apparently contacted a number of senators either in person or by telephone in order to drive home the Administration's argument that the Mansfield Amendment was likely to have damaging and possibly disastrous effects on the American position not only in Europe but also in the Middle East – with the latter argument probably being emphasised in discussions with senators known to be strongly pro-Israel.[41] The following day, 14 May, while testifying before the Committee on Foreign Relations on the proposed War Powers Bill, the Secretary of State reiterated his arguments and publicly denounced the Amendment as a 'mistake of historic proportions'.[42] Valuable though these activities were, Rogers was soon eclipsed by both a past Secretary of State and a future one – Dean Acheson and Henry Kissinger. Indeed, it was an apparently unsolicited offer of help from former Secretary Acheson which seems to have provided the impetus for a ruthless and sustained attempt to discredit and thereby defeat the Majority Leader's proposal.

According to Kissinger, Acheson had advised President Nixon privately on several previous occasions, but was prepared on the troops issue to assist much more openly.[43] Stirred by a desire to protect an alliance which he regarded not merely as one of the great monuments of US foreign policy but as one which he had played a vital part in creating, and perhaps with echoes of the 'Great Debate' of 1951 in mind, Acheson informed Kissinger that 'he would call any Senator where he could help, or any newspaper'.[44] In addition he gave Kissinger a list of eleven 'worthies' – John McCloy, George Ball, McGeorge Bundy, Cyrus Vance and others – whose support should be actively sought. Having contacted these former officials and received what he described as a divided response – but one which, in fact, seems to have been rather more positive than he suggests – Kissinger again discussed the situation with Acheson who suggested that maximum impact could be obtained by 'a little volley firing and not just a splattering of musketry'.[45] To accomplish this, Acheson urged that President Nixon gather together 'an array of former Secretaries of State, Secretaries of Defense, High Commissioners for Germany, NATO Commanders, and Chairmen of the Joint Chiefs of Staff. This embodiment of a bipartisan postwar foreign policy should issue a statement supporting the President's determination to maintain our present military strength in Europe.'[46] The idea evoked an enthusiastic response from both Nixon and Kissinger and a meeting was convened at the White House for the late afternoon of 13 May.

Among those present at what turned into a ninety-minute session were Acheson, Lucius Clay and Henry Cabot Lodge, all of whom had been involved in the controversy over sending troops to Europe in 1951. Other participants were Cyrus Vance, former Deputy Secretary of Defense, George Ball, former Under Secretary of State, John McCloy, a former High Commissioner in Germany, and three former Supreme Allied Commanders Europe – Alfred Gruenther, Lauris Norstad and Lyman Lemmitzer. Also present were General Goodpaster, the current SACEUR and Robert Ellsworth, the US Permanent Representative on the North Atlantic Council – both of whom had flown back from Europe to assist in the lobbying campaign against Mansfield[47] – as well as Kissinger, Rogers and the President. Although accounts of the discussions are fragmentary, it seems that it was, in essence, a meeting to devise methods and coordinate efforts aimed at defeating the troop reduction amendments. Three distinct strands of activity

emerged from this planning session: a continuation and inten-
sification of the private lobbying which had been initiated by
Kissinger and Rogers; an attempt to mobilise public and press
opinion behind a bipartisan statement of support for the President; and an effort to encourage the European allies to con-
demn the Mansfield Amendment as dangerous and destabilising.

Although it is impossible to assess fully its impact, the
personal lobbying of senators was probably the most significant
of the Administration's activities. The campaign was both
intensive and extensive. The State Department established a
forward base on Capitol Hill where the Assistant Secretary of
State for Congressional Relations, David Abshire, seems to
have played an effective coordinating role. Officials and military officers from the Department of Defense, and members of
the congressional liaison staff of the White House added their
weight to the effort, as did Rogers, Kissinger, General Goodpaster, George Ball and some of the other 'elder statesmen'.
More surprisingly, several United States ambassadors overseas were also involved. Ball in particular seems to have been
one of the most influential of the lobbyists, and Kissinger has
noted that although Ball believed that some form of compromise would probably be necessary 'he went to work with effectiveness and characteristic passion for the outright defeat of the
Mansfield Amendment'.[48] Ball's task was probably facilitated
by his reputation as a dove on Vietnam, a reputation which
particularly enhanced his credibility in dealing with those
liberal and moderate Democrats who were most critical of the
war.[49] Indeed, Ball may have concentrated his efforts on such
senators as part of an overall division of labour. General
Goodpaster in a similar way seems to have focused his attention
on the chairman and ranking minority members of each committee and subcommittee with some claim to jurisdiction on the
troops issue.[50] Thus one report noted that Goodpaster had met
with Stennis, Margaret Chase Smith of Maine and Bentsen of
Texas, while Ball had discussed the issue with Senator
Ribicoff.[51] Ribicoff, in fact, seems to have been one of the prime
targets of the lobbying and it was reported that Deputy Assistant Secretary of State Henry Symmes impressed on one of the
Senator's aides that 'Israel has a large interest in maintenance

of NATO because it is a back-up for the US Sixth Fleet in the Mediterranean.'[52] Another senator singled out for a great deal of attention was Senator Muskie, one of the candidates for the Democratic nomination for president. Muskie's position is especially interesting because he had been one of Mansfield's staunchest supporters on the troop withdrawal resolution, but had admitted to 'second thoughts' in January 1971 after a visit to the Federal Republic of Germany and discussions with Chancellor Brandt.[53] On his return to the United States Muskie acknowledged that the Ostpolitik, the negotiations on Berlin and the Soviet proposal for a European Security Conference were closely bound up with the US military presence in Europe. Given his presidential ambitions, Muskie could hardly have been insensitive to the need to project an image of sober statesmanship; nevertheless, it was his discussions with Brandt which seem to have been the major consideration in his reappraisal. Even so, there is some evidence that he remained ambivalent and that during the troop debate actively solicited advice from former officials in the Johnson Administration before finally coming down against the troop withdrawal proposal.[54]

Although much of the lobbying seems to have concentrated on the substantive case against substantial force reductions, an additional theme, which was propounded publicly by Ziegler and privately by Clark Macgregor and other officials involved in congressional liaison, was that the amendment was regarded in the White House as a direct challenge to the President's constitutional prerogative to make foreign policy.[55] The involvement of the congressional liaison officers of the White House and State Department was only to be expected on such a controversial issue. Much more unusual was the participation of American ambassadors overseas, which testified to both the vigour of the Administration's campaign and the way in which it was sustained. In a floor speech on 18 May, Senator Charles Percy of Illinois – who had been one of the most outspoken critics of the allies' failure to compensate the United States adequately for the costs incurred in deploying its troops in Europe[56] – disclosed that he had received several telephone calls regarding the pending vote. He remarked, somewhat ironically,

I have never been blessed with so many calls from friends overseas in any 24 hour period. I have heard from the distinguished American Ambassador in Belgium, Ambassador Eisenhower, with whom I have discussed the problem before. I have heard from by distinguished constituent from Illinois, the Ambassador to Iceland with whom I have not been privileged to talk since he went over there several years ago. The distinguished American Ambassador to the Netherlands called this afternoon. I was happy to talk to him, and yesterday to my distinguished friend, Ambassador Lodge.[57]

Percy also revealed that he had taken the initiative (deciding perhaps that it was more convenient) in contacting the American representative in France, Ambassador Watson, in order to discuss the matter further.[58] As someone who was an outspoken critic of the European record on burden-sharing yet not firmly committed to troop withdrawals, Percy may have been a particularly attractive and important target for Administration lobbying, with the result that his experience may have been atypical. Even if this is so, it nevertheless suggests the lengths to which the White House was prepared to go in order to chip away at Mansfield's support.

The private lobbying was only one facet of the onslaught. The second track was to use the 'elder statesmen' to mobilise editorial and public support behind the President's position. Once again Acheson seems to have been the decisive figure. Assigned the task of dealing with the press, he went to work immediately after the meeting of 13 May, not only informing reporters that President Nixon was adamant in his opposition to the Mansfield Amendment, but describing the proposal itself as 'asinine' and 'sheer nonsense'.[59] As Kissinger put it: 'Reticence was not his style.'[60] More important than these acerbic comments, though, was his suggestion during the meeting that the former officials sign a statement of support for President Nixon in his condemnation of unilateral troop reductions. Although planned in advance by Acheson and Kissinger and having Nixon's approval, the idea aroused some opposition from Secretary Rogers before he too joined the consensus.[61] It was agreed that the statement would be released on Saturday

15 May. With this decided, Nixon left Kissinger to manage the
situation and departed for Key Biscayne, Florida, and it was
from there that the President's statement was duly issued as
planned. Explaining that the troop deployment in Europe had
been maintained by five successive Presidents representing
both political parties, the statement was unequivocal. In language reminiscent of that used by Rogers before the Committee
on Foreign Relations, the President declared that for any
NATO members to reduce forces unilaterally would be an
'error of historic dimensions'.[62] Together with the statement,
Ziegler issued a list of former officials who fully endorsed the
President's views. The list was an impressive one. As well as
two former Secretaries of State, Acheson and Rusk, it included
three former Secretaries of Defense, Robert Lovett, Neil McEl-
roy and Thomas Gates, and two former Deputy Defense Secretaries, Roswell Gilpatrick and Cyrus Vance. Others who
endorsed the statement were Robert Murphy, Livingston Mer-
chant, Douglas Dillon, George Ball and Nicholas deB. Katzenbach, all of whom had been Under-Secretaries of State, and
four former SACEURs, Generals Ridgeway, Gruenther, Norstad and Lemnitzer. 'Completing the list were four former
United States delegates to NATO – Charles Spofford, W.
Randolph Burgess, Thomas Finletter and Harlan Cleveland –
and three former military governors, or High Commissioners
for Germany, Lucius Clay, John McCloy and James B.
Conant.'[63] It was also announced that although Robert
McNamara, former Secretary of Defense, had been unwilling
to associate himself formally with the President's declaration
because of his position as head of the World Bank, he did not
want his abstention to be interpreted as non-support.[64] There
was a bonus which may or may not have been expected, when,
almost immediately after the release of the statement, former
President Lyndon Johnson sent word from his ranch in Texas
that he was 'totally in accord' with its sentiments.[65] The
following day it was announced that another former President,
Harry Truman, also agreed with Nixon's statement – a message which had been relayed to the Florida White House by
Dean Acheson.[66]

Not everyone who had been approached had agreed to
endorse the statement. Ziegler announced that Clark Clifford,

who had replaced McNamara as Secretary of Defense, and James Douglas, Truman's Deputy Defense Secretary, had both declined – although no reason was given.[67] Unlike former Chief Justice Arthur Goldberg, who not only wrote to Mansfield to advise him of his support but came out publicly in favour of troop withdrawals,[68] both Clifford and Douglas maintained a discreet silence – and their non-compliance did little to undermine the Administration's tactic, which was designed to show that Mansfield was not only jeopardising the security policy of the current Administration but was also going against the accumulated wisdom, experience and advice of several generations of foreign policy-makers.

The third element of the Administration's approach was similar in that it too was meant to highlight the irresponsibility of Mansfield's actions – and involved soliciting statements from the European allies which again condemned the congressional pressure for troop withdrawals. This is to suggest neither that the European governments were apathetic about the fate of the American military presence, nor that they would have failed to make strong denunciations of the Mansfield Amendment without prompting from Washington;[69] but it is to argue that the President and his advisers were prepared to leave nothing to chance in their endeavours to defeat the amendment on the Senate floor. Accordingly, McCloy was assigned the task of persuading Brandt to issue a declaration of this kind – and succeeded in eliciting yet another statement warning of the dangerous consequences of troop withdrawals.[70] Furthermore, on 17 May, the White House released the text of a letter which Manlio Brosio, the NATO Secretary-General, had written to President Nixon saying that a reduction of United States troops would undermine the credibility of the alliance and make a return to the trip-wire unavoidable. Although the letter was officially described as 'unsolicited'[71] it is not unreasonable to speculate that Brosio may have been encouraged to write in such terms as part of the Administration's comprehensive efforts to undermine support for Mansfield.[72]

At one level the mobilisation of both domestic and international opinion against legislation mandating troop reductions was successful: warnings of the dangers attendant upon precipitate action came from all quarters, with both the *New York*

Times and the *Washington Post* joining the refrain.[73] Yet at another level, it is questionable how influential such activities were. In the last analysis the efforts to isolate Mansfield and defeat his amendment by first discrediting it were probably less significant than the more covert approaches made to senators. Mansfield himself dismissed the campaign as the Administration dredging up the 'old timers' in order to perpetuate old policies which had become outmoded.[74] While the Majority Leader seemed bemused rather than angered by these proceedings, amongst other senators there were several signs of disaffection with both the President's hard-line stance and the heavy-handed public posturing. Clifford Case, for example, a Republican senator from New Jersey, condemned Ziegler's 'no-compromise' statements as undiplomatic,[75] while Senator Pell, although having serious reservations about the scale and speed of the withdrawals contemplated in the Mansfield Amendment, suggested that the Administration's tactics were in danger of becoming counterproductive. Pell was particularly critical of Acheson and the other 'elder statesmen' and argued that 'When Dean Acheson describes Senator Mansfield's suggestion as "asinine" he turns off more members of our body than he would turn on.' He went on: 'In fact the way the administration is going, I would not be surprised to read in tomorrow's press of an ESP report from Woodrow Wilson to the effect that we should support the administration and maintain our 300,000 American troops in Europe.'[76]

Despite such reactions, the prognosis increasingly pointed towards the defeat of the amendment. Although Senator Griffin made clear on 14 May that he thought the vote would be very close, Administration forecasts gradually became more optimistic. By 16 May there was growing confidence that the President would win and one unofficial survey suggested that the amendment would be defeated by about 10 votes.[77] The increased optimism, however, probably owed less to the activities of the 'elder statesmen' than it did to a statement made by Mr Brezhnev – which prompted one commentator to refer to a 'Nixon–Acheson–Brezhnev Alliance'.[78] And it is to the Brezhnev intervention that attention must now be given.

On 14 May Mr Brezhnev made a speech at Tiblisi in Soviet Georgia in which he referred to the notion of mutual force reductions and suggested that if the West wanted to taste the wine, it was necessary first of all to open the bottle. Although there was nothing in the statement that was especially new or particularly different from earlier Soviet proposals on force reductions, its timing gave it a significance that earlier initiatives had lacked.[79] Preliminary feelers and diplomatic sparring about the possibility of negotiating a mutual withdrawal of forces from Central Europe had been going on for several years. The Soviet Union's initial response to the idea had been cool, but it had gradually come to see some advantage in such negotiations – if only to help build up the momentum of *détente* and facilitate progress in other areas such as a European Security Conference.[80] Accordingly, Brezhnev had made a positive statement on force reductions on 30 March 1971 at the 24th Party Congress. This had not aroused much interest in Washington, however, until the appearance of Mansfield's troop withdrawal proposal.[81] The introduction of the amendment precipitated an unprecedented burst of enthusiasm for mutual force reductions by the Nixon Administration. This was hardly surprising – after all, a mutual cutback was a preferable alternative to unilateral American withdrawals. Consequently, the Administration began to use the possibility of a reciprocal Soviet action as an argument against a premature United States move mandated by Congress. After Brezhnev's Tiblisi statement, the attractiveness of this argument increased enormously. The 14 May announcement was immediately 'picked up by the White House, hailed as an initiative for multilateral withdrawals and used as ammunition by the President against the Mansfield Amendment'.[82] This was to prove highly effective – and in the aftermath of Brezhnev's speech many observers discerned a transfer of support from Mansfield to the President, while White House forecasts of the eventual outcome became much more optimistic. There was far less talk of a presidential veto and far more of defeating the Mansfield Amendment in a straight up or down vote on the Senate floor.

The conventional interpretation of the Brezhnev speech, however, is that it was an essentially fortuitous event which caught President Nixon and his advisors by surprise but was nevertheless seized upon and used by the Administration in an opportunist but skilful manner. In other words, Soviet assistance in defeating the Mansfield Amendment was both unintentional and unexpected. It is sometimes argued that from the Soviet point of view Brezhnev's initiative was particularly ill-timed, that by helping the Nixon Administration contain the congressional pressures for US troop withdrawals, it prevented the attainment of a long-held and deeply-cherished Soviet goal – the weakening of both the American military presence and United States political influence in Western Europe. Henry Kissinger has certainly taken this approach and has suggested that the timing of the speech is evidence of the Kremlin's ineptness and lack of flexibility in foreign policy.

> What possessed Brezhnev to make his mutual force reduction offer on that particular day is not clear. The Mansfield Amendment must have caught the Kremlin even more than the Administration by surprise. Nor could Moscow have expected it to pick up such a head of steam. The Brezhnev proposal was undoubtedly planned to give impetus to the Berlin negotiations by suggesting that they could unlock the door to a hopeful future. Nothing illustrates better the inflexibility of the Soviets' cumbersome policy-making machinery than their decision to stick to their game plan even when confronted with the Mansfield windfall.[83]

While this analysis of the Brezhnev intervention can hardly be dismissed out of hand, there are problems with it. A central assumption is that Brezhnev was either ignorant of what was happening in the United States Senate, or, if he knew about the Mansfield Amendment, was certainly not aware of its implications, and in particular the potential opportunities its passage would offer to the Soviet Union. Yet it is equally plausible that Brezhnev not only had a clear notion of what was happening in Washington, but was sensitive to the possible consequences – and that far from providing opportunities to be exploited, the amendment posed problems to be preempted. The *status quo* in Europe had many advantages for the Soviet Union, and a substantial presence of American troops was an integral feature of the *status quo*. A rapid and large-scale reduction of these forces would prove destabilising. It would give the United States less control over events in Europe, elevate the Federal Republic to a preeminent military position in NATO (especially as the most likely compensation for a diminished American presence was an enlarged Bundeswehr) and possibly encourage the emergence of a more cohesive and far-reaching West European defence identity than had hitherto seemed feasible. In contrast the *status quo* appeared very attractive. The superpowers had established mutually acceptable 'rules' of behaviour which not only held out the prospect of managing or resolving any East–West crisis in Europe, but increasingly seemed to point to the prevention of crises in the Central Region. Furthermore, the existing security arrangements provided a framework within which the threat to the Soviet Union from the Federal Republic was minimised. To put it crudely, US troops in Europe helped to contain West Germany as well as the Soviet Union. The highly visible American connection also meant that the Europeans were both fragmented and fairly relaxed, not to say half-hearted, in their approach to security and defence. Not only did this offer distinct advantages to the Soviet Union, but it was also preferable to a more tightly-knit grouping which would almost inevitably be concerned with augmenting West European strategic nuclear capabilities. In other words, the fears of the Nixon Administration that passage of the Mansfield Amendment would result in an unravelling of NATO policy may have been shared by Moscow. Where the Soviet assessment could have diverged from Washington's, though, was in the probable consequences of this. American fears that troop withdrawals would be followed by the Finlandisation of Western Europe may have been mirrored in the Soviet Union by concern that it would result in the Europeanisation of Europe, especially in matters of defence.[84] It is at least conceivable, therefore, that Mr Brezhnev – albeit for different reasons – shared President Nixon's view of the Mansfield Amendment as an inescapable and potentially very dangerous proposal – and anything but a windfall.

To argue along these lines, of course, is necessarily to engage in speculation. Nevertheless, the conclusion to which it leads – that the Brezhnev statement was a deliberate and calculated attempt to undermine support for the Mansfield Amendment is at least as plausible as the suggestion that the Soviet leader was

unaware of the likely consequences of his speech. The implication is that there was a coincidence of interests between Brezhnev and Nixon in defeating the troop cut proposal. It is perhaps
not going too much further than this to suggest that there may
also have been a degree of collusion between Soviet and
American governments – a possibility that becomes less startling when it is remembered that May 1971 was also the time
when the crucial breakthrough was made on SALT by using
the back channel, and that the personal relations between the
key foreign policy decision-makers in Washington and those in
the Kremlin were remarkably close. There were certainly
diplomatic communications on mutual force reductions prior
to Mr Brezhnev's Tiblisi announcement. On 12 May Robert J.
McCloskey, a State Department press officer, noted that at the
24th Party Congress, Brezhnev had 'said something about
reductions in forces and armaments, particularly in relation to
Central Europe'. He added that the statement had been 'somewhat weak in absence of specifics, and we are interested in
clarification'.[85] The United States had asked for clarification
and elaboration of Brezhnev's proposal but had so far received
neither. Against this background the Tiblisi speech takes on
new significance as a response to the American request. Although the statement did not contain much in the way of
specifics, it was hailed as an important breakthrough and was
followed up almost immediately by talks between Jacob Beam,
the US Ambassador in Moscow and Soviet Foreign Minister
Andrei Gromyko. On 16 May, Secretary Rogers announced
that Beam had been instructed to seek further details,[86] and in a
meeting with the Ambassador the following day, Gromyko not
only confirmed Soviet willingness to consider troop reductions
but also offered to separate the talks from a European Security
Conference, the convening of which had been a Soviet goal for
some time.[87] Had the 14 May speech been a tactical error, as
Kissinger and others have suggested, it is unlikely that the
Soviet leadership would have been prepared to follow it up so
quickly – especially as the Nixon Administration had already
begun to make political capital out of it in the domestic debate.
On 14 May, for example, the same day as the speech itself,
Secretary Rogers, testifying on another matter before the Com-
mittee on Foreign Relations, had welcomed the initiative on

mutual force reductions and noted that unilateral measures by the United States would make it necessary to 'kiss that goodbye'.[88]

This theme was echoed in other statements by State Department spokesmen, in comments by Ziegler, and in pro-Administration speeches on the Senate floor. The impact of the Tiblisi announcement, however, went far beyond the provisions of an additional argument for the Administration to deploy. It fundamentally changed the context of the debate. From appearing a long overdue measure on 11 May, the Mansfield Amendment was transformed by Mr Brezhnev's intervention into what even some of its supporters felt was a tragically ill-timed initiative. Margaret Chase Smith, the Republican senator from Maine, probably spoke for a significant number of her colleagues in the Senate when she argued that although Mansfield was right in principle, the timing of his amendment could not have been more unfortunate.[89] Other senators reiterated this theme, arguing that negotiated cutbacks would be far more productive than unilateral withdrawals, while even fairly enthusiastic Mansfield supporters began to waver or defect. Gaylord Nelson of Wisconsin summed up the dilemma which the Brezhnev intervention had posed for pro-Mansfield senators when he stated that if the Soviet leader had 'not spoken on the subject . . . I would have been prepared to vote to cut our forces in half in accordance with the Mansfield Amendment'.[90] In the event, Nelson – after trying unsuccessfully to obtain the Senate's approval for a compromise measure – did vote for the amendment, but this was probably out of loyalty to the Majority Leader, and done with the knowledge that there was little chance of the proposal being accepted in light of the other defections which followed the Brezhnev initiative. The impact of the Soviet move, therefore, was very considerable. As Henry Kissinger has shrewdly commented, it offered 'a way out for uneasy supporters of Mansfield as well as for his . . . opponents. Both could unite behind the proposition that the imminence of negotiations made unilateral reductions untimely.'[91] Thus the prospects for the passage of the Mansfield Amendment receded rapidly after 14 May. Nevertheless, there was still a possibility that some form of compromise proposal might be approved which would placate the sentiment in favour of retrenchment while avoiding the drastic action contemplated in the initial Mansfield proposal. Indeed, this possibility gave the final stages of the debate and the votes on 19 May an added element of drama and unpredictability – and it is to the closing stages of the Senate's deliberations that attention must now be given.

3   THE AMENDMENT DEFEATED

The Brezhnev speech, although providing revised assessments of the outcome, did little to defuse the intensity of the arguments. Nor did it prevent a plethora of substitute and perfecting amendments from being introduced, as moderates on both sides of the issue tried to find the common ground which would appeal to a majority of senators. The perfecting amendment essentially contemplated less severe and more leisurely reductions than advocated by Mansfield. There were also attempts to devise a formula whereby unilateral cuts would be made only in the event that negotiations on mutual force reductions either failed to materialise or proved sterile. The substitute measures were rather more innocuous, and although urging the President to take action, were careful not to mandate cuts. As mentioned above, the major substitute, and the one which particularly worried Henry Kissinger, was the more or less bipartisan proposal devised by Javits, introduced by Mathias and backed by Hubert Humphrey. More akin in spirit to the Mansfield Resolution than to the Majority Leader's pending amendment, the proposal was anathema to the White House, largely because of its reporting requirement.[92]

Indeed, the hostility of the Administration to the various compromise measures – or as Senator Pastore, a strong Mansfield supporter, described them, 'the hocus-pocus amendments'[93] – was to play an important part in determining the pattern of voting on 19 May. It was not the only relevant factor though. Equally significant, if in a more mundane way, was the Senate procedure which determined not only that all substitute and perfecting legislation had to be addressed prior to the Mansfield Amendment, but also that if any of these alternatives was approved, then there would not be a vote on the Majority

Leader's initial proposal. Both sides were keen to avoid such a side-stepping of the issue, seeing it as an unsatisfactory out-come to a controversy in which the lines had been drawn very clearly. The Administration in particular regarded all the measures, to a greater or lesser degree, as restrictive of excecu-tive freedom of action and encroaching on the presidential prerogative. The White House was also confident that it had the votes to turn back the Mansfield Amendment. Having invested such a great deal of time, energy and prestige in mobilising opposition to the Mansfield Amendment, the Ad-ministration, quite understandably, did not want to miss the opportunity to display the extent of that opposition. Further-more, a vote by the Senate against the Majority Leader's troop cut proposal would reaffirm executive control over US foreign policy and signal to the European allies that the American commitment remained firm. By 18 May the Administration appeared to believe that such a victory was well within its grasp. Although an Associated Press poll showed 36 in favour of the Amendment, 42 against and 22 still undecided, it was reported that both sides were expecting it to be defeated by between 5 and 10 votes.[94] One White House congressional aide predicted confidently that the Administration could 'beat any-thing with a date in it'.[95] Consequently, the main thrust of executive branch activity on 19 May was reserved for the compromise proposals and it appears that there was fairly intensive lobbying by Kissinger and others to ensure that pro-Administration senators remained unyielding against all forms of compromise. Although Kissinger's memoirs contain only a brief and somewhat inaccurate reference to the various compromise proposals, his account of the Senate captures the spirit of the day's events. As he put it rather ruefully: 'The final vote came none too soon for our sanity . . . The mood in the Senate was revealed by one of our supporters who balked when I tried to brace him on the vote against another of the cascade of amendments: "How many times a day can a man vote no?"'[96] Kissinger's efforts to ensure that all the compromise proposals were thrown out were assisted by John Stennis, who emphas-ised frequently throughout the debate that he wanted a straight up or down vote on the Mansfield Amendment, so that there would be no ambiguity about the Senate's position.[97] Help also came from an unsuspected quarter in that, for the most part, Mansfield himself wanted to avoid an ambivalent compromise. The result, as John Finney of the *New York Times* had predicted, was that Administration supporters and pro-withdrawal senators teamed up to defeat the more moderate proposals, thereby ensuring a straight up and down vote on the Mansfield Amendment itself.[98]

This is not to suggest that there was no pressure on the Majority Leader to compromise and throw his weight behind a watered-down proposal. Senator McClellan, in particular, urged Mansfield to do this and thereby win over those senators like himself, who agreed with the principle of the amendment but were unhappy about the speed and scale of the proposed cutbacks.[99] Consequently, Mansfield, albeit without much enthusiasm or commitment, gave his support to a compromise proposal sponsored by Gaylord Nelson. Despite this there was an element of hasty and ill-considered improvisation about the Nelson substitute which attracted the hostility of several senators. Nelson had initially introduced an amendment on 17 May stating simply that the United States should, at the earliest possible opportunity, enter into negotiations for a mutual reduction of forces. The Wisconsin senator had then modified his proposal on 18 May in a way which combined his original wording with the Mansfield Amendment and added the proviso that if final discussions or negotiations between the Soviet Union and the United States had started by September 1971, the reductions clause would be inoperative. This was modified yet again on 19 May, so that it incorporated a phased withdrawal of troops rather than the more drastic reduction contemplated in the Majority Leader's proposal – the number of US troops in Europe would be cut to 250 000 by 1 July 1972, to 200 000 by 1 July 1973, and to 150 000 by 1 July 1974, unless negotiations on mutual withdrawals began by the end of 1971.[100] The result, however, was an unsatisfactory compromise which provoked considerable criticism. Described by Humphrey as 'the Mansfield Amendment on the instalment plan', the Nelson compromise was attacked by Stennis and Senator Griffin as a measure which would deny the Soviet Union any incentive to engage seriously in discussions about mutual withdrawals. Even Frank Church, a firm advocate of troop reductions, was unhappy about the proposal and, like the more conservative critics, argued that it would put the United States in an impossible negotiating position.[101] It was not surprising, therefore, that the amendment was defeated by 63 votes to 26. Although a hard core of Mansfield supporters had swung behind the proposal, with the 48 Democrats dividing in half as a result, little inroad had been made into Republican ranks, and only 2 out of 41 GOP senators lined up with Nelson. [102]

The next amendement dealt with by the Senate had been introduced on 17 May by Birch Bayh of Indiana in cooperation with William Saxbe (Rep. Ohio) and Abraham Ribicoff (Dem. Conn). The Bayh modification mandated a 50 per cent reduction in the US troop contingent in Europe by the end of 1972, unless the European allies, prior to the end of 1971, agreed to compensate the United States for half the currently uncompensated balance of payments outflow resulting from the presence on the continent. Although the proposal neatly encapsulated the Senate's resentment at the failure of the European allies to devise adequate burden-sharing arrangements – and was a forerunner of the Jackson–Nunn amendment of 1974 which linked a continuing military presence in Europe directly to satisfactory offset payments – in the context of the May 1971 debate, it had little appeal. There was widespread agreement that it did little to clarify the main issues involved, and with Mansfield, Symington, Cranston and other leading members of the pro-withdrawal coalition opposed to it, its fate was a foregone conclusion. The only uncertainty concerned the margin of defeat. In the event this was a hefty 68 votes as the amendment was rejected by 81 to 13.[103]

It was clear by this stage of the debate that the various attempts at compromise were finding little favour. The preference of many members was summed up by Senator Pastore, who argued that it was essentially a straight choice between Congress taking action through the Mansfield Amendment or the President doing something as urged by the Mathias compromise. Although admitting to reservations about the precise terms of the Majority Leader's proposal, Pastore nevertheless suggested that this was the more appropriate approach, given that the European allies had been derelict in their duty.[104] The proponents of the Mathias Amendment, in contrast, argued that this was a preferable option because it offered a remedial alternative without doing anything irrecoverable. By recommending the President to pursue negotiations with both the Soviet Union and the NATO allies, the proposal would put the Senate on record as favouring the principle of troop withdrawals, while leaving considerable scope for presidential discretion. By incorporating a requirement that the President report to Congress at intervals of six months on the progress of these discussions, Javits and Mathias had taken steps to ensure that it would not simply be ignored. Javits argued, in fact, that passage of the amendment would strengthen the President's bargaining position *vis-à-vis* the NATO allies: simple exhortation for the Europeans to do more was one thing; exhortation backed by congressional legislation, however discretionary, was something else.[105] Although vigorously opposed by the Administration and characterised by Stennis as a demand that the President pursue two mutually inconsistent approaches – unilateral and bilateral reductions – the proposal nevertheless appealed to Senators sympathetic to the principle of troop withdrawals but unhappy with either the terms of the Mansfield Amendment or the idea that Congress itself should mandate and oversee reductions. Its attraction was considerably greater than the roll-call vote, in which it was rejected by 73 votes to 24, suggested. It is significant, for example, that despite all the efforts of the Administration, 11 Republicans broke with their party colleagues and voted for the proposal.[106] Furthermore, many of the committed Mansfield supporters might well have been prepared to support such a measure, had the Senate's procedure not ruled that adoption of the Mathias substitute would have prevented consideration of the Mansfield Amendment itself.

Even with the Mathias Amendement defeated, there remained several other proposals which had to be dealt with before the Senate could turn to the Majority Leader's initial amendment. This did not take too long, however. A substitute Sense of Congress Resolution by Senator Dominick, recommending consultation with the Europeans on troop cuts, was withdrawn (and not, as Kissinger's account suggests, defeated in a formal roll-call),[107] while two other perfecting amendments, both of which were watered-down versions of Mansfield's proposal, were fairly rapidly disposed of. The first was a fairly simple modification, suggested by Senator Fulbright, which added the words 'unless hereinafter authorised' to the Mansfield Amendment. The Chairman of the Foreign Relations Committee argued that this would provide an opportunity for the Administration to present to Congress a case against the implementation of the legislation. Stennis suggested that this would only cloud the issue, and a majority of senators seemed to agree, as the Fulbright modification was rejected by 68 to 29.[108] The remaining modification, introduced by Frank Church, specified a 50 000-man reduction rather than the 50 per cent cut contemplated by Mansfield. Had this been the initial proposal, it might have received considerable support. As it was, even the Majority Leader voted against it and it was rejected with 81 votes against to 15 in favour.[109]

Having disposed of all the compromise attempts, the Senate finally moved on to consider the Mansfield Amendment itself. The debate itself was something of an anticlimax, with members on both sides merely reiterating familiar arguments or restating their positions. Aware that his amendment would be defeated, the Majority Leader emphasised that he had at least partially succeeded in his objective. Merely by introducing the amendment and pushing it to a vote, he had brought the matter to the attention of both the Administration and the European allies in a more pointed way than ever before. He suggested further that whatever the outcome of the vote, the issue would not go away.[110] Because of these comments, the Senate's rejection of the Mansfield Amendment by the unexpectedly wide margin of 25 votes in a 61 to 36 roll call was perhaps slightly less comforting to the Administration than would otherwise have been the case.[111]

This is not to suggest that the Administration had failed to achieve an impressive victory. On the contrary, the mobilisation of opposition to the troop withdrawal proposal had been a formidable display of political power. When the Mansfield Amendment was first introduced, the likelihood of defeating it seemed remote, the prospects for the White House daunting; yet just over a week later the Senate had rejected the measure with votes to spare. The intensive lobbying activities by leading officials and the 'elder statesmen', the Brezhnev intervention, and the skilful and energetic leadership of John Stennis in marshalling the counter-attack in the Senate, had all contributed significantly to this outcome. Nevertheless, there were several aspects of the proceedings which, from the President's point of view, were disquieting to say the least. In the first place, both the nature and the scale of the lobbying campaign would make it difficult to repeat, should there be a resurgence of the pressure for troop withdrawals. Secondly, although the Administration had succeeded in obtaining a clear margin of safety on each of the amendments, this had been artificially inflated by the tactical voting which took place. Only Senator Inouye voted for both the Mansfield and Mathias proposals and, as one commentator pointed out, there was every reason to believe that the other 35 senators who voted for the Mansfield Amendment 'would have voted for the Mathias substitute had it been left until last. But the 35 rejected the Mathias Amendment which their votes would have carried, so that they could bring the Mansfield Amendment to a final vote.'[112] In other words, there was a clear majority in favour of a reduction of the US military presence in Western Europe. The division in the Senate in May 1971 was not merely, and perhaps not even primarily, between those for and those against troop withdrawals; equally important was that between those who were prepared to impose such a reduction by 'legislative mandate' and those who were reluctant to do this, preferring, for the moment at least, to pressure the executive into taking action. How long the more patient and discretionary approach of this last group would retain its appeal, however, remained uncertain: if the Administration failed to move on the issue it was conceivable that these senators too would be prepared to take direct action.

In the light of all this, the decision of the White House to press for the defeat of the Mathias substitute may have been a tactical error. Although the decision was taken largely on the grounds that the reporting requirement would keep the troop issue alive, the result was a missed opportunity to establish an unprecedented degree of executive legislative cooperation on the troop deployment policy.[113] By choosing the path of confrontation and showing itself, for the most part, to be unresponsive to congressional demands, the Administration not only

missed an opportunity to strengthen its position *vis-à-vis* the
European allies in the burden-sharing arguments, but it also
ensured further congressional attempts to legislate withdrawals. Mansfield had succeeded in getting the donkey's attention,
but he had failed to make it move very far. Consequently,
further Mansfield Amendments were virtually inevitable.

4   POSTSCRIPT TO MAY 1971: THE NOVEMBER
DEBATE

The political shockwaves caused by the May 1971 debate on
US troop withdrawals from Europe had barely subsided before
Senator Mansfield began to hint at the possibility of further
attempts to legislate a reduction in the American contribution
to NATO's conventional forces. On 3 June, there was discussion of the issue in the Senate.[114] This was prompted by the
return of several members from a meeting of the North Atlantic
Assembly, at which, according to Senator Charles Percy, the
European parliamentarians had not only been unsympathetic
to the American position but had clearly failed to learn the
lesson of the May 1971 votes that a majority of senators, in
principle at least, favoured some reduction of US forces in
Europe. Percy, along with Mathias and several other senators,
warmly commended Mansfield's initiative for highlighting the
burden-sharing problem. Hubert Humphrey put it most
graphically when he stated that Mansfield had 'rung a bell' and
provided a warning that changes would have to be made in the
Atlantic relationship. This suggests that even senators who had
originally opposed the Mansfield Amendment nevertheless
recognised that its reappearance might have more value in
bringing home to the European allies the need for a fundamental readjustment of roles and responsibilities in NATO. For his
part the Majority Leader merely reaffirmed his determination
to pursue his objective with 'vigor, persistence and determination'. This was further underlined just over a month later when
Associated Press carried details of a Mansfield statement in
which he had discussed the drug and racial problems besetting
the Seventh Army in Europe, complained that the United

States was shouldering a lopsided burden and revealed that he planned to launch a new campaign for phased cutbacks in the American military contingent in Europe.[115]

One thing which may have encouraged Mansfield to carry on in this direction was the public reaction to his earlier amendment. The amount of mail received by the Majority Leader's office both during and immediately after the debate was considerable. Although some of the correspondents were sharply critical of the troops cut proposal, the vast majority overwhelmingly approved Mansfield's action. Nor was the mail confined to the senator's Montana constituency: letters and telegrams came from all parts of the United States. There were even letters from disgruntled servicemen in Germany complaining of the financial problems they faced because of the declining value of the dollar and the difficulties of finding employment for their wives and families.[116] The precise impact of this, of course, is impossible to evaluate, but it seems likely that it confirmed Mansfield in his belief that action had to be taken.

Once again though it was United States economic difficulties which helped to bring matters to a head. In August 1971 President Nixon announced major changes in American economic policy. Resulting primarily from continuing deterioration in the overall US balance of payments position, together with figures on the trade balance which 'increasingly indicated that the United States would show a trade deficit for the year for the first time in the twentieth century',[117] the President's package contained measures which the European allies regarded with trepidation and hostility. The decision to give up all efforts to maintain the dollar's exchange value, to end the convertibility of dollars into gold, and to impose a 10 per cent surcharge on certain import duties was bad enough; it was made worse by the fact that this departure from the practices and precepts of the Bretton Woods system was made with little or no consultation with the allies. Nor were the tensions in Atlantic relations eased by the Administration's demand for a general depreciation of the dollar, unilateral trade concessions and greater 'military burden-sharing' by Europe and Japan.[118]

It is not surprising, therefore, that when Senator Mansfield visited Western Europe in late August and early September to examine the allies' reaction to the New Economic Policy, he found 'stunned surprise'.[119] After returning to Washington the Majority Leader produced a report for the Foreign Relations Committee which was particularly critical of the import surcharge and warned of the damage to Atlantic unity that could result from increased economic confrontation.[120] Yet both the report and Mansfield's preliminary observations to the Senate suggest that he regarded the visit to Europe primarily as an opportunity to keep the troop issue in the forefront of attention – a consideration which made it even more inexplicable that Mansfield's trip had not included a visit to the Federal Republic (although an accompanying staff member of the Foreign Relations Committee had gone to West Germany). On his return, Mansfield argued that the Administration's economic initiatives merely underlined the need for a further reappraisal of the US military presence. While emphasising that Atlantic unity, as enshrined in the treaty of 1949, was essential, Mansfield described the US troop deployment in Europe as anachronistic. Among his specific suggestions was a graduated reduction in the military contingent, a transfer of command posts to the European allies and the 'development of techniques for keeping alive the initial concept of the North Atlantic Treaty while cutting NATO to streamlined essentials needed for prompt remobilization in the event of emergencies.' These and similar recommendations were made to the Senate on 14 September prior to the formal report which appeared the following month. When describing his preliminary observations, Mansfield announced his intention to reintroduce his amendment 'at an appropriate time in connection with an appropriate bill'.[121]

The appropriate legislation was the Defense Appropriations Bill (HR 11731) and on 17 November, the Defense Subcommittee of the Senate Appropriations Committee voted by 9 to 7 to attach to the bill an amendment prohibiting the use of funds to support more than 250 000 US troops in Europe after 15 June 1972.[122] This was much more moderate than the May proposal, requiring a reduction of between 50 000 and 60 000 troops. Even so, the Administration response was sharp and immediate. Although the executive branch seems once again to have been taken by surprise, Secretary of Defense Laird, in particular, reacted very quickly. On hearing of the proposal on the evening of 17 November, Laird at once issued a statement condemning it as dangerous, ill-timed and arbitrary.[123] The following morning the text of this statement was included in a letter to all members of the Appropriations Committee, exhorting them to kill the proposal. Laird outlined the debilitating consequences which, he felt, would follow passage of troop reduction legislation. As well as resurrecting all the well-known arguments about the need for the United States both to observe its commitment to the allies and to negotiate from strength with the Soviet Union, Laird also emphasised that NATO had selected former Secretary-General Brosio 'to explore the basis for negotiations with the Warsaw Pact and he is now anticipating his first meeting in Moscow'.[124] The mutual force reduction card was also played by Secretary of State Rogers in a statement issued through the department spokesman, Charles Bray.[125]

How much impact this had on the members of the committee is uncertain. The amendment came at a time of increasing tension over Vietnam, and there was a suggestion that many senators, especially those opposed to the war, 'had been angered by Nixon's announcement on 17 November that he would not consider another Mansfield Amendment asking the Administration to fix a date for withdrawal from Vietnam as binding'.[126] To some extent this may have offset the Laird appeal, as the committee voted 14 to 13 in favour of the subcommittee's recommendation. Although the positions of each individual were not reported, the full Senate vote suggests that the 24 members of the Appropriations Committee may have been evenly divided and that it was the votes of the 3 ex-officio members from the Committee on Armed Services which proved decisive.[127] Alternatively one or two senators may have taken a position in committee different to that they were to take in full public view on the Senate floor.[128]

One senator who was unequivocal in his stance was the Committee Chairman, Allan J. Ellender. In the late 1950s Ellender had been one of the first senators to complain about the US military presence in Western Europe, and he now dismissed Administration arguments against the Mansfield Amendment as 'hogwash'.[129] Mansfield too responded to Administration charges in a speech at Johns Hopkins University on 18 November, where he vigorously rejected the idea that US forces were a 'bargaining chip', arguing that there was no bargaining power in the irrelevant, excessive and antiquated deployment of such a large number of US troops in Europe.[130] Nevertheless, the Administration continued to lay emphasis on the progress being made towards negotiation on mutual force reductions. During the 80-minute debate on 23 May – in which both sides, for the most part, merely repeated well-rehearsed themes and familiar arguments – John Stennis read out a letter from President Nixon indicating that the Administration was expecting Mr Brosio to be received in Moscow the following week.[131] Although Mansfield's more pessimistic assessment, that the United States would be lucky to get mutual force reductions in *ten* years, was also very accurate, what *The Times* described as 'the first disclosure that the Russians had agreed to the Brosio mission' helped the Administration once again to characterise the amendment as ill-timed.[132] Senator Percy argued along similar lines, buttressing his case with the responses to cables he had sent to US ambassadors in NATO countries, requesting their assessment of the likely impact of unilateral troop cuts.[133] Although the cables may have been Percy's own idea rather than an Administration-inspired move – and were a follow-up to his experiences in May 1971 – the reactions of the ambassadors were predictable.

In spite of these efforts, the troop reductions cause gained some converts and the final roll-call vote, although still a clear victory for the Administration, represented a moderate gain for Mansfield. The 54 to 39 vote meant that the President's margin of advantage had diminished by 10 votes. Four Democrat senators, McIntyre of New Hampshire, Randolph of West Virginia, and Montoya and Anderson of New Mexico, had all changed position to support the Majority Leader, while Senator Bible of Nevada, who had been recorded against the amendment in May, also voted for the new proposal, as did Lee Metcalf, Mansfield's Montana colleague, who had been absent on the previous occasion. In addition, the Majority Leader picked up the vote of Senator Stafford of Vermont who had just been appointed to the Senate following the death of Winston Prouty. This more than compensated for the fact that four strong proponents of troop withdrawals – Church, McGovern, Saxbe and Hartke – were absent.[134] Thus, although the Administration succeeded in containing the pressure, the trend was clearly running against the *status quo*. There had not been a great upsurge of enthusiasm for Mansfield's more moderate proposal, but inroads had been made into the Administration's position and the accretion of support for the amendment was not insignificant. Thus the executive branch may have expected an even stronger challenge in 1972. In the event, however, the Senate did little as the issue moved from Capitol Hill into the presidential election contest, where George McGovern campaigned vigorously for military retrenchment overseas. With McGovern's defeat, the stage was set for another round of congressional pressure, and in 1973 the issue reemerged in the Senate more dramatically than ever before.

7 The Pressure Peaks: The 1973 Debate

1 INTRODUCTION

The controversy over US troops in Europe was more intense during 1973 than in any previous year. The main reason for this was the presence in the Senate of a profound and pervasive sense of dissatisfaction or, more accurately, a combination of impatience, disappointment, resentment and frustration – with the European allies, with the continuing high levels of defence expenditure in the United States, with the centralisation of power in the Presidency and, perhaps most important, with the attitudes, actions and policies of President Nixon. Nationalism, ideology, institutional pride and partisan considerations became inextricably bound up in ways which provoked a far more serious challenge to the American military presence in Western Europe than anything which had occurred hitherto.

The nationalist sentiments manifested themselves in a mood of anti-Europeanism. There was nothing new in this, of course: it had been an important factor in the congressional demands for troop withdrawals from the mid-1960s onwards. What was novel in 1973, however, was its strength and appeal. Indeed, the need to do something about the relationship with the West European allies was widely accepted in the executive branch as well as in Congress – as was reflected in Nixon and Kissinger's decision to launch the 'Year of Europe'. Central to this initiative was the notion of linkage between security and economic issues: the allies could not expect continued cooperation within NATO while the European Community was pursuing policies inimical to the United States. This theme was developed in both the President's Report to Congress on Foreign Policy and in Kissinger's Atlantic Charter speech of 23 April. Although

the Europeans tended to see this emphasis on linkage as a
calculated attempt by the Administration to extract economic
concessions from them, Kissinger emphasised that the 'political, military and economic issues in Atlantic relations are *linked
by reality*, not by our choice, nor for the tactical purpose of
trading one off against the other'.[1] In domestic political terms
Kissinger was right. Linkage was a reality because key figures
in Congress were increasingly making the connection – and
noting the discrepancy – between European security preferences and European economic practices. In relation to this it is
worth noting that on 28 December 1972 Charles Ferris, the staff
director and counsel of the Senate Democratic Policy Committee and one of Senator Mansfield's closest and most influential
advisers, submitted to the Majority Leader a six-page
memorandum outlining the conclusions he had drawn from a
recent visit to Europe. Among the points Ferris emphasised
was 'the intertwining rationales of the Common Market and
the US military force commitment to NATO'.[2] As he put it:

> The development of the Common Market and its policies . . .
> cannot be considered separately from the NATO and milit-
> ary aspects of the American presence in Europe. The notion
> of *interdependence* so articulately drawn by the Europeans and
> the Executive Branch on the issue of NATO should be
> applied to the economic and trade relationships between us.
> And conversely, if the Europeans do not accept a relation-
> ship of interdependence economically, then we should not
> accept the heavy burden that imposes upon the US by the
> heavy commitment of men in Europe.[3]

Furthermore, Ferris was far from certain that the Europeans
would accept the obligations of economic interdependence,
noting that he had been startled by the extent to which the
Common Market people wanted to 'reassert an autonomy from
the US' and either restrict American exports or compete more
vigorously with the United States, especially in the areas of
agricultural commodities, high technology and aerospace.[4] He
went on to contrast European willingness to depend on US
troops with its unwillingness to 'let that dependence demonstrate itself when it comes to economic areas where the United

States is most efficient'.[5] The whole thrust of these remarks underlines Kissinger's argument about the impossibility of compartmentalising Atlantic relations. Resentment at the policies of the Community inevitably spilled over and had an effect on congressional thinking about troops.

The prevailing attitude, however, was not simply one of anger. Annoyance was tinged with frustration and disappointment that the Europeans had not fulfilled either their own or American aspirations towards greater political unity. Yet this too lessened congressional tolerance, coinciding as it did with the disappearance of United States economic hegemony. Support for European integration had been a luxury that the United States could afford in the 1950s, but was far less attractive in the 1970s. The results of European efforts towards greater unity and self-reliance seemed rather meagre in political and security terms, and it appeared that the United States had succeeded solely in encouraging the emergence of a powerful economic competitor. Indeed, the United States now found itself with a Western Europe very different from that envisaged during the later 1940s. Then, the aim had been to recreate Western Europe's economic and military power. That there would be a natural harmony of interest and outlook between a reconstituted and more unified Western Europe and the United States was taken for granted. By the early 1970s, however, Western Europe was neither militarily strong enough nor sufficiently compliant to satisfy those Americans who increasingly were coming to regard the EEC as little more than 'a huge customs arrangement with an anachronistic agricultural policy which discriminates against American goods'.[6] Kissinger's call for a new 'Atlantic Charter' was simultaneously an expression of this disquiet and an attempt to eliminate the reasons for it. The Nixon Administration hoped to reorganise and moderate the Atlantic relationship before nationalist, protectionist and anti-European sentiment in the United States became overwhelming. The initiative, however, was rather late. By 1973 Atlantic relations had fallen into disrepair partly because of the inevitable structural changes in the international economy but also because of the Nixon Administration's neglect. A preoccupation with the war in Indochina and the desire to establish a *modus vivendi* with both Moscow and Peking, had relegated

Western Europe to a secondary role in the Administration's foreign policy. Although this period of neglect aroused anxieties in Europe, probably even more important was that it facilitated the development of congressional antipathies to a point where they could not be easily restrained or placated. The continued deficit in the balance of payments and the problems of the dollar – symbolised by the devaluation of February 1973 – only compounded the feelings of hostility. That the United States should continue to subsidise West European defence efforts by maintaining a substantial military presence on the continent – with its accompanying outflow of dollars – at a time when the European economies appeared to be more buoyant than that of the United States seemed anomalous if not intolerable.

If many Senators were dissatisfied with the NATO allies, they were equally unhappy with the limited congressional role in the making of foreign policy. The attempt to legislate troop withdrawals in 1973 can be seen, therefore, as part of the continuing executive–legislative struggle. The congressional backlash against both its own abdication of authority and the arrogation of power by the President had gathered momentum since 1971. The Case Act of 1972, for example, attempted to prevent any further abuse of executive agreements while in November 1973 the congress was finally to pass the War Powers Resolution over President Nixon's veto. Thus a mood of congressional defiance coincided with the congressional antagonism towards Western Europe. Even this convergence, however, does not fully explain the intensity of the 1973 controversy. Indeed, the strength of the Senate's challenge can only be fully understood against a background of events and issues which, superficially, appear to have little relevance to the troop question, but in practice did much to determine the form it took. It is arguable, in fact, that the outcome of the 1972 presidential election made both a further reassertion of congressional prerogatives and an upsurge of demands for troop withdrawals extremely likely. After all, McGovern's campaign platform had emphasised the need to 'bring America home', to reduce and rationalise American commitments overseas in order to release funds to meet pressing domestic needs. The failure of the Democratic candidate did nothing to alleviate

these concerns. Senator Mansfield, along with many of his
colleagues, remained unhappy both about the scale of the
American military presence in Europe and the consequent
drain on national resources. It was the attitudes and policies of
President Nixon though which transformed a probable confrontation into an inevitable one. Interpreting his reelection as
a mandate not only for imposing his own policy preferences
over those of his critics but for once again reasserting presidential prerogatives and privileges *vis-à-vis* an increasingly restive
and resentful Congress, Nixon continued in 1973 to take actions which were anathema to many members of the legislature. 'At the beginning of the year . . . President Nixon laid
down a dramatic challenge to Congressional authority by
refusing to spend appropriated money, refusing to let certain
members of his Administration appear before congressional
committees and refusing to stop the bombing of Indochina,
despite protests from both Houses that it was illegal.'[7]

What made this challenge even more serious was that
Nixon's victory had not been accompanied by comparable
Republican success in the congressional elections: not only did
the Democrats remain firmly in control of the House, but they
had increased their majority – albeit only slightly – in the
Senate. Mansfield, in a statement to the Democratic caucus on
3 January 1973, emphasised that the Senate too had been given
a mandate – to exercise its separate and distinct constitutional
role in the operation of the Federal government. Although
Mansfield, as usual, emphasised the need for cooperation
between the Administration and Congress, he also made clear
that the Democrats would be unwilling to defer to presidential
desires or dictates where these ran against their own preferences and principles.[8] Thus relations between the Republican
President and a Democratic Congress could hardly fail to be
characterised by a high degree of partisan conflict. Far from
trying to avoid this though, Nixon's actions seemed designed to
provoke it. They also ensured that the institutional and the
partisan aspects of congressional–executive relations became
inextricably linked. Nixon's impoundment of funds approved
by Congress intensified the already very acute fears about the
aggrandisement of presidential power. The practice of impoundment had only a 'minor status in law and custom',[9] but it

was now being extended to encompass what Senator Humphrey called 'policy impoundment' intended to thwart the will of Congress as expressed in appropriations.[10] Thus the concerns over the excesses of the 'Imperial Presidency' in foreign policy merged with anxieties about the actions of an imperious President in domestic policy. Furthermore the fact that the President's budgetary strictures were directed at programmes long favoured by the liberal Democrats provoked a hostile reaction on ideological grounds as well as underlining the need to rectify the constitutional imbalance. In short, substantive and procedural concerns became inseparable.

Anxieties about the expenditure ceilings and budgetary priorities imposed by the White House were apparent at the outset of the eighty-third Congress. They became even more pronounced when, at the end of January, the President's budget proposals for fiscal year 1974 were revealed, and the full effect of Nixon's actions on the fiscal year 1973 budget became clearer. It emerged that the President had cut $11.2 billion from the $261.1 billion approved by Congress for fiscal 1973. The reductions included a cut of $3.1 billion dollars in Department of Agriculture spending. Nor were the prospects for fiscal year 1974 much comfort to the Democrats, as the President emphasised the need to restrict overall spending to $268.7 billion, a ceiling which would be imposed largely by limiting domestic social programmes.[11] The defence budget, in contrast, emerged relatively unscathed from the President's review of spending priorities. Although the President's request for fiscal year 1974 was over $2000 million less than that for the previous year, it still represented the second largest figure ever placed before Congress. With American disengagement from the Vietnam War virtually completed, the expectation in Congress was for a much more substantial 'peace dividend' than the Administration seemed prepared to offer. If the substance of Nixon's budget message was unpalatable to many members of Congress, however, the manner of it was almost equally so. In a radio address on 28 January, Nixon justified cutting funds for hospital building and urban renewal on the grounds that these programmes had become 'sacred cows'. The response was immediate, sharp and widespread. Carl Albert, Speaker of the House, reflected the views of many of his Democratic colleagues in both chambers when he described Nixon's budget as 'nothing less than the systematic dismantling and destruction of the great social programmes and the great precedents of humanitarian government inaugurated by Franklin D. Roosevelt and enlarged by every Democratic President since then'.[12] As such it could not go unchallenged.

2 THE DEMOCRATIC CHALLENGE

This controversy over national priorities provided the immediate context within which the troop withdrawal issue developed during 1973. Indeed, the battle over priorities and the military presence in Europe were directly connected by the desire of the Democratic leadership in the Senate to establish a different set of budgetary priorities from that presented by the President. In order to fund domestic social programmes while remaining within existing expenditure ceilings – and thereby avoid any increase in taxation – it was decided to reduce the share of national resources devoted to defence. The next step was the logical progression from this. As Gelb and Lake suggested: 'Having decided to go after cuts in the defence budget, the Mansfield group had a further choice – to make the fight over weapons systems (aircraft, ships, missiles, etc.) or manpower (US troops stationed overseas). They decided, albeit not exclusively, to do the latter.'[13] This reflected Senator Mansfield's personal conviction that the time was long past for a substantial cutback in American forces overseas. It was also more expedient: cutting back on weapons systems had adverse consequences both for employment and for the technological balance between the two superpowers.[14] 'Foreign bases and stationings', on the other hand, 'are exposed. They are no-one's constituents.'[15] Accordingly, the Democratic Policy Committee drafted a resolution to reduce US forces in Europe. The initial proposal from Mansfield's office was for a 50 per cent reduction, but sentiment in the committee was so strong that the scope of the resolution was expanded to include all American forces overseas and the percentage reduction was increased to 66.[16]

It was this more far-reaching resolution which was considered in the Senate Democratic caucus on 15 March. The caucus meeting was 'stormy', and it appears that several senators dissented very strongly from the leadership's proposal.[17] A compromise was finally achieved, however, and the caucus voted overwhelmingly (with 48 votes in favour and only about 6 against) for a resolution calling on the President to reduce 'substantially' the size of the United States military presence in Europe and Asia by mid-1974. 'But the word substantially was reportedly inserted at the insistence of the moderates and conservatives ... by inserting a generality for a specific cut, the conservatives preserved their flexibility for later votes.'[18] A possible additional reason for this change was to allow the leadership to make exploratory contacts with the Executive regarding the issue.[19] If this is the case, it suggests that in spite of the pervasive dissatisfaction at least a few Democratic senators remained reluctant to challenge either the substance of the Administration's security policies or its exclusive control of military commitments.

Mansfield, however, was prepared to issue such a challenge and when announcing the caucus decision in the Senate, he not only identified the concerns which had motivated the conference action but also made clear the strength of his own feelings on the issue. Having acknowledged the seriousness of both domestic inflation and the decline in the value of the dollar, Mansfield attacked the Administration's decision to cut back on domestic expenditure while pouring money into the military budget. In the light of the financial problems facing the nation the $17 billion which was the cost of its contribution to NATO seemed an excessive drain on resources. So too did the balance of payments costs incurred as a consequence of the troop deployment in Europe, costs which had doubled in current dollars between 1969 and 1972. As Mansfield put it:

> Overseas there are still too many Americans, too many dependents, too many bases, too many facilities at too great a cost to the people of this nation, and at little or no cost to those whose security, presumably, is being defended ... As if to add insult to injury, the American taxpayer is forced to listen to a government which wastes billions for antiquated and irrelevant purposes of this kind tell him that the nation's

resources are just not big enough to provide adequately for domestic services – whether for health, education, welfare, or rural services – to the people of this nation.[20]

The Majority Leader's comments were endorsed by other prominent Democrats such as Fulbright, Pastore, Hart, Symington and Hollings.

That Mansfield's intention was to reduce defence expenditures in order to promote domestic welfare was underlined further a week later when he had a strategy meeting with Senator McClellan, Chairman of the Committee of Appropriations, and other leading Democrats. During the meeting Mansfield emphasised that if 'substantial' reductions in federal expenditures were to be made, 'the kind that would provide funds for essential purposes at home without feeding the inflation', it was not enough merely to withdraw troops from overseas: the overall manpower ceilings of the armed forces also had to be reduced.[21]

This meeting of 22 March was a preliminary to Mansfield taking up the matter with the Speaker of the House and the Director of the Office of Management and Budget – as he had been directed to do in the caucus resolution. The Democratic leaders though had few illusions about the Administration's response to the troop withdrawal pressure. Indeed, the Executive's position was unequivocal. It had also been swift in coming. Almost immediately after the caucus decision was announced it was criticised by spokesmen for the White House and the Department of State. Not only was the resolution characterised as 'unwise', but the estimates of the budgetary savings that would result from the cuts were also challenged. A much fuller riposte to the Mansfield pressure however came (as it had done in 1970) from Elliot Richardson who, in his new position as Secretary of Defense, testified before the Senate Armed Services Committee on 27 March. Richardson made use of the forthcoming negotiations on mutual force reductions to argue that unilateral reductions of the kind demanded by Mansfield would 'not only destroy the current tenuous military balance in Europe, but also destroy the prospect for orderly, balanced mutual force reductions'.[22] The possibility of mutual cutbacks had been a major factor in the defeat of the Mansfield

Amendment in May 1971 and it was both natural and inevitable that the Administration should now resort to it once again. Indeed, this had been anticipated by Ferris in his memorandum to Senator Mansfield the previous December, when he had forecast that

> any effort in this Congress to accelerate any timetable for a reduction outside the scope of MBFR will be greatly resisted. The same type of scare tactic will be deployed that was successful before, both with respect to the antiballistic missile effort in the Senate and the SALT negotiations – namely the bargaining-chip argument . . . that unilateral action will undermine these negotiations with the Russians and therefore will be irresponsible.[23]

That Richardson's argument was predictable, however, did not make it any the less attractive to the Administration. Even so, the Secretary of Defense did not rest his case solely upon the impending MBFR negotiations. As a former Secretary for Health, Education and Welfare, Richardson was able to confront the resource allocation problem directly and authoritatively. Emphasising that an extension of present HEW services 'equitably to all those meeting the eligibility standards' would cost an additional $250 billion a year, he noted that such a sum 'would consume not only the entire defense budget but the entire current budget as well. The obvious point is that with present technologies and resources we cannot now do all that we would like to do: choice is inescapable.'[24] And a cut in defence to benefit domestic social programmes was the wrong choice. Thus the expectations of the Democratic leadership about the Administration's unwillingness to accommodate its views on the issue seem to have been borne out.

The meeting with the Speaker of the House seems to have been more fruitful, although the extent to which the demand for troop reductions by the House of Representatives was the result of Mansfield's prodding is not entirely clear. It may well have been that concerns over national priorities and the balance of payments were sufficient to evoke such demands irrespective of any initiative by, or pressure from, the Senate leadership. Whatever its origin there was certainly much more sustained pressure for troop withdrawals in the House of Representatives during 1973 than in any previous year. Several amendments were introduced – including one by Majority Leader O'Neill – and although these were ultimately defeated by substantial margins, they helped to ensure that the possibility of reductions was fully ventilated.[25] Hearings were held by the Subcommittee on Europe of the House Foreign Affairs Committee, and with a subcommittee chairman, Benjamin Rosenthal of New York, who was sympathetic to Mansfield's ideas, it appeared possible that its activities would create a groundswell of sentiment in favour of reductions. It was to forestall this that the State Department pressed to have the hearings transferred to the full committee where it would have a better opportunity to present its case.[26] Accordingly, the committee, on 10, 11 and 12 July, heard a parade of Administration witnesses, the most effective of whom were Deputy Secretary of State, Kenneth Rush, and James Schlesinger, who had replaced Richardson as Secretary of Defense. Rush and Schlesinger were also the key spokesmen for the Administration at hearings held on 25 and 27 July before the Senate Foreign Relations Committee's Subcommittee on International Law, Arms Control and International Organisation – hearings at which Mike Mansfield also testified.

3 THE ARGUMENTS

Although a large part of Senator Mansfield's testimony merely reiterated familiar arguments, he provided the subcommittee with a comprehensive and clear statement of why, in his judgement, United States troop withdrawals from Western Europe were both feasible and desirable. Emphasising that he regarded NATO as the most important of all America's overseas commitments, Mansfield attempted to counter or forestall arguments about the inappropriate timing of a troop withdrawal amendment. After asserting that this excuse for upholding the *status quo* had been used frequently during the 13 years he had been campaigning for troop withdrawals, Mansfield suggested that the forthcoming negotiations on mutual force reductions should not rule out unilateral action. Expressing a scepticism of the 'bargaining-chip' argument which echoed the

analysis made by Ferris the previous December, Mansfield
argued with considerable prescience that the negotiations
would mean 'a postponement of significant action
indefinitely'.[27] What made this all the more irksome to the
Majority Leader was his belief that an American military
presence in Europe on the existing scale was superfluous. One
reason for this was *détente*. Mansfield cited 82 events since 1963
which suggested a change in East–West relations of sufficient
scope to make possible a change in the American military
posture.[28] A Soviet attack on the Central Front had become a
highly implausible contingency.

Although the *détente* argument gained credence from Mr
Brezhnev's visit to Washington the previous month, Mansfield
did not base his case solely on the assessment of Soviet political
intentions. He also suggested that, in the event of an attack,
United States conventional forces were unlikely to be particularly effective. With about 7000 nuclear warheads deployed in
Western Europe, many of them near the intra-German border,
it was difficult for Mansfield to 'envision any serious conventional war scenario that doesn't go nuclear in less than two
days. Our "tactical" nuclear weapons will be either "cap-
tured" or "detonated"'.[29] In other words, Mansfield rejected
both the feasibility of NATO's flexible response strategy, and
the need for American forces to be prepared for a 60- to 90-day
conventional war in Europe. Nor did he obtain much comfort
from the deployment of US forces in Southern Germany when
the most likely theatre of operations was the North German
plain. In the light of all this, he suggested, 'a properly structured United States military force of one or at the most two lean
mobile divisions, in a position to move rapidly along the
German frontier' would offer 'greater insurance against any
form of pressure from the East'.[30]

The other advantage of this system was that it would be less
expensive than the existing force. What Mansfield objected to
most, though, was not the expense *per se* of the troops in Europe,
but that they provided an *unnecessary* drain on resources – which
was all the more distressing now that the competition for
resources had become so intense. Although keen to reorder
national priorities, Mansfield was not demanding that security
needs be subordinated to domestic imperatives: the central

point was that money could be saved and the defence budget reduced 'not by trimming our sails or international obligations but by trimming the waste from years of inattention to a rational international policy'.[31]

These arguments were directly challenged by executive branch witnesses. Resting their arguments on judgements and assumptions very different to those made by Mansfield, they claimed that the troops in Europe remained vital to American security (and were there not just to protect the West Europeans), that their cost was neither unreasonable nor excessive, and that the allies, in spite of claims to the contrary, were taking their defence seriously and were willing to share burdens more equitably. Schlesinger, in particular – both in his prepared statement and his response to questions – made an explicit attempt to refute Mansfield's arguments. Although acknowledging that the forward deployment of tactical nuclear weapons was a problem which would have to be dealt with, the Secretary of Defense refused to accept the case for troop withdrawals. As he put it: 'I assure you our troops are still in Europe some 28 years after the end of World War II, not because the President wishes to incur the political costs of deploying major forces in Europe, not because of inertia or bad habit, not to save our European allies the trouble and expense of their own defense, not simply to maintain an American "presence", and not just to serve as a "tripwire".'[32] Schlesinger went on to argue that the troops were essential because they provided the United States with options for dealing with a large Soviet conventional threat which, in an age of nuclear parity, could no longer be offset by American nuclear advantage. The dichotomy was complete. Whereas Mansfield had concentrated on Soviet political intentions, Schlesinger focused on Soviet military capabilities. He also claimed that unilateral troop reductions would go a long way to fulfilling a major Soviet objective, which was a Western Europe devoid of a protective American military presence.[33] Additional arguments – and indeed recurring themes of all the Administration witnesses – were that such reductions would unravel the Atlantic Alliance (although precisely how was never made explicit), would lead to fragmentation rather than greater unity among the European allies (with 'Finlandisation' as the most probable

long-term consequence) and would undermine the mutual
force reduction talks by taking away any incentive the Soviet
Union might have to seek a negotiated withdrawal.

Arguments about the cost of the US commitment were also
prominent in the hearings, as executive officials tried once
again to defuse the criticisms made by Mansfield and his
supporters.[34] The balance of payments deficit of $1.5 million
associated with the troops was compared to the $1.2 billion
deficit resulting from American tourism in Western Europe; it
was also pointed out that the $1.5 billion was only one-sixth of
the overall balance of payments deficit for 1972. As well as
minimising the scale of the problem, however, the witnesses
also identified the steps which were being taken to eliminate it.
Schlesinger noted that as a result of his June meeting with other
NATO defence ministers, the alliance was exploring ways of
achieving a multilateral solution. Kissinger's 'Year of Europe'
initiative was also presented as evidence of the Administration's intention to eliminate the inequities which had developed
in Atlantic relations. At the same time, the witnesses emphasised that European defence efforts were far more substantial
than many Americans either realised or were prepared to give
them credit for. As Schlesinger pointed out: 'Most of the
deployed forces are supplied by our allies – something on the
order of 90 per cent of the ground forces, 80 per cent of the ships,
and 75 per cent of the aircraft.'[35] While this was an important
corrective to ideas that the Europeans had become 'free riders',
the Secretary of Defense was aware that it would not convince
those who felt that the allies were taking advantage of the
United States. It may well have been to appeal to such senators
and Congressmen that he promised to be tough in the burden-
sharing negotiations within the alliance. In this connection,
however, he also acknowledged that the pressure from Congress had been helpful in bringing home to the Europeans the
need to do more.

The emphasis on the financial aspects of the commitment –
the balance of payments difficulties and burden-sharing –
reflected the Administration's calculation that a great deal of
support for Mansfield was coming from those of his colleagues
who resented the costs of the US troops in Europe. This

calculation was also to prove influential in the period before the Military Procurement Authorisation Bill came to the Senate floor.

4 THE SENATE BATTLE

The decision to offer a troop cut amendment to the defence procurement bill seems to have been taken in mid-August partly as a result of prompting from Ferris. On 10 August, he suggested to Mansfield that the forthcoming bill would be the 'most appropriate and logical vehicle' upon which to attach the proposal for a 50 per cent reduction of US forces overseas, which had been considered by the Democratic Policy Committee and the caucus earlier in the year.[36] The reduction was to take place over three years and leave the Executive with discretion in determining where the troop withdrawals should occur. Ferris also argued that the proposal would complement the recommendation of the Committee on Armed Services to reduce the overall manpower levels by 156 000. Furthermore, since the Mansfield Amendment would not deal with the question of demobilisation – even though this had been discussed at the strategy meeting with Fulbright, McClellan and Symington on 22 March – it did not invade the jurisdiction of the Armed Services Committee. Ferris also recommended that the Policy Committee and caucus consider the proposal before its presentation on the Senate floor.[37]

It was not only the Mansfield forces which were preparing for a battle on the issue, however. Senator Henry Jackson, who had consistently been one of the leading critics of troop withdrawal proposals, was attempting to devise a measure which, by doing something to placate those whose major concern was the cost of the commitment, would help either to defuse the issue or, at a minimum, wean away some of the support from Mansfield. In August he announced his intention – along with Sam Nunn of Georgia, a freshman senator particularly interested in national security matters – of introducing what was to become known as the Jackson–Nunn Amendment to the defence procurement bill. Based on an idea that probably originated with Jackson's aide Richard Perle, the amendment stipulated that the President should seek to offset the balance of payments deficit resulting from the deployment of US forces in Europe: in the event that the United States failed to obtain a total offset, the American forces would be reduced by a percentage equal to the percentage shortfall. The second part of the amendment demanded that the allies substantially increase their contributions to assist the United States in meeting the added budgetary expenses incurred as a result of deploying forces in Europe rather than the United States.[38] Although the proposal was not welcomed by the Administration, at least initially,[39] it evoked an enthusiastic response in the Senate and, after a brief debate of 25 September, was passed by an overwhelming majority of 84 to 5. This was hardly surprising. The measure provided an opportunity for Southern senators and Midwest Republicans in particular to tell their people back home that they had put pressure on the European allies to do more – while at the same time allowing them to vote against the Mansfield Amendment. Thus, Jackson–Nunn was a tactical device intended to erode support for Senator Mansfield's more far-reaching and direct proposals. In the words of Senator Cranston of California – a vigorous supporter of troop withdrawals and a sharp critic of the idea that US troops in Europe were necessary as 'hostages' to ensure American involvement in hostilities – it was 'a defensive move to deprive us of some of our arguments', particularly those relating to the balance of payments and burden-sharing.[40]

Nevertheless, the immediate impact of the amendment was less pronounced than its sponsors had hoped or its critics feared. It was certainly not sufficient to satisfy the Majority Leader and on 26 September, Mansfield introduced his own amendment to reduce US troops overseas by 50 per cent over three years. Prior to this the Majority Leader had circulated a letter to his Senate colleagues explaining the purpose and scope of his proposal.[41] The letter set out clearly Mansfield's aims, but was an appeal for support rather than an attempt at pressurising other senators. In this, it was typical of Mansfield's gentle style of leadership, a style which during the events of 26 September was to put him at a serious disadvantage when challenging an Administration with far fewer scruples. The debate on the amendment was a fairly brief one, in which both sides did little more than reiterate the arguments for and against reductions. Just prior to the vote, however, Mansfield modified his proposal to encompass a 40 per cent rather than a 50 per cent reduction. With this change the measure passed the Senate by a vote of 49 to 46, a result which seemed to surprise its author almost as much as it surprised the executive branch.

The Mansfield Amendment was itself a substitute for an amendment proposed by Alan Cranston. Parliamentary procedure, however, required a second vote – on the initial Cranston Amendment as modified – before the measure could be formally attached to the defence procurement bill. In most circumstances, this would have been a mere formality accomplished without a second roll-call vote. In this instance, however, an objection from Senator Griffin, the Republican Whip, prevented its immediate consideration. The Senate continued with its next item of business and the executive branch was provided with an opportunity for some intensive lobbying in a bid to overturn the decision. The key figures in this seem to have been General Goodpaster, who apparently telephoned several senators from Belgium, Secretary of Defense Schlesinger, and Marshall Wright, Assistant Secretary of State for Congressional Relations. It was largely as a result of their efforts that when the Senate, six hours after the first vote, resumed consideration of the Cranston Amendment, it was rejected in a 51 to 44 split. The crucial difference between the two votes was a change of position by four senators: Aiken of Vermont, Magnuson of Washington, Young of North Dakota (all of whom had consistently voted for the Mansfield Amendment on earlier occasions), and Johnston of Louisiana all transferred their allegiance on the second vote.

Although there is no indication as to why Young switched, Johnston's change is more explicable. It came as a result of a meeting with Secretary of Defense Schlesinger, which apparently had been scheduled for 26 September a few days earlier, in order to give the senator an opportunity to discuss the forthcoming vote on Trident. As one of Johnston's aides emphasised: 'It wasn't a matter of Schlesinger rushing over here to twist the Senator's arm.'[42] Nevertheless, the Secretary used the meeting to present a powerful and, for Johnston, compelling case against troop withdrawals.[43] The timing of the meeting may have been fortuitous, but it was fully exploited by Schlesinger, who also used his presence in the Senate to lobby other Senators. These included Richard Schweiker who reported a hallway conversation with the Defense Secretary in which he had been urged – to no avail – to change his vote.[44]

Magnuson's defection from the troop withdrawal camp also seems to have been a response to lobbying, probably by Marshall Wright. Wright had discovered that Hubert Humphrey was planning to introduce a less drastic troop reduction amendment and, according to Charles Ferris, used this knowledge to sway those senators concerned that the cuts resulting from the Mansfield Amendment would be too severe. As Ferris put it: 'Humphrey tried to keep his intentions quiet and he was peeved when the State Department used the proposal to try to turn the Mansfield vote around.'[45] Whatever Humphrey's intent, details of his proposal seem to have been a major factor in inducing Magnuson to alter his position. Although the *Washington Post* reported that Magnuson had given no clear reason for his reversal other than to claim that he thought (wrongly) that the second amendment was a bit different in scope, his aides suggested that he decided to switch when he heard of Humphrey's proposal. As one of them put it: 'Magnuson thought that this was a more responsible way to achieve improvement in our balance of payments position.'[46]

Aiken's reversal is, if anything, even more interesting, not least because he was Mansfield's daily breakfast companion and his closest friend in the Senate. One possibility which has been suggested is that he was induced to change his vote in return for favourable legislation relating to a river within his own state of Vermont – a deal which was worked out with Senator Jackson, in his capacity as Chairman of the Committee on the Interior, and the White House, after an initiative by John Tower of Texas who was leading the opposition to the Mansfield Amendment on the Senate floor.[47] While this may have encouraged the switch, however, it seems unlikely that it was the main reason for it. In fact, Aiken may have traded a vote which he was going to change anyway. Although he had supported Mansfield on the first amendment, he made clear in the debate preceding it that his support was not unqualified.

Despite his concern that the amendment went 'too far too fast', however, he voted for it, almost certainly on the assumption that it would be defeated.[48] In his memoirs, Aiken suggests that he saw the amendment primarily as an opportunity to prod 'the European countries to carry a bigger load of the cost of their own defence. It also gave me a chance to support Senator Mansfield who had accommodated me so many times.'[49] In other words, Aiken seems to have seen his vote as essentially a gesture or token. Having made it, and discovered that its significance went far beyond anything he had anticipated, his natural inclination was to reverse his position – partly, as he himself explained, to give the force reduction talks a chance.[50] In this instance, therefore, any additional inducement may have been unnecessary. Nevertheless, it illustrates the lengths to which the Administration and its supporters in the Senate were prepared to go to defeat Mansfield's proposal.

Not all the lobbying was successful, however, and the anti-troop reduction forces may have remained uncertain of victory until the second vote was counted. The attempt to switch votes seems to have continued until the last possible moment. The *Baltimore Sun* reported that before the second vote, Senator William Scott, a freshman Republican from Virginia, was visited at his back row seat by John Stennis, Chairman of the Armed Services Committee, Strom Thurmond, the senior Republican on the Committee, High Scott, the Minority Leader, and Harry Byrd, the senior senator from Virginia.[51] In spite of this, Scott remained firm in his support for Mansfield.

This is not to suggest that the Mansfield forces did nothing during the period between the two votes. The Majority Leader's office called several senators, including Johnston, to thank them for their support and to express Senator Mansfield's hope that they would stick on the procedural motion. It seems probable that they also contacted Stevenson and Kennedy, both of whom had voted against the amendment and emphasised both the procedural aspect of agreeing to the Cranston Amendment as modified, and the fact that a large proportion of the troop cuts could be made in Asia, with only 25 000 being withdrawn from Europe, all in the third year in which the amendment was in effect. Furthermore, it was suggested that this figure would probably be far less after the

House–Senate Conference.[52] In addition, Senator Clark of Iowa, who was in his home state attending to his father's funeral arrangements, was flown back to Washington. Clark's vote, however, was more than offset by the presence of Stennis, who had been attending the trial of an alleged assailant and consequently missed the morning vote, and Bentsen of Texas (who was flown back from Alabama where he had been attending a governor's conference), both of whom were strong NATO supporters. Furthermore, Lowell Weicker and Robert Packwood, who had both decided for the amendment in the morning, did not vote in the afternoon. Along with the four reversals, this guaranteed victory for the Administration.

The 1973 battle over troops did not end with the second vote of 26 September, however. The following day there was a postscript when a more moderate amendment, introduced by Senators Humphrey and Cranston, mandating a reduction of 110 000 men overseas (i.e. a 23 per cent withdrawal as opposed to the 40 per cent demanded by the Mansfield Amendment) was passed by a vote of 48 to 36. Although the Administration was again active in its opposition to the proposal, its authors were determined to go ahead, partly in reaction to the events of the previous day when, it was felt, Senator Mansfield had been unnecessarily humiliated. While resentment at the Administration's tactics may also have contributed to the success of the amendment, a more important factor was probably the sponsorship of Senator Humphrey.[53] Although Humphrey was not prominent in the debate on troop withdrawals, in 1973 at least he was probably the single most influential member of the Senate on the issue, and the one to whom uncommitted or wavering senators looked for guidance on how to vote. Furthermore, the amendment itself was a moderate one – and was made even more so after a proposal introduced by Robert Byrd, the Democratic whip, to reduce the original figure of 125 000 by 15 000 had obtained Senate approval. In a further attempt to broaden support, the deadline for withdrawal was also extended from mid-1975 to the end of the year. The proponents of the bill also emphasised that the Executive had complete discretion in determining where the cuts should be made – and that there was sufficient scope for reductions in the Pacific and in Asia to enable the measure to be implemented without impinging on the American military presence in Western Europe. This, along with Humphrey's leadership and example, may well have been decisive in obtaining the support of senators such as Bentsen, Kennedy and Mathias who were reluctant to scale down the presence in Europe but felt that retrenchment elsewhere was both feasible and desirable. With Johnston, Aiken and Magnuson again voting for the amendment, the defection of these pro-NATO senators was sufficient to ensure victory.

Although the Administration had reluctantly accepted before the vote that the Humphrey–Cranston Amendment would pass the Senate, the President remained highly critical of it and, according to his Press Secretary, considered it a 'dangerous and serious impediment' to the attempt to negotiate withdrawals.[54] As such, the Executive branch wanted it dropped in the House–Senate Conference Committee on the defence procurement bill – an outcome which was highly probable in view of the decisive rejection by the lower chamber of troop cut proposals but which was facilitated by events in the Middle East. In a letter to Mansfield after the Conference Committee, Senator Stennis explained that House Conferees had refused to budge on the amendment and that the Senate's position had been undermined by the outbreak of the Middle East War.[55] The Yom Kippur War, of course, had far-reaching ramifications, affecting both Soviet–American relations and relations among the NATO allies in ways which were ultimately to make US troops withdrawals from Western Europe a less attractive option to many senators. Before examining the decline of congressional pressure in 1974 and 1975, however, it is useful to examine, if only in an impressionistic way, the votes of 26 September, 1973.

5   THE PATTERN OF VOTING

The first vote of 26 September 1973 represents the high water mark of support for Senator Mansfield's attempt to scale down the United States military presence in Western Europe. As such, it provides an appropriate opportunity to identify not only the kind of senator – in terms of party affiliation, ideological preference, regional origin and age – in favour of troop withdrawals, but also those who supported the Nixon Administration in its adherence to the *status quo*. The analysis is impressionistic rather than scientific and does not attempt to establish precise correlations between senators' voting positions on the troops issue and their other attributes. It does, however, attempt to build up a profile both of those senators who voted for the Mansfield Amendment and of those who were typically opposed to the measure.

The vote on the Majority Leader's proposal had a very clear partisan basis with 42 Democrats and 7 Republicans voting in favour and 12 Democrats and 34 Republicans coming out against it. In some respects, this division is hardly surprising: as discussed above, it was the Democratic leadership in the Policy Committee which had made all the running on the issue and the Democratic caucus which, in March, had approved the general principle of military retrenchment overseas. Furthermore, the division largely along party lines reflected the general trend of Senate voting in 1973 which saw a sharp rise in the number of 'party unity' votes in which a majority of voting Democrats opposed a majority of voting Republicans.[56] Even so, the degree of party unity was remarkably high with 78 per cent of the Democrats supporting Mansfield and only 22 per cent opposing. The Republicans provided a virtual mirror image of this split with 17 per cent supporting Mansfield and 83 per cent backing the Administration in its opposition to the proposal.

Of the 12 Democrats who were out of line with their party colleagues, 6 were Southern conservatives. This defection suggests another possibility to be considered – that the roll-call reflected the classic ideological split in the Senate between liberals and conservatives. There are, of course, sophisticated procedures which can be used to scale a senator's ideological position and preferences.[57] For present purposes, however, a somewhat cruder approach is sufficient. An individual senator's broad stance can be determined by the percentage of the votes he casts which are in accordance with the position taken by the conservative coalition of Southern Democrats and Republicans – the lower the percentage the more liberal the senator, the higher the percentage the more conservative.[58]

Although this method involves some dangerous oversimplification, it does provide a broad indication of each senator's ideological position and is used in Table 7.1. Several observations arise from this. The first is that there was a clear and fairly dramatic ideological cleavage on the issue. Categorising senators as either conservative or liberal on the basis of the predominant tendency in their voting yields an interesting result: 82 per cent of those voting in favour of the Mansfield Amendment were liberal and 18 per cent were conservative, while of those opposing, 74 per cent were conservative and 26 per cent liberal. This, of course, goes hand in hand with the

TABLE 7.1   *Ideological positions of senators voting on Mansfield amendment*

	For the amendment		
Democrats	*% support for cons. coalition*	*Democrats*	*% support for cons. coalition*
Abourezk (SD)	2	McIntyre (NH)	24
Bayh (Ind)	7	Metcalf (Mont)	17
Bible (Nev)	42	Mondale (Minn)	2
Biden (Del)	9	Montoya (NM)	33
Burdick (ND)	16	Moss (Utah)	6
Byrd (WVa)	47	Muskie (Me)	7
Chiles (Flo)	33	Nelson (Wis)	4
Church (Idaho)	11	Pastore (RI)	19
Cranston (Cal)	13	Pell (RI)	11
Eagleton (Mo)	7	Proxmire (Wis)	11
Fulbright (Ark)	25	Randolph (W Va)	45
Gravel (Alaska)	14	Ribicoff (Conn)	10
Hart (Mich)	3	Symington (Mo)	14
Hartke (Ind)	13	Talmadge (Ga)	85
Haskell (Colo)	14	Tunney (Cal)	15
Hathaway (Me)	6	Williams (NJ)	7
Hollings (S C)	53		
Huddleston (Ky)	25	*Republicans*	
Hughes (Iowa)	3		
Inouye (Haw)	23	Aiken (Vt)	70
Johnston (La)	65	Hatfield (Ore)	37
Long (La)	59	Packwood (Ore)	41
Magnuson (Wash)	24	Schweiker (Pa)	24
Mansfield (Mont)	8	Scott (Va)	86
McClellan (Ark)	89	Weicker (Conn)	63
McGovern (SD)	2	Young (ND)	80

TABLE 7.1   *(continued)*

	Against the amendment		
Democrats	*% support for cons. coalition*	*Republicans*	*% support for cons. coalition*
Allen (Ala)	89	Cotton (NH)	17
Byrd (Va)	89	Curtis (Neb)	84
Cannon (Nev)	42	Dole (Kan)	89
Eastland (Miss)	85	Domenichi (NM)	89
Ervin (NC)	74	Dominick (Colo)	82
Humphrey (Minn)	10	Fannin (Ariz)	93
Jackson (Wash)	33	Fong (Haw)	79
Kennedy (Mass)	4	Goldwater (Ar)	60
McGee (Wyo)	29	Griffin (Mich)	80
Nunn (Ga)	85	Gurney (Flo)	81
Sparkman (Ala)	76	Hansen (Wyo)	93
Stevenson (Ill)	9	Helms (NC)	98
		Hruska (Neb)	91
Republicans		Javits (NY)	20
		Mathias (Md)	31
Baker (Tenn)	59	McClure (Idaho)	72
Bartlett (Ok)	90	Percy (Ill)	35
Beall (Md)	74	Roth (Del)	79
Bellmon (Ok)	65	Saxbe (Ohio)	47
Bennett (Wash)	76	Scott (Pa)	75
Brock (Tenn)	85	Stafford (Vt)	50
Brooke (Mass)	18	Stevens (Al)	71
Buckley (NY)	80	Thurmond (SC)	94
Case (NJ)	8	Tower (Tex)	93
Cook (Ky)	74		

high degree of partisanship, but it also gives credence to the argument that the troops issue was inextricably bound up with the dispute over national priorities. It also seems to have been part of the broader pattern which emerged in the late 1960s and early 1970s, whereby the liberals, and especially the liberal Democrats, took the lead in demanding both military retrenchment and greater restrictions on presidential power. In the vote on the national commitments resolution of 1969, for example, 'the primary empirical cleavage . . . occurred along the liberal–conservative line, with liberals supporting restrictive measures and conservatives opposing them'.[59] The implication is that liberalism no longer went hand in hand with internationalism, in so far as this involved the retention of a large military establishment overseas. Just as the Democrats had changed from the party which, in the 1950s, had been most strongly committed to higher defence expenditures, to the party which contained the most vociferous critics of what were seen as an unnecessarily bloated defence budget, so liberal support for a strong presidency and an activist foreign policy had been transformed into opposition to the 'Imperial Presidency' and a global foreign policy. This is not to suggest that the liberals had become isolationist. For the most part they were not demanding a retreat to 'Fortress America'; but they did want what Senator Mansfield described as a 'more discerning internationalism'.[60] Demilitarisation of United States foreign policy was deemed essential, both for its own sake and to facilitate the diversion of attention and resources to serious domestic problems.

Not all the liberals voted for the Mansfield Amendment, of course. Those liberal Democrats who opposed the proposal were by and large in favour of overseas troop withdrawals but thought that Europe should be exempt. Humphrey, for example, had always been a strong NATO supporter, while Henry Jackson combined his sympathies for the alliance with militant anti-communism and scepticism about *détente*. Senator Edward Kennedy, in contrast, had supported the Mansfield Amendments on both occasions in 1971 but believed that the force reduction talks had to be given an opportunity to bring about mutual withdrawals.[61] If the few liberal Democrats who opposed Mansfield were out of line with most of their party colleagues, the same cannot be said of the liberal Republicans, whose position may have owed as much to party and allegiance to the President as to their ideological convictions. Yet it is important not to exaggerate the influence of party on their position. It is perhaps significant that several of the liberal Republicans – Javits, Mathias, Brooke and Case – were from the East Coast with its traditional ties to Europe. Indeed, Javits and Mathias were part of the collegiate Republican leadership group which played an important part in opposing the successive amendments. So too was Percy of Illinois, another liberal Republican, who had been prominent during the late 1960s and early 1970s for his attempts to devise schemes whereby the Europeans could engage in greater burden-sharing, but who had consistently taken the position that troop withdrawals were not the best way to ensure this. For the most part, therefore, the liberals of both parties who did not support Mansfield had a clear, unequivocal and very public commitment to NATO which seems to have been an important, and perhaps the decisive, factor in determining their position.

As well as explaining the actions of liberals who deviated from what was a liberal stance, it is necessary to try to account for the small group of conservatives who voted with Mansfield. Although not all these senators have provided public explanations of their vote, personal conviction seems to have been important once again. For Democrats McClellan and Talmadge, disquiet over the scale of American military expenditures overseas and concern over European lack of effort seem to have been important considerations – as they were for one or two conservative Republicans such as Aiken.[62] Milton Young of North Dakota, in contrast, was one of the few real isolationists in the Senate (and also, along with McClellan, one of the few senators to have experienced the 'Great Debate' of 1951 at first hand) and, on the first vote at least, was probably doing no more than expressing long-held beliefs about the American role in the world. The point about these convictions, however, is that they were idiosyncratic. Most conservatives were unalterably opposed to the Mansfield Amendment, a position which almost certainly reflected their broad outlook on international politics as well as their preference for the *status quo*. Such attitudes included a profound antipathy towards the Soviet Union, scepticism about the depth or durability of East–West *détente*, an unwillingness to relinquish positions of strength and a belief that national security should usually have the first claim on American resources. As one analyst has summarised it, congressional conservatives 'saw Communism as an implacable, unceasingly expansionistic force, capable of tipping the balance of power until the United States has retreated before falling dominoes into Fortress America. Not only did they perceive a US posture as requiring an ever-superior US military force, but also the necessity of continuing present levels of military aid to promote "stability" in vulnerable countries.'[63]

Support for troop withdrawals from Western Europe – with its attendant dangers and uncertainties – was hardly consistent with such a set of attitudes.

Conservatism also seems to be related to the regional variations displayed in Table 7.2.[64] What is most striking about this is that, with the exception of the Pacific States and the South, there do not appear to be any pronounced regional biases. The Midwest, the Plains states and the Northeast were marginally in favour of the amendment, while the Mountain states were slightly against it – and the Border states senators, voting completely along party lines, were equally divided. The desire for troop reductions in Europe, therefore, seems to have had little to do with insularity. The Midwest, which had once been the centre of opposition to American involvement in Europe, no longer had that distinction. On the other hand, the voting of senators from the Pacific States suggests that the traditional West coast orientation towards Asia rather than Europe may have been a factor, especially when it is kept in mind that of the seven Republicans supporting the amendment, two were from Oregon. The vote of the Southern senators is even more interesting as without their support the Nixon Administration would have been defeated much more easily and would consequently have found it much more difficult to reverse the outcome of the first Senate vote. Indeed, the Southern bias is, if anything, understated in the table, as on the second roll-call the South provided an additional two votes against the amendment, both from Democrats. The opposition of the Southern

TABLE 7.2   *Breakdown of votes by region*

Region	For the amendment	Against the amendment
South	8 (7 Dem, 1 Rep)	12 (6 Dem, 6 Rep)
Border	6 (6 Dem)	6 (6 Dem)
Pacific	7	3
Mountain	7	9
Midwest	7 (7 Dem)	5
Plains	4	3
Northeast	10	8

Democrats to the Mansfield Amendment can be explained partly in terms of their conservatism, as suggested above. But it also reflects a distinctively Southern approach, with its emphasis on a strong defence posture both at home and overseas. As Charles Lerche has noted, the South supports 'the armed forces with its sons as well as with its votes, the poor white no less than his higher status brethren. Here real tradition and immediate regional interest neatly coincide, because (in spite of a heavy shift towards the West) a large share of the defense dollar has tended to be finally spent in the South either for wages or for procurement.'[65]

Southerners have also played an important role in the Senate Committee on Armed Services which provided one of the major focal points of opposition to the Mansfield Amendment. Indeed, it is tempting to interpret the battle over troops in Europe as essentially a conflict between two standing committees – Foreign Relations and Armed Services – on an issue in which responsibility is divided and unclear. The pattern of votes on the amendment, however, suggests otherwise. Although some of the senior members of the Foreign Relations committee were among the leaders in the campaign for troop withdrawals, the committee as a whole split largely, although not exclusively, along party lines, with eight members voting for, eight against, and one not voting. The Armed Services Committee was more cohesive, with 10 of the 15 members opposing the measure, only 4 supporting it, and the Chairman, Senator Stennis, not present for the first vote. Nevertheless, it is clear that there was no unanimity on either committee. Indeed, if any committee was important in generating the momentum and coordinating the legislative strategy for withdrawals it was the Democratic Policy Committee and not Foreign Relations. And even here one has to look primarily to individuals rather than to the committee as a whole.

While it was the senior members of the Senate who provided the leadership on both sides of the argument, the outcome of their efforts depended in part on the reaction of the younger and newer members. Indeed a *New York Times* article by John Finney a few days after the 26 September votes suggested that the result demonstrated that the 'Senate Guard' was changing, that the younger generation of senators was fairly solid in its

TABLE 7.3   *Breakdown of votes by age*

Age group	For the amendment	Against the amendment
30–39	2	1
40–49	14	11
50–59	17	14
60–69	10	14
70 +	6	6

support for Mansfield and that the intermediate generation of men in their fifties was hovering between acceptance of past policy and the search for a new one.[66] There is at first sight something to this: although the three freshmen Republicans voted with the majority of their party colleagues, seven of the eight freshmen Democrats supported the Majority Leader. (The other Democrat, Sam Nunn, was to emerge as one of the key figures in the Senate's consideration of the troops issue in 1974.) Table 7.3, however, suggests that such assertions need to be treated with caution.[67] The margin of support for Senator Mansfield among senators under 50 was not as great as Finney suggests, while senators between 50 and 59 were also divided fairly evenly. Nevertheless, there does appear to be a pattern in that 33 of the senators under 60 voted for the amendment while 26 voted against it. For those over 60 the split was 20 to 16 against the Majority Leader. Thus, there was some justification for the comment of one senator who warned Secretary Schlesinger that the Administration was on the 'losing end of the age spectrum'.[68]

Indeed, the prospect for the Administration was an exceedingly worrying one. The typical senator voting for Mansfield tended to be a Democrat, liberal and under 60 – all factors which seemed to portend even greater support for the Majority Leader's stance in the future. The liberals had consolidated their position as a powerful legislative force in the Senate and were in an aggressive mood. The Democrats as a party faced a Republican President increasingly bogged down by Watergate. And the younger and newer members of the Senate were increasingly independent and outspoken now that the norm of apprenticeship had been relaxed.[69] Thus expectations were widespread that support for American troop withdrawals from Western Europe would increase: the Administration had won the battle in 1973 but seemed unlikely to prevail in the future. In the event, however, Senate demands for reductions abated rather than intensified. The reasons for this are examined in the following chapter.

8 The Decline of Pressure, 1974-5

1 THE CONTEXT

In June 1974 Senator Mansfield, in what was coming to be regarded as an annual event, introduced yet another troop withdrawal amendment. By this time, however, some of the favourable conditions of 1973 had disappeared and the Senate gave less support to the Majority Leader's proposal than it had nine months earlier. This change of mood resulted from developments in both domestic and international politics.

One of the most important of these developments was the Yom Kippur War of October 1973. The immediate impact of the war was to undermine the Senate's position on overseas troop withdrawals in the House–Senate Conference Committee. Its long-term importance, however, was far greater, as the hostilities precipitated both an 'adversary' and an 'intra-mural' or 'intra-alliance' crisis. The Soviet–American confrontation was in many respects the less serious of the two and involved little more than a series of abrasive communications between Washington and Moscow which, by preparing the way for final agreement on supervision of the ceasefire, helped to defuse the situation. Nevertheless, its legacy was far-reaching. The episode provoked the beginning of an American reappraisal of *détente* which was to culminate, several years later, in a new foreign policy consensus based on a hard-line stance towards the Soviet Union and intense opposition to the SALT II Treaty. This is not to suggest that there were no opponents or critics of *détente* prior to the confrontation. There obviously were. By and large though they were fighting a rearguard action as the Nixon Administration established what appeared to be a solid and fairly durable basis for superpower cooperation. After the Yom Kippur War this changed: the proponents of *détente* were increasingly placed on the defensive, while Soviet actions were construed in a way which gave the 'non-trusters' a degree of legitimacy and credibility that had hitherto been lacking.[1] As one commentator has observed, in the aftermath of the war anti-Communism became respectable once again.[2]

To some extent, this shift is understandable. Soviet behaviour both prior to and during the war was sufficiently ambiguous to give at least some credence to charges that Moscow was deceitful, unreliable and irresponsible, if not downright aggressive. The Soviet Union had given Washington no forewarning of the Arab attack despite superpower agreements pledging consultation over any situation liable to exacerbate their relations.[3] Furthermore, it had supplied the Arab belligerents with arms, thereby enabling them to continue the war in the face of high attrition rates, while its rhetoric, both in relation to the fate of Israel and the use of the oil weapon, was unrestrained to say the least. Most important of all, the Soviet leaders had threatened unilateral intervention, knowing that such action would almost inevitably bring them into direct confrontation with the United States in a highly volatile region – with unpredictable and possibly disastrous consequences. The fact that the Soviet Union had scrupulously avoided anything which smacked of a *fait accompli*, and that its threats of intervention were designed essentially to render American decision-makers more sensitive to Soviet anxieties over the fate of Egypt, were deemed to be less significant than messages from Mr Brezhnev which were variously described as 'tough', 'brutal' and 'leaving little to the imagination'.[4] Part of the problem, of course, was that the Nixon Administration had created expectations about Soviet behaviour which appeared to preclude or prohibit such conduct. Thus Moscow's threats of intervention were widely – although perhaps unjustly – interpreted as a breach of trust. At a minimum they appeared to be inconsistent with the Administration's assertions that the 'era of confrontation' had been replaced by an 'era of negotiation'. Against a background in which the improvement in superpower relations had been oversold, Kissinger's claim that the events of 24 and 25 October had validated rather than undermined *détente* were treated with considerable scepticism. Those who had been critical of the Administration's policy towards Moscow were, inevitably, confirmed in their prejudices, but even some of those who had looked upon it more favourably began to reconsider. The implications for the troop withdrawal debate were far-reaching. The proponents of reductions had started from the premise that the Soviet threat had subsided to such an extent that the United States could carry out a policy of military retrenchment with impunity. The 'non-trusters' on the other hand had consistently argued that troop withdrawals would increase the vulnerability of the United States and its allies. Their problem had been in proving this. After Yom Kippur, however, the burden of proof shifted to those who wanted to reduce the US military presence in Europe. Not only did Senator Mansfield and his supporters have to contend with renewed doubts about Soviet intentions but also with the fear (sparked off by the Arab success in launching a surprise attack on Israel) that the assumption of 'political warning time' on which NATO military planning was based might be erroneous.[5]

It was not only the crisis in superpower relations which changed the context of the troop withdrawal debate from 1973 to 1974. The rupture in Atlantic relations was equally, if not more, significant. Indeed, the crisis in the Western Alliance was deeper, more intense and much longer-lasting than that between Washington and Moscow. Perhaps the main reason for this was that the Yom Kippur War and the energy crisis provided the occasion for, rather than the cause of, the breach. Divisions and issues which had been simmering below the surface for several years were accentuated and brought into the open. The effect of this was to render the difficulties more intractable as competing conceptions about the future of Europe became entangled with more immediate calculations of national advantage and disadvantage. Thus, as well as the manifest divergence of interests stemming from differing degrees of dependence on Middle East oil, there was the more fundamental and long-term issue of whether Western Europe was to develop into a 'European Europe' or an 'Atlantic Europe'.[6] The controversy took the form of an argument over consultation: should the members of the European Community consult with the United States before or after reaching a collective decision? In reality, though, this was merely part of the more basic issue as to whether a West European identity was to be submerged in a broader Atlantic framework in which Washington remained the dominant partner or was to be sought, in Kissinger's words, 'in opposition to the United States'.[7] The problem had been defined most ruthlessly by President de Gaulle in the 1960s and it was not coincidental that the most intractable European policy-maker was the French Foreign Minister, Monsieur Jobert – whose position was clearly within the tradition established by the General.

While these conceptual differences were at the heart of the controversy, they were given a particular acerbity in the atmosphere of mutual animosity and recrimination which followed Yom Kippur. Complaints by the allies that the United States had not consulted them before putting its forces on alert and had generally treated Western Europe like a 'non-person' were parried by accusations that the Europeans had deserted Washington in order to seek temporary and parochial advantages. Similarly, arguments that the United States was more concerned with avoiding conflict with the Soviet Union than with maintaining the nuclear guarantee to Western Europe were matched by assertions that the Europeans regarded economic competition with the United States as more important than security cooperation. As discussed in the previous chapter, it was this American resentment at the European Community's discriminatory trade practices which had prompted the Nixon Administration to formulate its linkage strategy – and it is hardly surprising, in the circumstances of late 1973 and early 1974, that even greater emphasis was put on this theme. Although considerable pressure was exerted on the Europeans in both the Washington Energy Conference and in the discussions about a new Declaration on Atlantic Relations, it was the increasingly abrasive public statements of both President Nixon and Secretary of State Kissinger which brought matters to a head.[8]

The theme of these speeches was a familiar one – that the Europeans could not have economic and political confrontation with the United States and still expect security cooperation – but the tone was much more strident and insistent than in the past. Kissinger's remark about the lack of legitimacy of existing

European governments,[9] together with his rather pointed comment that although the Administration 'under present conditions' was opposed to a reduction of American forces in Europe, these 'conditions include compatability of foreign policies',[10] foreshadowed even more hostile statements by the President. During a press conference in Chicago on 15 March 1974, Nixon suggested that the Europeans avoid 'ganging up' on the United States if they wanted to retain an American military presence in Western Europe. As he put it:

> I have had great difficulty in getting the Congress to continue to support American forces in Europe at the level that we need to keep them there. In the event that Congress gets the idea that we are going to be faced with economic confrontation and hostility from The Nine, you will find it almost impossible to get Congressional support for continued American presence at present levels on the security front.[11]

The threat which had been present – albeit in more muted form – during 1973 was now made brutally explicit. A few days later at another presidential press conference in Houston, Nixon returned to the theme. Although the Houston statement was widely regarded as being more conciliatory, Nixon did little more than clarify his earlier position, and in essence did not retreat from a hard-line stance. He emphasised that his Chicago comments did not imply – as some commentators had observed – that he would now back the Majority Leader's proposal 'regardless of what happens in terms of the economic and political arrangements'.[12] At the same time, he reiterated the point that if the Europeans persisted in their present course, congressional willingness to retain troops on the Continent would be seriously undermined. The threat was all the more potent because it did not require that the President himself do anything – he was merely identifying potentially uncontrollable forces in Congress which would respond to continued European intractability by mandating troop cuts. Thus the difference between Chicago and Houston was one of subtlety and nuance: the pressure on the Europeans was being maintained, at least for the moment.

After Houston, however, this pressure did begin to ease. The main reason for this was the success of the Administration's approach in making the Europeans aware of just how dependent they were on continued American assistance and goodwill. Indeed, there had been signs of this even before Houston, with both Jobert and British Foreign Secretary James Callaghan making conciliatory statements. Even more important was a meeting between American Secretary of the Treasury George Shultz and Helmut Schmidt which resulted in an agreement in principle on new arrangements to offset the balance of payments cost of US troops in Germany.[13] Although it is difficult to establish a direct and unequivocal connection between this diplomatic breakthrough and Nixon's comments at Chicago a few days earlier, it is almost certain that the growing rift in Atlantic relations put additional pressure on the Federal Republic to accommodate United States demands. If nothing else, the timing of the announcement was fortuitous and it almost certainly contributed to the abatement of tensions which occurred after Houston. There were several indications of this improvement in Atlantic relations. On 6 and 7 April, Nixon met with European leaders in Paris after attending a mass for the late President Pompidou, while at the end of May the United States and the European Community agreed to major tariff reductions. Thus by early June 1974, when the Mansfield Amendment was once again introduced into the Senate, Atlantic animosities had diminished considerably. Indeed, there was a greater recognition on both sides that the alliance remained essential and that the difficulties which had surrounded the 'Year of Europe' initiative, the Middle East War, the energy crisis and the activities of the European Community, should not be allowed to jeopardise any further the underlying framework of Atlantic cooperation. Indeed, it is one of the ironies of the 1974 debate on troop withdrawals that had it taken place three or four months earlier, when Atlantic relations were at their most strained, the outcome could well have been different. As it was, NATO's 'intra-mural' crisis seems to have had a salutary affect, and in its aftermath there was a feeling on the part of at least some senators that it was an inopportune time to bring about reductions. Although the alliance had displayed considerable resilience, an overwhelming vote in favour of substantial reductions would impair the recovery process, with dangerous and perhaps irreparable consequences.

The other important change between September 1973 and June 1974 was in the American balance of payments position. There were several reasons for this. The first was that the increases in oil prices had hit the West Europeans far more severely than the United States. Indeed, in the aftermath of the war, the United States balance of payments improved spectacularly and the United States ended 1973 with a surplus of about $2 billion, the first surplus for years. It was not merely this overall improvement which took the heat out of the issue. The conclusion of the new offset agreement with the Federal Republic in March and April 1974 (to cover the two years from mid-1973 to mid-1975) was widely seen as part of a serious attempt by the Europeans to meet the requirements of the Jackson–Nunn Amendment. The negotiations, though, had not been without difficulties and were described by Nixon (in his message to Congress on the extent to which the stipulations of Jackson–Nunn were being met) as 'unusually complex and time consuming'.[14] Among the reasons for this was the belief of the Germans that they were being asked to make inordinate sacrifices. As a report prepared by Richard Moose and James Lowenstein, two members of the staff of the Senate Foreign Relations Committee, put it:

> They have become increasingly sensitive on this issue ... because they feel themselves being squeezed, on the one hand, by the United States for expenditure on a number of accounts simultaneously – in NATO for additional budgetary support, in the offset negotiations for balance of payments assistance and in the European Defense Improvement Program for the upgrading of their own forces – and, on the other hand by the constraints of their own defense budget.[15]

Indeed, the existence of the NATO burden-sharing exercise – following Schlesinger's initiative of June 1973 and the creation of a study group in August – actually complicated the bilateral exchanges. This, together with arguments over the amount to be offset and differences over the proportion to come from military equipment made the negotiations particularly difficult.[16] Nevertheless, the final agreement, announced on 25 April 1974, was presented as a major step towards the solution of the foreign exchange drain. As the US Embassy in Bonn put it:

> Cognizant of the requirements of the Jackson–Nunn amendment, the American side views the agreement as a major component of the NATO-wide effort to share more equitably the common burden of alliance defense.
>
> We anticipate sufficient military procurement from our other European allies so that, together with the German offset, we expect to meet the requirement of this amendment and to maintain our forces in Europe at present levels.[17]

The consequence of this was that by June 1974 the balance of payments problem had lost much of the urgency of the previous year. In so far as it had contributed to defusing the issue, therefore, the Jackson–Nunn Amendment had gone a long way towards achieving the objectives of its authors. Indeed, those senators whose prime concern had been the balance of payments costs of American forces in Europe would no longer find it necessary to support troop reduction amendments.

The other major change from 1973 was the existence of the mutual force reductions talks in Vienna. After years of preparatory manoeuvres, the negotiations had begun in October 1973 and although there was still some scepticism about their prospects, their very existence militated against support for the Mansfield Amendment. It was one thing to vote for unilateral reductions before talks on mutual withdrawals had been formally initiated (particularly when it was widely – and correctly – anticipated that the negotiations would be both complex and protracted); it was another to undermine the American negotiators in their attempt to obtain a *quid pro quo* from the Soviet Union. Thus it is hard to avoid the conclusion that the Administration's policy of emphasising mutual and negotiated cutbacks as an alternative to unilateral action by the United States once again paid substantial dividends – just as it had done in May 1971. At the very least it contributed to the sentiment that 1974 was the wrong year for the passage of the

Mansfield Amendment. Indeed, it is apparent that the major changes in the international environment between September 1973 and June 1974 all worked in the same direction – in favour of maintaining the *status quo* in Western Europe. Perhaps equally significant, though, were those changes which had taken place in United States domestic politics, especially, although not exclusively, in the Senate.

2 DOMESTIC OPPOSITION TO THE AMENDMENT

In contrast to the previous year when the challenge to Mansfield's troop withdrawal proposal from *within* the Senate had been relatively ineffectual, the opposition in 1974 was better prepared and equipped than ever before for what was now widely regarded as an annual legislative battle. Part of the difference was that Senator Stennis was fully restored to health. Perhaps even more significant was the emergence of a freshman senator, Sam Nunn of Georgia, as the 'resident expert' on NATO issues. Nunn had come to the Senate in 1972 and in his electoral campaign had promised to follow the traditions of previous Georgian senators such as Richard Russell by trying to obtain a seat on the Committee on Armed Services. Having accomplished this, Nunn seems fairly quickly to have obtained the approval and patronage of several of the more senior committee members. His association with Jackson on the offset legislation in September 1973 was one manifestation of this. It was the Committee Chairman, Senator Stennis, however, who was perhaps most instrumental in facilitating Nunn's rise to prominence after what was at most a minimum apprenticeship.[18] Anticipating further battles over the troops, Stennis – probably with considerable encouragement from Nunn, who in November 1973 reportedly made it clear that he would like to undertake a study tour to Western Europe – assigned the Georgian senator to examine the issue. Prior to the trip Nunn apparently spent something like 100 hours informing himself of the problems and almost certainly worked closely with analysts at the Brookings Institution.[19] Having briefed himself thoroughly, the Senator, along with Frank Sullivan, a very knowledgeable member of the Committee Staff, not only made the trip, but subsequently produced an influential report to the Committee on Armed Services.

Entitled *Policy, Troops and the NATO Alliance*, the report was important both politically and as an early indication of Nunn's ideas on the need for rationalisation and reform of the defence posture. The document was frank and thorough in its apprais-als, while its conclusions challenged not only the arguments of Senator Mansfield but also some of the practices and precepts of the US military establishment in Europe. As well as being highly critical of the French stance, with its emphasis on limited cooperation with NATO and maximum manoeuvrabil-ity, the report also suggested that there was excessive reliance on the 'nuclear crutch in Europe'.[20] To minimise this depen-dence on nuclear weapons it was not necessary to provide more manpower. There was already a rough parity of personnel between NATO and the Warsaw Pact; the problem was that despite this, the alliance generated substantially less combat forces than its adversary. What was required, therefore, was a restructuring of US forces in particular to produce more com-bat capability out of available resources. As the report stated: 'United States forces in Europe are structured for a longer war than the European and Warsaw Pact forces. Therefore, they have relatively more support troops than other forces. A U.S. division plus its support slice, has about 45,000 troops com-pared with about 25,000 for the Allies and 12–15,000 for the Warsaw Pact.'[21] In Nunn's view, restructuring was a far more prudent approach than reduction. Indeed, the report con-cluded that there was an urgent need to refocus the congres-sional debate: the previous arguments had not always dealt with what Nunn regarded as the key issues and had not given sufficient attention to the impact of US troop withdrawals on the nuclear threshold or the problems of Germany filling the vacuum that would be left. Furthermore, the question of what long-range commitment to NATO the US was prepared to make had not been fully ventilated.[22]

Nunn's arguments were given additional impact by this recognition that to be effective, the report had to be followed by specific legislation designed to implement some of its recom-mendations. Accordingly he introduced three committee amendments which were intended to initiate a process of rationalisation in NATO. One of the amendments set a limit on the number of tactical nuclear weapons deployed in Europe, while a second focused on the need for greater standardisation in the alliance. The most important, however, was a measure requiring a cut of 23 000 (reduced to 18 000 after the House–Senate Conference Committee) US non-combat troops in Europe – while allowing the Secretary of Defense to replace them by combat units if he deemed it necessary. It seems likely in fact that Nunn's initiative was worked out in consultation with the Department of Defense. At the very least the amendment seems to have had the full backing of Secretary Schlesinger who visited the Federal Republic in April 1974 and discussed with German officials the various ways in which the teeth-to-tail ratio of American forces might be improved.[23] During his trip, Schlesinger also stated that the prognosis was far more favourable than in the recent past for continued political support of the United States troop deployment in Europe.[24]

This assessment may have been based in part on a shrewd assessment of the impact of Nunn's activities in the Senate. Yet Nunn's opposition to Mansfield was neither total nor indiscriminate. Indeed, it was all the more effective because of this. Although Nunn argued very strongly that the troop withdrawal advocates were trying to extricate the United States from the problems of NATO rather than confronting these problems, he recognised that some of the Majority Leader's grievances and frustrations were justified. This was reflected in the support troops amendment. The strength of this proposal was precisely that it went some way towards meeting the long-standing complaint of Mansfield and other liberal Democrats that the United States military presence in Europe had excessive fat. What Nunn claimed to be offering was a more constructive approach than Mansfield, and by emphasising reform rather than reduction *per se* he was able to gain support right across the political spectrum. As one observer has noted, the Nunn amendments had broad political support because they promised greater military efficiency to defence conservatives, while simultaneously offering the possibility of lower costs to defence liberals.[25] In line with this conciliatory approach the Committee on Armed Services made another genuflection in Mansfield's direction by proposing a reduction of 49 000 personnel in overall American troop strength. Although this reflected a genuine desire for a smaller military establishment in the aftermath of Vietnam, it was also a shrewd political tactic. The members of the committee could not only argue that they had tried to meet Mansfield's concerns, but could present themselves as moderate reformers opposed to the Majority Leader's 'meat-axe' approach.

Thus the opponents of troop withdrawals in the Senate were clearly in a stronger position in 1974 than at any previous juncture. Not only were their arguments more sophisticated and better articulated than ever before, but their tactics were also most effective. Having done much to defuse the balance of payments issue, they had also gone a long way to disarming criticisms that the United States military structure in Europe was top-heavy and inefficient. What made all this particularly significant was the position of the Administration – which was far weaker in June 1974 than the previous September. Watergate, by then, had taken a severe toll of the President's authority and it was only a short time before his enforced resignation. Yet it is another of the paradoxes surrounding the troops issue that this did not invariably work in Mansfield's favour. The demand for troop cutbacks in 1974 lacked the bitterness and intensity of the previous year precisely because the President was in such a difficult position: the additional momentum which, in 1973, had come from the desire to restrain the Imperial Presidency and to reorder national priorities had been lost. At the same time, the executive branch was not wholly without influence. The prestige and authority of Secretary of State Kissinger was probably at its height in mid-1974 – both because he appeared to be a powerful force for stability in a period of domestic political turmoil and because of his successful diplomatic initiative in the Middle East. Thus despite the political incapacity of the President, the Administration was again able to mount a serious – if on this occasion less frenetic – lobbying effort to minimise support for Mansfield. Kissinger naturally played a role in this, with a letter to Stennis highlighting the destabilising consequence of unilateral reductions. An important part was also played by Stanley Resor, the head of

the American delegation to the MBFR negotiations in
Vienna.[26] Several senators, including Edward Kennedy, had
apparently been impressed by Resor and when he too wrote to
Stennis to say that the Soviet Union, although adhering tena-
ciously to its position, was approaching the talks in a business-
like way and had shown signs of serious interest in reaching
agreement, it was not a claim that senators were willing to
dismiss.[27] Furthermore, there seems once again to have been a
certain amount of personal lobbying of senators, with James
Schlesinger, as in the previous year, playing an important part.
How extensive this was in 1974 is difficult to assess, but it was
certainly sufficiently evident to provoke Mansfield, in the
debate of 6 June, to complain that representatives from the
Pentagon, the State Department and the AFL-CIO had all
been prowling the corridors of the Senate in an attempt to wean
away support from his amendment.[28] Press opinion too –
especially that of the Eastern seaboard – was hostile to Mansfield's position. The *New York Times* claimed that unilateral
troop reductions would lead to 'nuclearisation' or 'Finlandisation' and described the proposal as 'the wrong battle in the
wrong place at the wrong time'.[29] The Senate floor debate
suggested that this view evoked considerable sympathy from a
majority of the senators present – and it is to this debate that
attention must now be given.

3 THE DEBATE AND THE VOTES

After the dramatic events of 26 September 1973, the debate on
the Mansfield Amendment on 6 June 1974 was something of an
anticlimax. To some extent this may have been the result of the
proposal itself: the Majority Leader's amendment, by prohibiting the use of funds to maintain over 312 000 personnel at land
bases outside the United States, required a reduction of 125 000
troops overseas by the end of 1975. Furthermore, the troops
were to be demobilised after their return to the United States.
Although the executive branch would have discretion about
where the reductions should be made, it was clear that a
substantial diminution of the American military presence in
Western Europe would be unavoidable should the amendment

pass. Consequently, the proposal received considerable criticism on the Senate floor prior to its formal rejection in a roll-call
vote.

The major critic, as expected, was Senator Nunn who, in
several direct exchanges with the Majority Leader, attempted
to refute the arguments for the amendment. In doing this,
Nunn drew heavily not only on his report to the Armed Services
Committee, but also on the committee amendments which, he
claimed, were a constructive alternative to the 'negative knee-
jerk' reaction to executive inertia symbolised in Mansfield's
proposal.[30] The other point emphasised by Nunn and other
opponents of the amendment was its unfortunate timing given
the recent developments in both domestic and international
politics. The idea that superpower accommodation permitted
American military retrenchment from Europe was strongly
attacked. As Nunn put it: 'Soviet actions in the Yom Kippur
War put to bed any hope that detente might substitute for
deterrence.'[31] At the same time, Nunn and other senators such
as Roth emphasised the damage that passage of the amendment would do to the MBFR talks. It is ironic, in fact, that
whereas Mansfield was hopeful about *détente* but sceptical
about the force reduction talks, his opponents were pessimistic
about, if not hostile to, *détente*, while adopting a much more
positive position on the negotiations. Another of Nunn's arguments concerned the need to maintain a relatively high
threshold for nuclear use. Based on assessments made in his
report, the senator rejected worst-case thinking about the
inferiority of NATO forces compared to those of the Warsaw
Pact. He also resisted suggestions that NATO either could or
should rely upon early use of nuclear weapons. As he stated:
'NATO's conventional inferiority is neither clear nor necessary. With better coordination, streamlining, and some change
in doctrine, NATO can establish a solid defence and deterrent
essentially with present resource levels.'[32] The implications
were far-reaching: instead of replacing a large token force by a
smaller and less expensive token force, the Mansfield Amendment would change the nature of the commitment by under-
mining the prospects for a strong conventional defence. The
result would be a dangerous and unnecessary reversion to the
trip-wire strategy. In other words, Nunn presented a much

more formidable array of arguments for maintaining the US military presence in Europe than had been deployed the previous year. It was obvious too that his contribution to the debate was based on meticulous preparation – an impression which was not unimportant in light of the Senate's tradition of specialisation and its respect for expertise. Indeed, Nunn received not only the approbation of his colleagues, but also that of outside observers. As one commentator noted: 'His was as solid and deft a parliamentary performance in the national security area as Congress has seen in years.'[33] Nunn's tactics were equal to his knowledge: although there is not much evidence of strong constituency pressure for troop withdrawals, any senator who nevertheless felt vulnerable on the issue but was reluctant to vote for Mansfield could say that he had voted for the Nunn amendments. At the same time, it is worth emphasising that Nunn was not giving a solo performance: opposition to troop withdrawals was led by a small collegial group of senators in which more senior Democrats such as Stennis and Jackson played an indispensable part. The importance of these three Democrats lay not only in what they did, however, but also in who they were. The fact that members of his own party were so prominent in opposing the Majority Leader's proposal almost certainly helped to defuse the issue of any partisan overtones it might otherwise have had. Once again the contrast with the bitterly partisan split of 1973 is marked.

In short, the opposition to the proposal was better prepared, better organised and more bipartisan than the previous year. Mansfield, on the other hand, seems to have done even less than usual to mobilise support. Apart from himself and Cranston there were few speakers in favour of the amendment – and certainly nothing like the steady stream of senators who argued against it. It was no surprise, therefore, when the Senate rejected the amendment by a vote of 54 to 35 – a comfortable margin of victory for the Administration.[34] The size of the gap resulted from the defection of a significant number of Democrats who had all voted for troop reductions on the previous occasion: Whereas the party had split 42 to 12 in Mansfield's favour in 1973, in 1974 they divided 30 to 20. Although a lone Republican, Senator Mathias of Maryland, had transferred his allegiance the other way, this did nothing to offset the decline in the level of support amongst the Democrats. Yet Democratic enthusiasm for the measure was not especially low in 1974; it was rather that it had been unusually high in 1973. By voting against Mansfield in 1974, Senators Tunney (Col), Chiles (Flo), Muskie (Ma) and Pell (RI) were merely reverting to their pre-1973 stance in which they had decided in favour of the *status quo*. For these four senators it seems probable that the extraordinary political circumstances of 1973 – in which the troops issue had become an integral part of the wider dispute over national priorities and institutional prerogatives – had brought about an important but temporary shift. In the very different conditions of 1974 they no longer felt the same compulsion to vote against the Administration. Two other senators who altered their position, McClellan (Ark) and Mondale (Minn), had hitherto been consistent supporters of the Mansfield Amendment. The reason for their change probably lay less in the circumstances of 1973 than in those of 1974 – which made it a particularly inopportune time for troop reductions. Mondale especially was forthright in his criticism of the amendment, arguing that it was 'not the time to administer yet another shock to transatlantic relations', not least because the crisis in the alliance had been accompanied or followed by several changes of government in Europe.[35] Furthermore, Mondale suggested, the President's domestic difficulties resulting from Watergate made it impossible for him to compensate for a smaller United States military presence by strengthening the political commitment.[36] Whereas presidential dominance had helped to generate support for Mansfield in 1973, presidential weakness contributed to its reduction in June 1974.

Important though these defections were, they do not account completely for the fall-off in the number of votes favouring troop reductions. An additional factor was the absence of several senators, including Fulbright and Symington, who would almost certainly have supported the Majority Leader. It is interesting too that both Milton Young of North Dakota (who had changed his position between the two votes on 26 September 1973) and Lowell Weicker (who had supported Mansfield on the first vote the previous year but had not participated in the second roll-call) were absent. Whether this was accidental or expedient is impossible to establish. Whatever the case, it appeared that sentiment in the Senate had changed and that the groundswell in favour of military retrenchment had subsided.

Yet the extent of the decline should not be exaggerated. Substantial troop withdrawals from Europe were certainly regarded by a clear majority as inappropriate to the circumstances of 1974. At the same time there was still a feeling that the American military presence overseas remained too extensive. Consequently a more moderate Mansfield Amendment, mandating a reduction of 76 000 overseas troops, was defeated only very narrowly – with 44 votes in favour and 46 against.[37] The increase in the number of senators supporting the proposal stemmed from the belief that it was sufficiently modest and flexible to allow its stipulations to be met without diminishing the American military presence in Europe. The higher level of support also reflected the influence of Senator Humphrey, who had voted against the previous amendment but now made an impassioned plea to his colleagues to back the new and more judicious proposal. The effect seems to have been particularly pronounced on those liberal or moderate Democrats who had a pragmatic approach to the issue and judged each specific amendment on its merits. Thus, along with Humphrey came Kennedy, McClellan, Muskie, McIntyre, Mondale, Tunney, Stevenson and Pell. The opponents of the proposal, however, not only argued that its passage would give the wrong signal to Europe but managed to retain enough strength to ensure that this did not occur. Nevertheless, the result was sufficiently close to dispel hopes that the issue would disappear. In fact, the controversy lingered on, albeit in more muted and less visible form, throughout the next few months. The discussion arose primarily in the Senate Appropriations Committee which, after considering troop cuts in Europe ranging from 15 000 to 100 000, decided 'with deep reluctance and some scepticism to concede' to Administration wishes and leave the presence in Europe intact.[38] The committee opted instead for a mandatory reduction of 25 000 troops deployed anywhere overseas, a figure which was reduced by half by the House–Senate Conference Committee.

In the final analysis, therefore, the proponents of troop

withdrawals had succeeded in bringing about only marginal changes during 1974. Nevertheless, when both McClellan and Nunn warned that without some progress in the MBFR negotiations, congressional support for the current troop levels would probably diminish further, this was not a claim that could be easily dismissed by either the Administration or the Europeans.[39] Although Schlesinger's prognosis of April 1974 had been correct for the short term, there were some signs – including growing, albeit still minority, pressure from the House of Representatives for withdrawals – that congressional patience was wearing thin and that 1975 might not only see Mansfield regaining the lost ground of 1974 but going beyond this to repeat and finally consolidate the victory of 1973. In the event, however, there was nothing more than a minor congressional skirmish on the issue.

4   THE 1975 DEBATE

Congressional enthusiasm for troop withdrawals from Western Europe receded dramatically in 1975. There were several reasons for this. In the first place, the need for reductions no longer seemed as urgent as it had been two years, or even a year, ealier. The United States had shed some of its overseas commitments and the policy of 'discerning internationalism' advocated by Mike Mansfield was in the ascendancy. Although the battle over national priorities had not been won outright by the liberal Democrats they had made a series of incremental gains which robbed the issue of much of its salience. Similarly, the arguments over both the balance of payments and the budgetary costs of the troop deployment in Europe had diminished further in intensity since 1974. Indeed, Jackson–Nunn continued to have the impact its proponents had hoped for by stifling any impetus for troop withdrawals which might have arisen from concern over the foreign exchange drain. In accordance with the stipulations of the amendment, the President, at the end of May, sent to Congress his final report on progress that had been made towards offsetting the balance of payments deficit incurred through stationing troops in Europe during fiscal year 1974. The conclusion was that the allies had met the requirement of Jackson–Nunn and had fully covered the deficit. During fiscal 1974 the agreement with the Federal Republic had yielded $1.150 billion to set against the $1.997 billion outflow. The rest of the offset had come from the purchases of American military equipment by other European allies. As the report stated: 'They have been able to identify 1.016 billion dollars in such procurement of which 917 million can at this time be applied against fiscal year 1974 expenditure. The NATO allies and the NATO Economic Directorate deserve our special recognition for that cooperation in establishing a liaison mechanism for identifying these purchases.'[40] This rather bland comment masks what had been a vigorous and sustained attempt by NATO – beginning in 1973 under pressure from Schlesinger – to examine comprehensively the balance of payments problem. Having done this it was apparent that Washington had little cause for complaint once European purchases of American equipment were taken into account. On top of this, of course, measures had been taken by the Federal Republic (as part of the April 1974 agreement) to reduce some of the incremental budgetary costs of stationing forces in Europe rather than the US. Thus the Jackson–Nunn Amendment had worked well, both in concentrating European minds and efforts on the problem and in placating congressional opinion. Indeed, the implication of all this is that the incentives for troop reductions had declined. On the other hand, the incentive for maintaining the *status quo* had increased.

The MBFR negotiations had not made much progress. Even so, their continued existence militated against unilateral action. The situation in Europe also suggested the need for caution: the Greek–Turkish conflict had erupted during 1974, and with an additional question mark over the political future of Portugal, the southern flank was in considerable disarray. Inevitably this led to renewed anxiety about European security and stability. Indeed, such concerns replaced – at least temporarily – the dissatisfaction and irritation with the allies which had been so pronounced little more than 15 months earlier. The improvement in Atlantic relations, however, had been accompanied by a further deterioration of superpower *détente*. Anxieties over Soviet policies increased during 1975 and although several senators such as Mansfield remained hopeful about the prospects for *détente*, they were unimpressed by the results. Others were not even hopeful and argued that the process had become a 'one-way street' with virtually all the benefits accruing to the Soviet Union. Yet this sentiment was not entirely new, and although it had intensified since 1974, it was hardly such as to persuade Mansfield to acquiesce in the maintenance of the large US military presence in Europe. Events in South East Asia had precisely this effect, with the fall of Saigon proving particularly traumatic.

Accordingly, on 2 June, the Majority Leader announced that he did not intend to reintroduce his amendment for overseas troop reductions. Although there had been no change in his fundamental approach, he acknowledged that 'because of the confusing and chaotic situation that exists in the world following the Indochina debacle' it was the wrong time for such an initiative.[41] Yet there is some evidence that Mansfield reached this conclusion only very reluctantly. During May 1975 he had a speech prepared which argued that the end of the Vietnam War provided 'a unique opportunity to re-evaluate international policy in an atmosphere free of battlefield events', and went on to reiterate the need for further US troop withdrawals from both Europe and Asia.[42] In Mansfield's view, the post-Vietnam period was 'the time to reflect, to re-evaluate and to redirect. To miss this historic opportunity can result in continuing out-dated Empire policies.'[43] As part of this reappraisal, it was essential to ask how many troops were necessary to manifest the United States commitment to Western Europe. And Mansfield's response was both familiar and unequivocal: 'The answer to that question . . . is the same as it was a decade ago: fewer combat forces are needed today to manifest the U.S. commitment. The recent events in Indochina do not change that view in any way.'[44]

This unyielding stance gave way to a more flexible approach by the Majority Leader and the prepared speech was not used. This is accounted for partly by the intervention of Secretary of the Senate, Frank Valeo, who was one of Mansfield's most trusted advisers and who had serious reservations about the wisdom of the speech in the current circumstances, let alone about introducing any legislation to mandate troop reductions.[45] In addition, Mansfield almost certainly realised that the timing was not propitious for such a move and that it would receive the endorsement of very few senators.

The accuracy of this assessment became clear during the Senate debate on the future course of United States foreign and defence policy which took place from 2 June to 6 June. The prevailing sentiment was best summed up by Alan Cranston who had consistently proven himself one of Mansfield's staunchest allies on the troops issues. As he stated:

> Prior to the events accompanying the collapse in Vietnam and Cambodia, I was an advocate of a cut of at least 100,000 in overseas troops and of reducing our Armed Forces level by that amount. However, in the aftermath of Vietnam, Cambodia, Mayaguez, and other developments and reactions to them, I reluctantly came to the conclusion that it would be unwise at this particular time to make any such reductions because it might give others the mistaken impression that we are on the run and turning inward and becoming isolationist. We are not doing that.[46]

The overwhelming majority of senators seem to have felt that a vote for troop withdrawals would encourage both allies and adversaries to accept the 'defeat and retreat of America' theme propounded by segments of the European press. Even the proponents of troop withdrawals in the Senate accepted this. They could not agree completely with Representative Wayne Hays when he argued that the summer of 1975 was 'the wrong time of the wrong year of the wrong century' for such a course, but for the moment they disagreed only with the third and final part of his proposition.[47]

Thus, when Senator Mike Gravel of Alaska introduced an amendment to reduce troops overseas by 200 000, the outcome was a foregone conclusion. Not only was Gravel one of the Senate's mavericks or outsiders who lacked the status, prestige and influence of someone like Mansfield, but the amendment itself was sufficiently far-reaching to invite rejection even in less exceptional circumstances. Gravel realised this and requested a unanimous consent agreement to modify his proposal to require only a 10 000 reduction. Objections by Nunn and Goldwater prevented this and the Senate continued with a meaningless debate on a proposal with virtually no support. Only Cranston gave Gravel any backing, and this was a result of personal loyalty rather than genuine conviction. It was not surprising, therefore, that the Senate did not even observe the formality of a roll-call and rejected the proposal by voice vote.[48]

This was a somewhat inauspicious ending for a movement which, on several occasions, had thrown the Nixon Administration into a frenzy, and had been a pervasive source of anxiety for the Europeans. Yet the sentiment for troop withdrawals had diminished so dramatically since the high point of 1973 that the option was not even discussed in 1976. And with Mansfield's retirement from the Senate at the end of the ninety-fourth Congress it appeared that the subject had been removed from the political agenda. Yet the assumption that it had become a dead issue was almost certainly premature. The persistence of the debate from 1966 through to the mid-1970s undoubtedly owed a great deal to Mansfield's convictions and leadership; yet it is arguable that the American military presence in Europe has an inherent potential for controversy. The political alignments on the issue had changed since the 'Great Debate' of 1951 but many of the basic questions about stationing US troops in Europe which had been raised by Robert Taft remained. This became clearer in an exchange between Nunn and Mansfield during the 1974 Senate floor debate. Under prodding from the Majority Leader, Nunn accepted the argument that the United States should not keep troops in Europe indefinitely. He also acknowledged that the US would be unable to support NATO in the future 'to the extent we have in the past'.[49] If one of Mansfield's strongest opponents could take this position, then those who were less firmly committed might well be prepared at some point in the future to challenge the *status quo*. Much, of course, would depend on both the broader international climate and the domestic political situation. Changes in these areas since 1973 had done much to reduce support for force reductions; yet it was not certain that existing trends would continue. And just as changing circumstances had made Mansfield's proposals less attractive, so future changes could encourage and facilitate a resurgence of pressure for US troop withdrawals from Europe. In this event, what was generally interpreted in the mid and late 1970s as the final demise of 'Mansfieldism' could appear as another in a series of reprieves for Western Europe.

9 Conclusions

The controversy which has surrounded the deployment of American troops in Europe is very revealing not only about some of the substantive problems involved in Atlantic relations but also about the role of the Senate in the formulation of American foreign and military policy. It is illustrative too of some of the changes which occurred between the late 1940s and late 1960s in the approach of Republican and Democratic senators to American commitments overseas. Consequently, this assessment of the controversy is divided into several sections. The first examines the attitudes in the Senate to the American commitment to Europe: it focuses on questions about burden-sharing and responsibility-sharing in the alliance, questions which for a variety of reasons came to the fore once again in the first half of the 1980s. The second section takes this a little further and assesses the changes which took place between 1951 and the early 1970s in the attitudes of both Democrats and Republicans to the American deployment of ground troops in Western Europe. The third section looks at the controversy in terms of the relationship between the President and Congress. It not only considers why the congressional protests occurred over the troops but also assesses the reactions these elicited from the Executive, and tries to explain why, in both 1951 and the 1966 to 1975 period, presidential policies ultimately prevailed. The final section considers the prospects for another resurgence of the pressure for troop reductions.

1 THE SENATE AND WESTERN EUROPE

The Senate's attitude to Western Europe since the inception of the Atlantic Alliance has been characterised by considerable ambivalence. A recognition that the continued independence of

259

Western Europe is of crucial importance to the security of the United States has been tempered by a residue of distrust towards the allies, and a suspicion that they may not be worth defending. Along with this lingering suspicion has gone a belief that the Europeans are exploiting the United States security guarantee and obtaining, if not a 'free ride', then at least security on the cheap. These attitudes go a long way towards explaining the sentiment in favour of greater burden-sharing efforts which ran through the deliberations on the North Atlantic Treaty, the 'Great Debate' and the troops controversy of the latter half of the 1960s and the first half of the 1970s. Indeed, it is no exaggeration to suggest that certain groups and individuals in the Senate have attempted to make the commitment to Europe conditional upon satisfactory defence efforts by the European allies. From the outset there was considerable emphasis on self-help, and this concept was enshrined in both the Vandenberg Resolution and Article 3 of the North Atlantic Treaty itself. The attempts to send troops to Europe on a ratio basis, although abandoned, were symptomatic of the desire to ensure that these self-help provisions were carried out. Indeed, the strict arithmetical ratios were replaced by language which reiterated the principle of self-help, especially in relation to the European creation of combat forces. If anxieties over the size of the European defence effort helped to fuel the Senate debate, concerns over burden-sharing also played a part in the subsequent demands for troop withdrawals. Mansfield was able to tap a substantial reservoir of dissatisfaction with European defence efforts among his Senate colleagues. This is not to say that the Europeans were as feckless and unreliable as many of the critics argued. In fact, part of the problem stemmed from the absence of generally accepted criteria for assessing whether or not burdens were being shared equitably amongst the members of a large, unwieldy mutilateral alliance. The main point, however, is that the perception that the United States was bearing an inordinate share of the burden was a significant element in both the arguments about sending troops to Europe and the pressure for reductions. Indeed, this perception was shared by many of those who supported the military presence as well as those who wanted to reduce it. In 1951, Henry Cabot Lodge was as concerned about European defence efforts as was Robert Taft, while in 1967 a major point of agreement in the *ad hoc* subcommittee on troops in Europe chaired by Mansfield was that the allies should be doing more for their own defence. While these concerns were both widespread and fairly consistent, however, they were intensified at certain times by events outside Europe or what in the 1980s has been termed the out-of-area problem. It is no coincidence that in 1951 the United States was fighting in Korea and in the latter half of the 1960s and the first part of the 1970s it was involved in Vietnam. In both instances the Europeans appeared to be doing little to help, and in the case of Vietnam were openly critical of the American involvement. This almost certainly intensified the concerns of many senators, especially those who saw the Cold War in global terms and were not convinced that Europe was necessarily the most important theatre in the East–West struggle.

If burden-sharing considerations led a significant number of senators to support Mike Mansfield in his campaign for troop reductions, however, Mansfield himself had a somewhat broader vision, and thought as much in terms of sharing responsibilities as sharing burdens. His thinking was five to ten years ahead of the Nixon Doctrine, with its emphasis on partnership, and unlike Nixon himself, Mansfield did not balk at the idea of applying the Nixon Doctrine to Europe. He believed that the large military presence encouraged the allies to depend excessively on the US; and he felt that the only way to transform this dependency was to bring home some of the troops. This, he believed, would remove the crutch and make the Europeans stand on their own feet to a much greater extent. Although Mansfield was not convinced that in these circumstances the allies would necessarily do more for their own defence, this was not the crucial point. After all, it was up to the Europeans themselves to decide on the priority they would give to defence. Indeed, when Mansfield objected to the United States taking the security of Western Europe more seriously than the Europeans themselves, his target was the United States government rather than the allies. Although he was not averse to the Europeans doing more, his real concern was that the United States should do less. Mansfield's position on this was in many ways reminiscent of Robert Taft's arguments during the 'Great Debate'. Although Taft was prepared to support a limited deployment of American troops to Europe, any suggestion that the United States should run the show was anathema to him. The difficulty with this, of course, was that Taft was denying the United States a leadership position when there was no alternative. Mansfield's argument in the 1960s and 1970s was that conditions had changed to such an extent that this leadership was no longer necessary or desirable. Mansfield, implicitly at least, seemed to have a conception of a pluralistic world order in which Western Europe could play a major part. The emergence of such a structure, in his view, was inhibited by a lack of imagination on the part of European and American policy-makers, who had failed to adapt to either the economic resurgence of Western Europe or the limits of American power.

At the same time Mansfield emphasised that a smaller American presence in Western Europe was in no way intended as a weakening of the American commitment. For the Democratic Majority Leader the essence of the commitment was political rather than military, and was enshrined in the North Atlantic Treaty rather than in the presence of a particular number of American troops in Europe. Since the function of the troops was primarily symbolic, a smaller number would suffice. This argument did not convince a majority in the Senate, however, partly because it was believed that the symbol had become the substance: any reduction of troops would be interpreted as a weakening of the American commitment. This was certainly the theme propounded by successive Administrations and it was one which the Senate, in the last analysis, was prepared to accept. Indeed, the President, throughout both the 1951 debate and the later controversies, was able to count upon a considerable body of support in the Senate. The source of this support, however, did not remain constant. Indeed, the alignments on the troops issue changed very considerably – and these changes must now be examined.

2   DEMOCRATS, REPUBLICANS AND TROOPS IN EUROPE

In 1951 the opposition to sending troops to Europe came primarily from a group of conservative Republicans, predominantly from Midwest states. They were supported in their attempt to restrict presidential power by a group of southern Democrats who defected from the bulk of the party in the crucial vote on the McClellan Amendment to the Connally–Russell Resolution. Indeed, one commentator at the time argued that the passage of the McClellan Amendment represented a victory for the conservative coalition which had consistently opposed Truman's, and indeed Roosevelt's, domestic policies.[1] Although support for the McClellan Amendment should not necessarily be construed as a vote against involvement in Europe, it does help to highlight the contrast with the divisions on the Mansfield Amendment. As discussed in Chapter 7, the support for Mansfield came primarily from liberal Democrats while the opposition came from the Republicans, supported by a small but significant number of conservative Democrats. Although this may be attributable partly to Republican support for a Republican President in 1973, the change had been apparent even during the Johnson years. In 1966 one of the strongest critics of the Mansfield Resolution was Everett Dirksen, who in 1951 had joined Senator Wherry and his group in voting against Senate Resolution 99 approving the deployment of troops to Europe. On the other side, the Democratic Policy Committee, which, in 1966, initiated the congressional pressure for troop reductions, included amongst its members Richard Russell, who had worked extremely hard in 1951 to get Senate approval for the Truman Administration's troops to Europe decision. It is difficult to disagree, therefore, with the conclusion of one analyst that 'as American foreign policy . . . evolved in the 1950s and 1960s the Democrats and Republicans shifted their orientations' to the point where each embraced 'beliefs about commitments policy and the policy process similar to those identified with the other party in 1951'.[2]

As this suggests, the change was evident not only on substantive issues but also on questions relating to the role of Congress in the policy-making process. It was typified by the transformation in the thinking of William Fulbright: the senator who had refused to vote on Resolution 99 in 1951 because of its claim to restrict presidential power had by the late 1960s become the great champion of congressional prerogatives and one of the

leading critics of presidential power. Fulbright's conversion
was probably more dramatic than that of most other Democrats but was not atypical. To a large extent this shift by
Democrats on both substance and process was a result of
American involvement in Vietnam. Not only did the war
destroy the faith of the Democrats in the Presidency but it also
brought home to them the dangers of an indiscriminate internationalism for the American political system – dangers which
had so concerned Robert Taft and other Republicans in 1951.
Republican demands during the 'Great Debate' were criticised
at the time as an indiscriminate assault on presidential prerogatives; in retrospect they appear as one of the last attempts
to limit the powers of what would develop into the 'Imperial
Presidency'. And Taft, instead of being dismissed as an old-
fashioned obstructionist, appears to be an incisive and far-
sighted commentator whose claims about the excesses of the
presidency were amply justified by subsequent events.

Another interesting parallel between the conservative Republicans of 1951 and the liberal Democrats 20 years later is
exemplified by the concerns of both Taft and Mansfield about
the impact of American security on domestic politics. They
approached this problem from very different perspectives, of
course, with Taft starting from an abiding belief in 'fiscal
conservatism' and Mansfield from the ideals of liberal interven-
tionism. Nevertheless, they converged on the principle that
foreign policy should be subordinated to the needs of the
American economy and American society – and both attacked
policies which they felt sacrificed national welfare (albeit defined rather differently) on the altar of national security.

Indeed, it is one of the ironies of the American political scene
in the late 1960s and early 1970s that the arguments of Robert
Taft, the senator who had been known as Mr Republican, had
far more appeal to Democrats than to members of the GOP
itself. This suggests that the changed attitudes in the Republican Party were as far-reaching as those which had taken place
amongst the Democrats. Most of these changes, in fact, had
taken place in the 1950s when Eisenhower had offered the
Republicans internationalist policies on the cheap and thereby
made internationalism far more palatable than it had appeared
under Truman. Although this goes part of the way towards
explaining the Republican stance on the military presence in

Europe from 1966 to 1975, it does not provide the whole explanation. The additional point which needs to be made is that the Republicans were still predominantly conservative, and as Michael Oakeshott has pointed out, conservatism is a disposition rather than a doctrine. It is 'to prefer the familiar to the unknown ... the tried to the untried'.[3] From this perspective the fact that the conservative Republicans supported a *status quo* in the 1960s and 1970s which was very different from the *status quo* in 1951 is not surprising. What mattered was the familiarity of the *status quo* not the arrangements themselves. In 1951, the idea of deploying forces to Europe, although the logical culmination of American policy towards Western Europe in the previous three or four years, was also a radical departure from anything that had gone before. The potential consequences were uncertain and it was believed that the costs and risks of embarking upon such a venture were enormous. By the mid-1960s, of course, the American military presence in Western Europe had become a familiar element in the political and strategic landscape. Attempts to initiate major changes in this presence – with incalculable consequences – had little appeal for conservatives who had gradually and reluctantly come to recognise the benefits of the security arrangements in Western Europe established by the Truman Administration. Similarly many conservatives had come to acknowledge the benefits of a strong Presidency. The desires of 1951 to restrain the President were understandable when that President was embarking on new and untried policies; there was less inclination by conservatives to challenge the White House when the incumbent (whether Democrat or Republican) was attempting to preserve the existing policies and commitments against substantial pressure for change. In both cases, however, the President was ultimately successful in preserving his policy and defeating the congressional challenge. Some of the reasons for this must now be examined.

3 THE PRESIDENT, THE SENATE AND TROOPS IN EUROPE

Although disputes between the President and Congress are sometimes portrayed as if the Congress is a monolith, this is rarely the case. More often than not the President is able to muster considerable support on Capitol Hill in defence of his policies and programmes – even when these are opposed by other members of the legislature.[4] This was certainly the case in the dispute over sending troops to Europe and in the later arguments over troop reductions. In both cases there was considerable sentiment in favour of the stance adopted by the Administration. In 1951, the troops decision became a symbol of internationalism and was regarded by many Democratic senators as well as the East Coast Republicans as the inevitable concomitant of American power and European weakness in the face of the Soviet threat. In the 1960s and 1970s Johnson and Nixon could count upon support from senators such as Henry Jackson, Jacob Javits and (from 1973) Sam Nunn – all of whom were strongly committed to the Western Alliance and automatically opposed to any proposals which appeared to weaken it. Indeed, broad agreement on policy made it possible for the Johnson Administration to work closely with Republican, Jacob Javits, in drawing up a substitute for the Mansfield Resolution in 1967; while in 1971 and 1973 Senator John Stennis, the Democratic Chairman of the Armed Services Committee, was one of the key figures in helping a Republican Administration defeat troop withdrawal legislation sponsored by the Democratic leadership.

As well as the natural coincidence of interest and outlook between the President and certain members of the Senate, the President also has considerable resources for mobilising support and deflecting or defeating opposition. The Truman Administration resorted to almost every one of the available techniques for building a winning coalition in the period from 1947 to 1949. In 1951, however, it paid the price for the overselling of its European policies in the previous two or three years. The 'Great Debate' was in part a protest over the fact that despite the Marshall Plan, the North Atlantic Treaty and the military assistance programme – and all the claims that had been made for them – the Truman Administration still found it necessary to send American troops to Europe. And the feeling that the Senate had been misled was intensified by the statement made in 1949 that there was no intention of sending troops. Yet Truman's response to this challenge was almost one of indifference. This became particularly noticeable after several statements by the White House asserting the President's power to send troops wherever he wanted, far from dispelling the opposition, actually increased it. If Truman subsequently relied on the Democratic leadership in the Senate to fight his battle for him, however, he eventually recognised the advantages in a positive resolution, which would satisfy those who felt that Congress, or at least the Senate, should have a say on the issue, but which would not seriously affect his power or his policy.

Lyndon Johnson's response to the Mansfield pressure for troop reductions was in certain respects even more conciliatory. Although Johnson in 1966 was unequivocal in his condemnation of the troop withdrawal resolution, in 1967 he sanctioned the Trilateral Agreement with its redeployment of 35 000 troops back to the United States. This was accepted by Mansfield as an important step in the right direction, and as such led to a temporary easing of the pressure for troop cuts.

Nixon, in contrast, adopted a confrontation policy almost from the outset. Whereas Johnson had attempted to find a formula which would satisfy Mansfield (as well as some members of the Administration itself), Nixon was not prepared to adopt this course, and decisively rejected suggestions by the Secretary of Defense Laird favouring token reductions as a way of placating Mansfield. To some extent this reflected Nixon's general response to pressure. Despite his distaste for face-to-face conflicts, the President was more than willing to countenance political confrontations, especially with those he regarded as his political enemies. And although he does not seem to have been extensively involved himself in the subsequent lobbying, Nixon was willing to use all the resources at his disposal to ensure that the challenge to his policies were defeated. During May 1971 and September 1973, the Administration engaged in intensive lobbying efforts which played a significant part in beating back the pressure for American troop reductions in Europe.

In some ways, of course, this contest was a very unequal one. Whereas the President and his advisers had no compunction about twisting arms or providing inducements to wean senators from Mansfield, the Majority Leader himself had a very different approach. Mansfield's attitude to his troop withdrawal proposals was almost one of scholarly detachment. As far as he was concerned, his proposals should stand or fall on their merits. As a result Mansfield was reluctant to lobby other senators. Indeed, apart from circulating a letter to all his colleagues in January 1967 informing them that he intended to reintroduce his resolution and making clear that he would welcome their co-sponsorship, there is no evidence that Mansfield ever attempted to mobilise support in favour of American troop withdrawals from Europe. Although this may appear surprising given that it was an issue on which he obviously felt very strongly, it fits in with Mansfield's approach to leadership in the Senate. His leadership style – in marked contrast to his predecessor as Majority Leader, Lyndon Johnson – was not only extremely gentle, but was based on the assumption that the Senate was composed of 100 individuals, each of whom should be allocated maximum discretion in deciding how to vote on any issue.[5] As a result of this approach Mansfield was universally admired for his fairness, and earned considerable respect from Republicans who had been far less well disposed towards Johnson. It did mean, however, that Mansfield was at a considerable disadvantage when dealing with political adversaries who had far fewer scruples about supplementing rational argument with political pressure.

For all this, the fact that Mansfield was prepared to push this issue in 1966 was significant. The pressures for troop reductions in Europe symbolised the end of an era in which Congress had played a very minor role in foreign policy, doing little more than acquiesce in presidential decisions about which it was informed and not consulted. This is not to argue that the troop issue was the only manifestation of the new congressional disquiet about either the substance of American foreign policy or the way this policy was formulated. Indeed, the period 1966 to 1970 can be understood as one of both ambivalence and acrimony in congressional–executive relations: the deferential approach of Congress to the President was coming to an end, but Congress was still reluctant to embark on direct confrontation with the President. By 1970, however, these rather tentative moves had given way to a new assertiveness, and once again it is not coincidental that in 1971 there was a much more direct attempt by Mansfield to deal with the troop issue. The fact that Nixon was a Republican made it easier for a Democratic Senate to oppose the White House, while the President's high-handed approach to domestic and foreign policy provoked a series of confrontations that a more conciliatory approach might have avoided. Although the Mansfield Amendments were ultimately defeated, they were part of the same congressional resurgence which resulted in legislation such as the War Powers Resolution and the Budget and Impoundment Control Act, both of which were designed to ensure that in the future Congress would not be excluded from the policy-making process.

The irony, of course, is that the 'Great Debate' of 1951 was itself a manifestation of congressional concerns over the accretion of power to the President. Furthermore, the failure of this revolt contributed to the long period of unchallenged presidential dominance between 1952 and the mid-1960s. Apart from the Bricker Amendment in 1954 – which was designed to give Congress a role in dealing with executive agreements – there was little attempt to protect congressional prerogatives. As Arthur Schlesinger pointed out, a critical international environment helped to create an uncritical consensus, in which untramelled presidential power was widely regarded as the key to America's salvation.[6] The view which prevailed was that embraced in 1951 by William Fulbright; the arguments of Robert Taft were relegated to the sidelines. In response to presidential aggrandisement, however, Fulbright gradually adopted an approach which was closely akin to that enunciated by Taft 15 to 20 years earlier. Indeed, the legislation of the early 1970s attempting to ensure the capacity of Congress to 'co-determine' foreign policy was as much a vindication of Robert Taft as it was of the senators and representatives who actually initiated the congressional revolt.[7]

Even in a period of congressional reassertion, however, there are certain things that the legislature remains reluctant to do. One of these is the determination of troop levels. In the last analysis, even Senator Mansfield recognised that such adjustments as were necessary could best be made by the executive branch. His main concern, therefore, was to put the issue on the policy-making agenda in the hope that the executive branch itself would take action. Although the Mansfield pressure had a significant affect on European burden-sharing efforts, however, it did not succeed in bringing about anything more than marginal changes in the size of the American military presence in Europe. Indeed, in the years after Mansfield's retirement from the Senate, the number of American troops in Europe actually increased. And in the early 1980s there were once again murmurings from the Senate about the desirability of reducing force levels in Europe. The nature of these pressures must now be examined and the prospects for a further resurgence of what is somewhat indiscriminately called 'Mansfieldism' briefly assessed.

4   THE FUTURE

During the early 1980s there were some indications that an embryonic coalition in favour of US troop reductions was once again developing in the Senate.[8] To some extent this movement was a result of the strains and tensions in Atlantic relations which became apparent in the aftermath of the Soviet invasion of Afghanistan. Differences over the nature of the threat to Atlantic security and the appropriate response by the members of NATO were not new; but in the aftermath of the Soviet action they took on an urgency and an intensity which had hitherto been lacking.

Inevitably, much of the argument revolved around burden-sharing. The American response to Afghanistan was much more vigorous than that of the European allies whose main concern was to ensure that whatever happened elsewhere the hard-won benefits of *détente* in Europe were retained. Inevitably, the Americans pointed not only to the increases in their defence budget of 5 to 7 per cent but also to the fact that the Europeans were not meeting the real increase of 3 per cent per annum that had been agreed upon in 1978. An agreement which had been intended to symbolise alliance cohesion and determination became, instead, a symbol of the growing discord between the two sides of the Atlantic. The European unwillingness or inability to live up to the expectations generated by the 3 per cent agreement caused considerable consternation on Capitol Hill. Senator Carl Levin of Michigan introduced legislation mandating the Secretary of Defense to submit to the Congress an annual report assessing the performance of the allies in sharing the burdens of the common defence. The effect of this was to institutionalise the issue in a period when the discrepancy between European and American defence efforts appeared to be increasing.

If the Europeans fail to respond to the Senate demands for greater defence efforts, one possible consequence will be an upsurge of the pressures for troop withdrawals from Western Europe. Indeed, this is an issue which conceivably could unite the liberals and conservatives in common cause. Although conservative senators will prove reluctant to relinquish positions of strength at a time of concern over both the Soviet threat and a low nuclear threshold in NATO, this may be offset by a desire for retribution against allies widely regarded as increasingly unreliable. At the same time, liberals concerned over the size of the budget deficit may see an opportunity for financial savings in a smaller American military presence in Western Europe.

There were some signs of this nascent coalition in the support given by the members of the Senate Subcommittees on Defence Appropriations to moves in 1982 by Senator Ted Stevens of Alaska to establish a ceiling on the number of US troops in Europe. It was even more evident in June 1974 when Senator Nunn introduced a proposal to cut US troops in Europe by 90 000 over three years unless the Europeans fulfilled their commitment to increase defence budgets by 3 per cent per annum in real terms, or took other steps to strengthen conventional forces. Superficially this appeared to be a marked shift from Nunn's position in the early 1970s. In fact, he was consistent in his approach. By linking the existing level of US troops to more substantial burden-sharing efforts by the allies, Nunn hoped to reduce NATO's reliance on nuclear weapons. In other words, he was merely attempting to establish the conditions on which American troops would remain in Europe. Even so, his amendment aroused considerable anxiety amongst the allies and prompted the Reagan Administration to embark on a lobbying campaign reminiscent of those conducted by Nixon against the Mansfield Amendment. This contributed to the rejection of Nunn's proposal by 55 votes to 41. Despite this, the Nunn Amendment may well mark a new phase in the controversy over US troop levels in Europe. Nunn himself is still a committed Atlanticist concerned with maintaining the viability of the alliance. Future Nunn Amendments, however, will almost certainly obtain support from senators who are far less sympathetic to the Europeans. Indeed, there are several developments which seem likely to accentuate the existing dissatisfaction with the European allies and with the existing level of American troops in Europe.

One of these is the juxtaposition of soaring budget deficits and new security commitments. The United States in 1980 made an unprecedented commitment to the security of the Persian Gulf. The early 1980s was also a period of growing preoccupation with Central America. Should either of these commitments result in large-scale military intervention, the implications for the American presence in Europe could be far-reaching. As argued above, the 'Great Debate' was related in part to Korea, while considerable support for the Mansfield proposals came from those senators who were unhappy about the American over-commitment resulting from the involvement in Vietnam. American involvement in hostilities in either the Gulf or Central America would almost certainly generate strong pressures for reducing troops in Europe.

Even without military action, the very existence of these other commitments may itself put pressure on the presence in Europe. Despite the Reagan Administration's massive military build up, American capabilities may still be insufficient to fulfil America's global role. Should such a perception become widespread, it can only strengthen the position of those who argue that Western Europe has been the recipient of American protection for long enough and that priority should now be given to other areas and other obligations.

Indeed, there is an important school of thought which argues that the emphasis on coalition defence which has been the main theme of American security policy throughout the postwar period needs to be abandoned or at least regulated in favour of a strategy based on 'maritime supremacy', a 600-ship navy and forces which are highly mobile and capable not only of rapid deployment to cope with emergent threats but of equally rapid withdrawal in their aftermath. Static defence lines and permanent deployments are regarded as undesirable strategically, and as a wasteful diversion of resources from roles and missions necessary to contain what has become a global threat by the Soviet Union. In many respects this approach harks back to some of the ideas proposed by Herbert Hoover and Senator Robert Taft during the 'Great Debate' of 1951. Although the 'maritime supremacy' strategy goes well beyond the Fortress America concept advocated by Hoover, it reiterates the emphasis on control of the sea found in Taft's and Hoover's prescriptions and shares the same antipathy to the notion of substantial ground forces permanently deployed on the Eurasian land mass.

Should this unilateralist approach become more widespread then the pressures for change in America's military posture overseas will almost certainly increase through the 1980s. And whereas in the past there were always committed Atlanticists who were prepared to do battle on behalf of the Europeans, this group is unlikely to have the same kind of influence in the future as it did in the past. The days when the 'Old Guard' of diplomatic and military officials could come out of retirement to help defeat a Mansfield Amendment are over. The implications of the decline of the Atlanticists are significant in the sense that this provides a more permissive environment for proposals to reduce American forces in Europe. A closely related consideration is that this trend away from Atlanticism is likely to be accompanied, and indeed encouraged, by long-term demographic changes. The emergence of Hispanics as perhaps the leading ethnic group in the United States will almost certainly require that greater attention be given to the needs of Central and South America, while an increasing Asian population could encourage a growing preoccupation with the Pacific.

In addition to these trends in American opinion, there are equally significant changes in European approaches to the Alliance. This is most obvious in the emergence of the peace movement, many members of which reject not simply the close connection with the United States but the dominant position of both superpowers in Europe. The idea of lessening Western Europe's dependence on the United States, however, is not confined to the supporters of disarmament. The argument that

Western Europe should be capable of providing for its own security appears to be gaining increased respectability in elite circles throughout the continent. And although such an approach is still somewhat tentative, it may well be that many Europeans are now asking the same question as was asked by Senator Mansfield about their need to depend on 200 million Americans to defend them from 200 million Russians with 800 million Chinese at their back. During the 1970s Mike Mansfield appeared to be threatening security and stability in Europe. Increasingly, though, his ideas about Western Europe taking greater responsibility for shaping its own destiny may be regarded as a source of inspiration. And if the successors of Robert Taft are becoming more prominent in shaping American policy, they may well find themselves having to deal with a generation of Europeans who embrace the kind of hopes for Europe that were evident in Mike Mansfield's thinking. In these circumstances a reduction in the number of American troops deployed in Europe would no longer be seen as a threat but as an opportunity. And the consideration given to the question by the American Senate would not have been in vain.

Notes and References

CHAPTER 1

1. An extremely good analysis which deals with these arguments is M. Foley, *The New Senate: Liberal Influence on a Conservative Institution, 1959–1972* (New Haven and London: Yale University Press, 1980).
2. D. R. Matthews, *US Senators and their World* (New York: Vintage Books, 1960) p. 247.

CHAPTER 2

1. Quoted in L. S. Kaplan, *A Community of Interests: NATO and the Military Assistance Program, 1948–1951* (Washington: Office of the Secretary of Defense, Historical Office, 1980) p. 17.
2. This is one of the main themes of T. Ireland, *Creating the Entangling Alliance: The Origins of the North Atlantic Treaty Organisation* (London: Aldwych Press, 1981).
3. See S. M. Hartmann, *Truman and the Eightieth Congress* (Columbia: University of Missouri Press, 1971) and W. C. Cromwell, 'The Marshall Non Plan, Congress and the Soviet Union', *Western Political Quarterly*, vol. 32 (1979) 422–43.
4. See *The Vandenberg Resolution and the North Atlantic Treaty: Meetings held in Executive Session before the Committee on Foreign Relations, United States Senate, Eightieth Congress, Second Session on S. Res 239*, Historical Series (Washington: Government Printing Office, 1973) especially pp. 1–29. Kaplan, *Community of Interests*, p. 20 offers a very similar interpretation.
5. A good account can be found in J. Eayrs, *In Defence of Canada: Growing Up Allied* (University of Toronto Press, 1980) pp. 89–96.
6. See E. Reid, *Time of Fear and Hope: The Making of the North Atlantic Treaty* (Toronto: McCleland and Stewart, 1977) p. 143.
7. Ibid., p. 54.
8. The text is contained in T. H. Etzold and J. L. Gaddis, *Containment: Documents on American Policy and Strategy 1945–50* (New York: Columbia University Press, 1978) pp. 144–53.
9. Ibid., p. 146.
10. Ibid., p. 152.
11. See ibid., pp. 147, 151.

12. Ibid., pp. 151, 152.
13. See Reid, *Time of Fear and Hope*, p. 88.
14. I am grateful to Peter Foot of Dartmouth Naval College for this point regarding the presence of Lodge.
15. Reid, *Time of Fear and Hope*, p. 91.
16. Eayrs, *In Defence of Canada*, p. 107.
17. Reid, *Time of Fear and Hope*, p. 63.
18. On the decline of bipartisanship, see H. B. Westerfield, *Foreign Policy and Party Politics* (New Haven: Yale University Press, 1955) pp. 326–30.
19. The rivalry is discussed in D. Acheson, *Sketches From Life of Men I have Known* (New York: Harper & Row, 1961) pp. 123–32.
20. For an account of the meeting see D. Acheson, *Present at the Creation* (London: Hamilton, 1970) p. 281.
21. Ibid., p. 280.
22. Eayrs, *In Defence of Canada*, p. 110. See also ibid., p. 281 and Reid, *Time of Fear and Hope*, pp. 92–3.
23. Quoted in Reid, *Time of Fear and Hope*, p. 94.
24. D. S. McLellan, *Dean Acheson: The State Department Years* (New York: Dodd, Mead, 1976) p. 151.
25. T. Connally, *My Name is Tom Connally* (New York: Crowell, 1954) pp. 332–3.
26. See *The Vandenberg Resolution and the North Atlantic Treaty*.
27. Ibid., pp. 98–100 in particular.
28. Ibid., p. 108.
29. Ibid., p. 157.
30. Quoted in Reid, *Time of Fear and Hope*, p. 93.
31. D. N. Farnsworth, *The Senate Committee on Foreign Relations* (Urbana: University of Illinois Press, 1961) p. 71.
32. *The Vandenberg Resolution and the North Atlantic Treaty*, pp. 202–4.
33. Connally, *My Name is Tom Connally*, p. 335.
34. J. Reston, 'Isolationism is not Main Factor in Pact Debate', *New York Times*, 20 Feb 1949. Section 4, p. 3.
35. See *The Vandenberg Resolution and the North Atlantic Treaty*, p. 87.
36. J. J. McCloy, *The Atlantic Alliance: Its Origin and Future* (New York: Columbia University Press, 1969) p. 25.
37. *The Vandenberg Resolution and the North Atlantic Treaty*, p. 159.
38. *Hearings before the Committee on Foreign Relations, United States Senate 81st Congress, First Session on Executive L, the North Atlantic Treaty. Part I: Administration witnesses, April 27, 28 and 29 May 2 & 3, 1949*, p. 296. Hereafter cited as *Open Hearings on Executive L*.
39. Acheson testimony in ibid., p. 10. See also Harriman testimony in ibid., p. 224.
40. *The Vandenberg Resolution and the North Atlantic Treaty*, p. 99.
41. *Open Hearings on Executive L*, p. 47 for the Acheson–Hickenlooper exchange. For Lovett's statement see p. 265 and for Bradley's, p. 333.
42. The report is reproduced in *The Vandenberg Resolution and the North Atlantic Treaty*, pp. 357–87. See p. 373 and p. 378 in particular.
43. Ibid., p. 378.

44. *Congressional Quarterly Almanac 1949* (Washington: Congressional Quarterly 1950) p. 344. Pages 343 to 349 contain a useful summary of the debate.
45. A. H. Vandenberg Jr (ed), *The Private Papers of Senator Vandenberg* (Boston: Houghton Mifflin, 1952) p. 493.
46. Ibid., p. 494.
47. For further details of the reservations see *Congressional Quarterly Almanac 1949.*
48. Ireland, *Entangling Alliance*, p. 147.
49. *Open Hearings on Executive L*, pp. 13–14.
50. Connally did acknowledge though that the United States was under an obligation to consider requests for aid. See *The Vandenberg Resolution and the North Atlantic Treaty*, p. 176. See also *Congressional Record*, 21 July 1949, p. 9894.
51. See *Congressional Record*, 21 July 1949, p. 9886.
52. Ibid., p. 9898.
53. Ibid., p. 9908.
54. R. E. Osgood, *NATO: The Entangling Alliance* (University of Chicago Press) p. 45.
55. The significance of Article 3 in this respect is discussed in Ireland, *Entangling Alliance*, p. 224.
56. J. L. Bryniarski, 'Against the Tide: Senate Opposition to the Internationalist Foreign Policy of Presidents Roosevelt and Truman' (University of Maryland, PhD diss, 1972) pp. 279–80.
57. *The Vandenberg Resolution and the North Atlantic Treaty*, p. 187.
58. Ibid., p. 195.
59. Ibid., p. 237.
60. See *Military Assistance Program 1949: Joint Hearings held in Executive Session before the Committee on Foreign Relations and the Committee on Armed Services, United States Senate, Eighty-First Congress, First Session on S.2388.* Historical Series (Washington: Government Printing Office, 1974) hereafter cited as *Military Assistance Program 1949.*
61. *The Vandenberg Resolution and the North Atlantic Treaty*, p. 215.
62. Ibid., p. 217.
63. Ibid., p. 218.
64. *Open Hearings on Executive L*, p. 190.
65. *The Vandenberg Resolution and the North Atlantic Treaty*, p. 213.
66. See Bradley's comment in *Military Assistance Program 1949*, pp. 87, 102.
67. Ibid., p. 357.
68. See General Lemnitzer's statement in ibid., pp. 157–8.
69. Acheson in ibid., p. 30.
70. Lemnitzer in ibid., p. 158.
71. The phrase 'liberating a corpse' was that of French Premier, Henri Queuille, and is quoted in Osgood, *NATO*, p. 37.
72. *The Vandenberg Resolution and the North Atlantic Treaty*, p. 237.
73. *The Private Papers of Senator Vandenberg*, p. 511.
74. Ibid., p. 504.
75. Acheson, *Present at the Creation*, p. 309.

76. Ireland, *Entangling Alliance*, p. 155.
77. George's comment is quoted in *Congressional Quarterly Almanac 1949*, p. 359.
78. C. V. Crabb, *Bipartisan Foreign Policy: Myth or Reality* (New York: Harper & Row, 1957) p. 86.
79. Acheson, *Present at the Creation*, p. 354.
80. Osgood, *NATO*, p. 30.
81. The text of NSC-68 is reproduced in Etzold and Gaddis, *Containment*. See p. 399 in particular.
82. See ibid., p. 428.
83. M. Bundy (ed), *The Pattern of Responsibility* (Boston: Houghton Mifflin, 1952) p. 76.
84. L. S. Kaplan, *Community of Interests*, p. 105.
85. Ireland, *Entangling Alliance*, p. 191.
86. Quoted in R. Wahner, *The Stationing of United States Troops in Europe: A Background Study* (Washington: Library of Congress Legislative Reference Service, 1967) p. 8.
87. Ireland, *Entangling Alliance*, p. 207.
88. T. Lowi, 'Making Democracy Safe for the World' in J. Rosenau (ed), *The Domestic Sources of Foreign Policy* (New York: Free Press, 1967) p. 315.
89. Ibid., p. 320.

CHAPTER 3

1. R. J. Caridi, *The Korean War and American Politics* (Philadelphia: University of Pennsylvania Press, 1968) p. 94.
2. Ibid., pp. 100–1.
3. For a fuller account of Taft's position see J. T. Patterson, *Mr Republican: A Biography of Robert Taft* (Boston: Houghton Mifflin, 1972) especially pp. 474–96.
4. Quoted in M. Bundy (ed), *The Pattern of Responsibility* (Boston: Houghton Mifflin, 1952) p. 86.
5. H. B. Shill III, 'Senate Activism and Security Commitments: The Troops-To-Europe and National Commitments Resolutions', PhD dissertation (Chapel Hill: University of North Carolina, 1973) pp. 149–51.
6. Ibid., p. 155.
7. For details of Hoover's October address see *New York Times*, 20 October 1950, p. 12.
8. Hoover's statement is reproduced in N. Graebner (ed), *Ideas And Diplomacy* (London: Oxford University Press, 1964) pp. 742–5. See p. 744.
9. Ibid, p. 744.
10. Ibid, p. 745.
11. *The 'Great Debate' On American Foreign Policy: Issues, Pros, Cons, And Agreement.* Compiled for the Duke University Consensus Project by

Hornell Hart, Professor of Sociology (mimeographed at Duke University, 1 March 1951) pp. 4–5. Many of the citations in this document actually refer to the Hoover–Kennedy proposals.

12. Shill, 'Senate Activism', p. 154 discusses Dulles's position while details of Dewey's speeches can be found in Hart, *The 'Great Debate'*, p. 5.

13. W. Lippmann, 'Mr Truman and the Constitution' reproduced in *Congressional Record*, 16 January 1951, pp. 313–14.

14. It is significant, for example, that Senator Knowland, one of the leading figures in the Asia First Group, was in favour of sending troops to Europe.

15. See A. Schlesinger Jr, 'Congress and the Making of American Foreign Policy', *Foreign Affairs*, vol. 51, no. 1 (October 1972) 78–113 at p. 95.

16. See *Congressional Record*, 82nd Congress, 1st Session, 5 January 1951, especially pp. 55–61.

17. J. P. Armstrong, 'The Enigma of Senator Taft and American Foreign Policy', *Review of Politics*, vol. 17 (April 1955) 206–31 at p. 223.

18. *Congressional Record*, 5 January 1951, pp. 60–1.

19. Ibid., p. 57.

20. This was clear in Taft's book *A Foreign Policy for Americans* (New York: Doubleday, 1951).

21. *Congressional Record*, 5 January 1951, p. 60.

22. Ibid., p. 59.

23. Ibid., p. 60.

24. Ibid., p. 59.

25. Ibid., p. 56.

26. Ibid., p. 59.

27. Shill, 'Senate Activism', pp. 156–7.

28. The comments of Senator Douglas can be found in *Congressional Record*, 5 January 1951, p. 62 while those of Senator Morse are on pp. 65–6. Connally's are in *Congressional Record*, 11 January 1951, p. 144.

29. *Congressional Record*, 11 January 1951, p. 145.

30. *Congressional Record*, 5 January 1951, p. 66.

31. *Congressional Record*, 11 January 1951, p. 145.

32. *Congressional Record*, 8 January 1951, pp. 98–101.

33. *Congressional Record*, 11 January 1951, p. 147.

34. Ibid., p. 154.

35. Ibid., p. 158.

36. 'Poll Indicates Congress Views on Aid to Allies Sharply Divided', *New York Times*, 7 January 1951.

37. Quoted in ibid.

38. *Congressional Record*, 15 January 1951, p. 239.

39. *Congressional Record*, 22 January 1951, p. 498.

40. *Congressional Record*, 16 January 1951, p. 322.

41. Shill, 'Senate Activism', pp. 160–1.

42. E. Corwin, *The President: Office and Powers, 1787–1957* (New York University Press, 1966) p. 171.

43. See W. B. Truitt, 'The Troops to Europe Decision: The Process, Politics and Diplomacy of a Strategic Commitment', PhD dissertation (New

York: Columbia University, 1968) p. 349.

44. *Congressional Record*, 11 January 1951, p. 142.
45. Ibid.
46. Lodge's comments are from *Congressional Record*, 11 January 1951, p. 147, while Fulbright's are from *Congressional Record*, 22 January 1951, pp. 520–1.
47. *Congressional Record*, 22 January 1951, p. 485.
48. *Congressional Record*, 16 January 1951, p. 325.
49. For the exchange see *Congressional Record*, 16 January 1951, pp. 330–1.
50. Ibid.
51. See, for example, *Congressional Record*, 17 January 1951, pp. 382–5.
52. *Congressional Record*, 15 January 1951, p. 229.
53. Ibid., p. 230.
54. M. Jewell, *Senatorial Politics and Foreign Policy* (Lexington, Kentucky: University of Kentucky Press, 1961) pp. 127–8. George's statement, reported in the *Washington Star*, was quoted by Wherry, *Congressional Record*, 16 January 1951, p. 329.
55. Truitt, 'Troops to Europe Decision', pp. 347–9 summarises Truman's early statements on the congressional debate.
56. Shill, 'Senate Activism', p. 162.
57. Jewell, *Senatorial Politics*, pp. 100–1.
58. The difficulties in the Policy Committee during the 'Great Debate' are discussed in ibid., pp. 90–1.
59. R. L. Strout, 'Direct Test By-passed', *Christian Science Monitor*, 23 January 1951.
60. Ibid.
61. Truitt, 'Troops to Europe Decision', p. 348.
62. *Congressional Quarterly Almanac 1951* (Washington: Congressional Quarterly, 1952) p. 223.
63. Ibid., P. 224; Shill, 'Senate Activism', pp. 176–80 also contains a useful discussion of the Eisenhower testimony.
64. *Assignment of Ground Forces of the United States to Duty in the European Area*, Hearings before the Committee on Foreign Relations and the Committee on Armed Services, United States Senate, 82nd Congress, 1st Session on S. Con Res. 8, 1, 15, 16, 19, 20, 21, 22, 23, 24, 26, 27 and 28 February 1951 (Washington: Government Printing Office, 1951) pp. 1–8. Hereafter cited as *Assignment*.
65. Ibid., p. 4.
66. Ibid., p. 5.
67. Ibid., p. 5.
68. Ibid., pp. 10–12.
69. Ibid., p. 19.
70. Ibid., p. 19.
71. Ibid., pp. 20–1.
72. Ibid., p. 34.
73. The reaction is discussed in *Congressional Quarterly Almanac 1951*, p. 224.
74. *Congressional Record*, 5 February 1951, p. 952.
75. *Congressional Quarterly Almanac 1951*, p. 224.

76. *Congressional Record*, 8 February 1951, p. 1117.
77. Ibid., p. 1120.
78. Ibid., p. 1120.
79. Ibid., p. 1123.
80. See R. Taft, 'Address to Executives Club of Chicago' reprinted in the Appendix to the *Congressional Record* (1951) pp. 418–20.
81. *Congressional Record*, 8 February 1951, p. 1123.
82. Shill, 'Senate Activism', p. 185.
83. Ibid., p. 186.
84. Ibid., p. 186.
85. Ibid., p. 190.
86. See *Congressional Record-House*, 14 February 1951, pp. 1256–66 for the text, the signatories and a brief debate.
87. *Executive Sessions of the Senate Foreign Relations Committee (Historical Series) Vol III Part I Eighty-Second Congress, First Session (made public August 1976)* (Washington: Government Printing Office, 1976) pp. 53–62. Hereafter cited as *Executive Sessions*.
88. Ibid.
89. Truitt, 'Troops to Europe Decision', p. 358.
90. This would certainly be consistent with Connally's attempt to stage manage the hearings to obtain maximum benefit for the Administration.
91. *Assignment*, p. 81.
92. Ibid., p. 85.
93. Ibid., p. 80.
94. Ibid., p. 79.
95. Ibid., pp. 126–52, pp. 153–97 and pp. 221–36.
96. Shill, 'Senate Activism', p. 134.
97. *Assignment*, pp. 325–6.
98. For the testimony of Wherry, Hoover, and de Seversky see the relevant sections in ibid.
99. Ibid., p. 40.
100. Ibid., p. 45.
101. Ibid., p. 45.
102. This is related to the problems of oversell discussed in Chapter 2 above.
103. Truitt, 'Troops to Europe Decision', p. 386.
104. Knowland was especially concerned over the imbalance of effort in Korea. See, for example, his questioning of Taft in *Assignment*, p. 650.
105. Ibid., p. 747.
106. Ibid., p. 426.
107. See ibid., p. 612 for Taft's comment on this point.
108. See, for example, ibid., pp. 167 and 210.
109. Ibid., pp. 720–5.
110. See, for example, Hickenlooper's comments in ibid., p. 110.
111. Ibid., p. 112.
112. Ibid., p. 112.
113. D. S. McLellan, *Dean Acheson: The State Department Years* (New York: Dodd, Mead, 1976) p. 155.

114. *Assignment,* pp. 604 and 639.
115. For Dewey's testimony see ibid., pp. 525–34.
116. For Byrd's comment see *Executive Sessions,* p. 145.
117. Ibid., pp. 101–29.
118. Ibid., pp. 1–10.
119. Ibid., p. 3.
120. Ibid., p. 3.
121. Ibid., p. 4.
122. Ibid., p. 5.
123. Ibid., pp. 131–2.
124. The text is reproduced in ibid., pp. 584–7.
125. Ibid., pp. 172–6.
126. Ibid., p. 175.
127. Ibid., pp. 244–5.
128. Ibid., pp. 256–7 and pp. 257–8 for the vote on the motion to approve the concurrent resolution.
129. For Fulbright's statement see ibid., p. 137.
130. Ibid., pp. 190–5. There was no record of the voting positions of the members.
131. Ibid., p. 196.
132. Ibid., p. 201.
133. Ibid., pp. 202–3.
134. See ibid., pp. 236–41.
135. Ibid., pp. 204–6.
136. Ibid., p. 204.
137. Ibid., p. 214.
138. Ibid., pp. 234–5.
139. R. L. Strout, 'Troops to Europe Backed in Senate: New Bout Looms', *Christian Science Monitor,* 19 March 1951.
140. Ibid.
141. Ibid.
142. *Executive Sessions,* p. 334.
143. Ibid., p. 333.
144. Ibid., pp. 339–41.
145. R. L. Strout, 'Troops to Europe Backed in Senate'.
146. *Congressional Record,* 16 March 1951, p. 2540.
147. For Cain's views see *Congressional Record,* 21 March 1951, p. 2740.
148. *Congressional Record,* 16 March 1951, p. 2547.
149. *Congressional Record,* 16 March 1951, p. 2556.
150. *Congressional Record,* 16 March 1951, p. 2577.
151. Truitt, 'Troops to Europe Decision', p. 411.
152. *Congressional Record,* 21 March 1951, pp. 2769–72.
153. *Congressional Record,* 28 March 1951, p. 2956 and *Congressional Record,* 29 March 1951, p. 2967.
154. For Bricker's comments see *Congressional Record,* 29 March 1951, p. 2970, while Dirksen's can be found on p. 2980.
155. *Congressional Record,* 29 March 1951, p. 2974.
156. W. S. White, 'Democrats Wary of Vote on Troops', *New York Times,* 30 March 1951.

157. *Congressional Record,* 2 April 1951, p. 3065.
158. For the discussions see ibid., pp. 3065–75.
159. The reference to Article 3 was added in the debate. See ibid., pp. 3075–7.
160. Ibid., pp. 3075–83.
161. Shill, 'Senate Activism', p. 261.
162. Truitt, Troops to Europe Decision, p. 410 makes the point that this final phase saw a near breakdown of the Senate's leadership.
163. *Congressional Record,* 2 April 1951, p. 3095.
164. Ibid., pp. 3095–6.
165. Ibid., pp. 3096–104.
166. W. S. White, 'First Vote Reversed: Chamber Rejects Curb by McClellan, Then Adopts Declaration', *New York Times,* 3 April 1951.
167. Ibid.
168. *Congressional Record,* 3 April 1951, pp. 3145–60.
169. Ibid., p. 3190.
170. Ibid., p. 3194.
171. *Congressional Record,* 2 April 1951, pp. 3083–8.
172. *Congressional Record,* 3 April 1951, pp. 3161–73.
173. *Congressional Record,* 4 April 1951, pp. 3254–69.
174. For Taft's announcement see *Congressional Record,* 4 April 1951, p. 3272.
175. See ibid., pp. 3270–84 for the debate and the reaction to Taft's announcement.
176. Ibid., pp. 3288–93.

CHAPTER 4

1. It is significant that in 1966 former President Eisenhower suggested that the deployment of US troops to Europe had been designed as an 'emergency measure' to create confidence and to provide Western Europe with a 'breathing space in which to produce, train, and deploy the troops that were deemed necessary for initial defence'. When this was completed 'the major portion of the American contingent would be returned to the United States' although some ground forces would remain in Europe. See letter from Dwight D. Eisenhower to Senator Henry Jackson (17 May 1966) in *The Atlantic Alliance,* Hearings before the subcommittee on National Security and International Operations, of the Committee on Government Operations, United States Senate, 89th Congress, Second Session, 15 August 1966, Part 7 (Washington: Government Printing Office, 1966) pp. 223–7.
2. R. F. Grimmett, 'The Politics of Containment: the President, the Senate and American Foreign Policy, 1947–1956' (Kent State University: PhD diss, 1973) pp. 167–8.
3. Ibid., p. 181.
4. Ibid.

5. The best analysis of the 'new look' remains that by Glenn Snyder in W. Schilling, P. Hammond and G. Snyder, *Strategy, Politics and Defense Budgets* (New York: Columbia University Press, 1962).
6. R. A. Divine, *Foreign Policy and U.S. Presidential Elections: 1952, 1956* (New York: Franklin Watts, 1974) p. 24.
7. T. Hoopes, *The Devil and John Foster Dulles* (Boston: Little, Brown, 1973) p. 199.
8. See R. Morgan, *The United States and West Germany, 1945–1973* (London: Oxford University Press, 1974) pp. 63–5.
9. Hoopes, *John Foster Dulles*, p. 313.
10. Grimmett, 'Politics of Containment', p. 269. See also pp. 291–336.
11. M. Jewell, *Senatorial Politics and Foreign Policy* (Lexington: University of Kentucky Press, 1962) p. 35.
12. Ibid., p. 52.
13. Ibid., p. 36.
14. Ibid., p. 48.
15. S. W. Reichard, 'Divisions and Dissent: Democrats and Foreign Policy, 1952–1956', *Political Science Quarterly*, vol. 93, no. 1 (Spring 1978) 51–72, especially pp. 55–6.
16. See Jewell, *Senatorial Politics*, pp. 23–8. For the pressures from the Democrats for the Administration to expand the defence budget see ch. 6 of E. A. Kolodziej, *The Uncommon Defense and Congress, 1945–63* (Columbus, Ohio: Ohio State University Press, 1966).
17. W. S. White, 'Ellender Charges Aid Waste Abroad', *New York Times*, 21 December 1951.
18. See, for example, Ellender's statement on Mutual Security Appropriations for Fiscal Year 1959 on 23 August 1958. *Congressional Record*, 85th Congress, Second Session, p. 19397.
19. See his comments on 9 March 1959 in *Congressional Record*, 86th Congress, First Session, p. 3502. That he was not a great supporter of conventional forces earlier in the decade is suggested by Reichard, 'Divisions and Dissent'.
20. S. Strange, *International Monetary Relations* (London: Oxford University Press for the Royal Institute of International Affairs, 1976) p. 40.
21. Ibid.
22. Quoted in G. Hodgson, *America In Our Time* (New York: Vintage Books, 1978) p. 256.
23. See C. S. Raj, *American Military in Europe: Controversy over NATO Burden-sharing* (New Delhi: ABC Publishing House, 1983) p. 208.
24. The figures are taken from the tables in the 7 July 1959 *Congressional Record*. See p. 12807.
25. See the debate on the Mutual Security Act of 1959, *Congressional Record*, 7 July 1959, pp. 12800–10.
26. The following account rests on Raj, *American Military in Europe*, pp. 201–5.
27. On the Anderson–Dillon Mission see ibid., pp. 205–7, Morgan, *United States and West Germany*, pp. 82–3, and E. L. Dale, 'Bonn Rebuffs US on Aid Now to cut Dollar Outflow', *New York Times*, 23 November 1960.

28. Raj, *American Military in Europe*, p. 207.

29. The most comprehensive and detailed assessment of Mansfield's career is C. E. Hood, '"China Mike" Mansfield: The Making of a Congressional Authority on the Far East' (Washington State University: PhD diss, 1980). Also useful is L. Baldwin, *Hon. Politician: Mike Mansfield of Montana* (Missoula, Montana: Mountain Press, 1979).

30. The fleeting sympathy for Wallace is suggested by A. L. Hamby, *Beyond the New Deal: Harry S. Truman and American Liberalism* (New York: Columbia University Press, 1973) p. 124. For Mansfield's thinking on the Cold War in the early 1950s see Hood, '"China Mike" Mansfield', pp. 20–3.

31. M. Mansfield, *The Foreign Policy of the United States*, Speech before the Bar Association, Butte, Montana, June 1951, p. 4.

32. This emerges in many of Mansfield's speeches and statements in the early 1950s. See, for example, ibid., p. 25, and M. Mansfield, *International Policy, 1950–52* (undated speech found in the Mansfield Collection, University of Montana, Missoula).

33. M. Mansfield, *Europe After the Geneva Conference*, Report to the Committee on Foreign Relations, 19 October 1955 (Washington: Government Printing Office, 1955) p. 2.

34. *Review of Foreign Policy ix: The United States and the Soviet Union*, speech released 24 July 1956, p. 4.

35. M. Mansfield, *The Foreign Policy of the United States*, p. 5.

36. M. Mansfield, *A Survey of Political and Economic Developments During 1949 in France, Western Germany, Austria and Italy*. Report to the House Committee on Foreign Affairs, 10 December 1949 (Washington: Government Printing Office, 1950) p. 16.

37. See, for example, Mansfield's 'Statement Before Foreign Affairs Committee re Atlantic Treaty' (Mansfield Collection: Series on Speeches) and *The Foreign Policy of the United States*.

38. This was one of the main themes of *Europe After the Geneva Conference*.

39. Ibid., p. 3.

40. M. Mansfield, *Foreign Policy and Security*, Statement of 18 November 1953, p. 1.

41. M. Mansfield, 'Statement Before Foreign Affairs Committee re Atlantic Treaty'.

42. This is a recurring theme in Mansfield's speeches of the early 1950s. *The Foreign Policy of the United States*, is a typical example.

43. M. Mansfield, *A Survey of Political and Economic Developments During 1950 in Western Germany, Austria, Trieste, Italy, Spain and Portugal*, Report to the House Committee on Foreign Affairs (Washington: Government Printing Office, 1951) p. 3.

44. Ibid., p. 1.

45. See M. Mansfield, *Prospects for Western Unity*, Report to the Committee on Foreign Relations on a Study Mission to France, Western Germany and Italy, 4 November 1954 (Washington: Government Printing Office, 1954) p. 1.

46. Ibid., p. 8.

47. *Europe After the Geneva Conference*, p. 7.
48. *The Foreign Policy of the United States*, p. 2.
49. Ibid., p. 15.
50. Ibid., p. 8.
51. This theme was expressed particularly forcefully in M. Mansfield, *Pressures, Politics and Partnerships*, Speech before Annual World Affairs Conference, Asilomer, California, 7 May 1955.
52. M. Mansfield, *United States Foreign Policy Today and Tomorrow*, Address in Father Edmund A. Walsh Lecture Series, Georgetown University, 25 February 1957, p. 12.
53. For a comparison of the ideas of the two men, see P. Williams, 'Isolationism or Discerning Internationalism: Robert Taft, Mike Mansfield and US Troops in Europe', *Review of International Studies*, vol. 8 (1982) 27–38.
54. This again is a recurring theme in Mansfield's speeches. For two typical examples see *Foreign Policy and the Democratic Majority*, released 30 January 1957, and *The Democratic Party and Foreign Policy*, speech at Pomona College, Claremont, California, 15 December 1955.
55. See *The Democratic Party and Foreign Policy*.
56. *Review of Foreign Policy ix: The United States and the Soviet Union*, p. 3.
57. Ibid., p. 16.
58. M. Mansfield, *The Next Stage in Foreign Policy*, released 14 July 1957, p. 11.
59. Ibid., p. 14.
60. Ibid., p. 15. See also M. Mansfield, *A Time for Decision in Foreign Policy*, Address to Convention of Montana State Press Association, Great Falls, Montana, 17 August 1957, pp. 18–19.
61. M. Mansfield, *National Security and International Peace*, released 22 July 1960, p. 6.
62. M. Mansfield, *A Third Way on Berlin*, released 15 June 1961. See p. 6 in particular.
63. Ibid., p. 2.
64. M. Mansfield, *Review of Foreign Policy vii: U.S. Policy and a Changing Europe*, released 2 July 1956.
65. *The Next Stage in Foreign Policy*, p. 20.
66. Ibid., p. 20.
67. Memo to Honourable Michael J. Mansfield, Attention: Mr Valeo. From Foreign Affairs Division, Library of Congress, regarding *Military Costs of American Participation in NATO*, 27 March 1959 (Mansfield collection).
68. M. Mansfield, 'Foreign Relations: Late Summer 1959', *Congressional Record*, 14 September 1959, 86th Congress, 1st Session, vol. 105, pt. 14, pp. 18038–40, at p. 18040.
69. J. Bell, 'Mansfield Sees Demand For Troops Return', *Montana Standard*, 14 December 1959.
70. Valeo's influence on Mansfield was very considerable. Although Mansfield developed his own ideas these were often reinforced and refined by Valeo. Personal interview with Valeo, Washington DC, 6 July 1983.

Valeo's influence is also discussed in 'Senate Staffs: A Separate, Second Layer of Governance', *Washington Post*, 24 December 1972.
71. Raj, *American Military in Europe* p. 141.
72. M. Mansfield, *Personal Opinion*, released 2 January 1961.
73. Ibid.
74. Ibid.
75. M. Mansfield, *Address to the Springfield Adult Education Council*, Springfield Public Forum, The Phillips Lecture, Technical High School, Springfield Mass., 10 October 1962, p. 4.
76. Ibid., p. 6.
77. Ibid., p. 17.
78. *Europe After the Geneva Conference.*
79. M. Mansfield, *Address to the Springfield Adult Education Council*, p. 17.
80. *Berlin in a Changing Europe.* Report of Senators Mike Mansfield, J. Caleb Boggs, Claiborne Pell, and Benjamin A. Smith to the Committee on Foreign Relations, United States Senate (Washington: Government Printing Office, 1963) p. 13.
81. Ibid., p. 16.
82. The term 'transatlantic bargain' was not used by Mansfield but by former American Ambassador to NATO, Harlan Cleveland, as the title to his book, *NATO: The Transatlantic Bargain* (New York: Harper & Row, 1970). It does, however, highlight the approach adopted by Mansfield and has been used here accordingly.
83. Ellender's remark about 'paper divisions' can be found in *Congressional Record*, 6 June 1958, 85th Congress, Second Session, vol. 104, pt. 8, p. 10428.
84. 'Report by Senator Ellender on U.S. Foreign Operations' in *Congressional Record*, 13 February 1961 (daily edition) p. 2111.
85. Ellender's resentment was also apparent in statements on the Senate floor. See in particular *Congressional Record*, 15 August 1961, pp. 15915–21.
86. This idea of the forces of tradition against those of modernity was central to Symington's thinking. This was emphasised in a personal interview, 16 September 1975.
87. The change in Symington's thinking about Vietnam is traced in F. Lewis, 'The Education of a Senator', *Atlantic Monthly* (December 1971) pp. 55–64. See also M. Hirschman, *Stuart Symington: Democratic Senator From Missouri*, Ralph Nader Congress Project: Citizens Look at Congress (Washington: Grossman, 1972).
88. See S. Symington, *The Balance of Payments Deficit*, released 18 November 1963; *The Causes of the Balance of Payments Deficit*, released 20 November 1963; *Various Proposals Suggested to Remedy the Continuing Problem of Balance of Payments*, released 22 November 1963; and *Suggested Monetary Solutions for Unfavourable Balance of Payments – The Dangers in Continuing Deficit Financing*, released 5 December 1963.
89. S. Symington, *Recommendations for Overcoming the Continuing Unfavourable Balance of Payments*, released 16 September 1965, p. 2.
90. See *Congressional Record*, 16 January 1963, pp. 421–44; and *Congressional*

Record, 14 February 1963, pp. 2329–37, especially p. 2330.

91. *Congressional Record*, 14 February 1963, p. 2334.
92. *Congressional Record*, 16 January 1963, p. 437. See also *Congressional Record*, 21 May 1963, pp. 9136–9.
93. *Congressional Record*, 14 February 1963, p. 2334.
94. A useful account of the distribution of power in the Senate and the way this has changed can be found in N. J. Ornstein *et al.*, 'The Changing Senate: From the 1950s to the 1970s', in L. D. Dodd and B. I. Oppenheimer (eds), *Congress Reconsidered* (New York: Praeger, 1977). See also M. Foley, *The New Senate: Liberal Influence on a Conservative Institution, 1959–1972* (New Haven and London: Yale University Press, 1980).
95. Raj, *American Military in Europe*, p. 142.
96. For a brief but useful discussion of these agreements see G. Treverton, *The 'Dollar Drain' and American Forces in Germany* (Athens, Ohio: Ohio University Press, 1978) pp. 32–4.
97. On 'Big Lift' see Raj, *American Military in Europe*, p. 98.
98. Senator Talmadge, 'Reduction of U.S. Military Strength in Europe', *Congressional Record*, 28 October 1963, p. 20315.
99. This is suggested in 'Growing Pressure in U.S. to Cut Europe Garrisons', *The Times*, 23 November 1963.
100. German sensitivities are discussed in M. Kandel, 'Bonn asks U.S. about "Big Lift"', *New York Herald Tribune*, 22 October 1963. For Rusk's position see Raj, *American Military in Europe*, p. 217; and 'Found: A Secretary of State', *New York Times*, 29 October 1963.
101. M. Frankel, 'President Gives Bonn Assurance on Combat Force', *New York Times*, 1 November 1963.
102. The importance of this was emphasised by Valeo in a personal interview with the author on 6 July 1983. Details of Eisenhower's comments in the *Saturday Evening Post* can be found in Raj, *American Military in Europe*, pp. 216–17. See also 'Growing Pressure in U.S. to Cut Europe Garrisons', *The Times*, 23 October 1963 and 'Eisenhower Urges Troop Cut Abroad', *New York Times*, 8 November 1963.
103. See 'Growing Pressure in U.S. to Cut Europe Garrisons'.
104. Raj *American Military in Europe*, pp. 216–17.
105. See D. Acheson, 'Withdrawal from Europe? "An Illusion" ', *New York Times Magazine*, 15 December 1963. Also useful is 'Mr Acheson's Plea for Germany', *The Times*, 19 November 1963; and 'Acheson Bids U.S. Remain in Europe', *New York Times*, 19 November 1963.

CHAPTER 5

1. See, for example, D. Watt, 'Will McNamara Stick to his Guns', *Financial Times*, 10 June 1966. In addition see 'Case for U.S. Cutting Forces in Europe', *The Times*, 6 June 1966 and 'U.S. Garrison in Europe to be Reduced', *The Times*, 25 May 1966.
2. A useful summary of these statements can be found in *Congressional*

Quarterly Almanac 1966 (Washington: Congressional Quarterly, 1967) pp. 434–5.

3. See B. Welles, '15,000 U.S. Troops to Leave Europe', *New York Times*, 8 April 1966.

4. That it did not provide the cause was emphasised by Mansfield in a personal interview with the author on 17 September 1975.

5. M. Mansfield, *Congressional Record*, 25 April 1966, p. 8874.

6. M. Mansfield, *Congressional Record*, 27 July 1966, p. 17338.

7. Quoted in 'America's Presence in Europe', *New York Herald Tribune*, 23 May 1966.

8. J. Pastore, *Congressional Record*, 31 August 1966, p. 20559.

9. S. Symington, *Congressional Record*, 6 September 1966, p. 21832.

10. M. Mansfield, *Congressional Record*, 7 September 1966, p. 21885.

11. Quoted in 'Slash Forces in Europe Sparked by Symington', *New York Herald Tribune*, 2 September 1966.

12. F. Valeo in a personal interview with the author, 6 July 1983. See also ibid.

13. For Mansfield's comments on, and the dates of, these meetings see *Congressional Record*, 31 August 1966, p. 20555. Raj, *American Military in Europe* (New Delhi: ABC Publishing House, 1983) pp. 152–6 is also useful on the meetings.

14. C. M. Roberts, 'Mansfield's Blockbuster', *New York Herald Tribune*, 5 September 5 1966.

15. The text is reproduced in *United States Troops in Europe: Hearings Before the Combined Subcommittee of Foreign Relations and Arms Services Committees on the Subject of United States Troops in Europe, United States Senate Ninetieth Congress, First Session on S. Res 49 and S. Res 83*, 26 April and 3 May 1967 (Washington: Government Printing Office, 1967) pp. 1–2. Hereafter cited as *United States Troops in Europe*.

16. *Congressional Quarterly Almanac 1966*, p. 430.

17. 'Democrat Leaders Ask Deep G. I. Cut in Europe', *New York Herald Tribune*, 1 Sept 1966.

18. Letter from Senator Fulbright to Senator Mansfield dated 1 Sept 1966 (Majority Leader File, Mansfield Collection, University of Montana, Missoula). Hereafter cited as Mansfield Collection.

19. Ibid.

20. E. W. Kenworthy, 'Senate Bloc Assaults Troop Cut Proposal', *New York Times*, 2 Sept 1966.

21. Quoted in J. Herbers, 'Senators Assail Proposed Troop Slash in Europe', *New York Times*, 7 September 1966.

22. For Dirksen's position see J. Herbers, ibid. and 'Dirksen Opposes Cutback of U.S. Forces in Europe', *New York Herald Tribune*, 3/4 September 1966.

23. See, for example, 'Sen. Morton: Cutback Plea is Embarrassing Johnson', *New York Herald Tribune*, 6 Sept 1966.

24. The Legislative Reference Service of the Library of Congress provided several memos to Mansfield and Valeo. These included *U.S. Troop Consignments to Europe Since World War II*, 30 August 1966; *U. S. Military*

Expenditures in Europe, 13 Sept 1966; *Questions on Senate Resolution 99, 1951 on Troops to Europe,* 13 Sept 1966; and *Changed Basic Factors Since 1951 which can be cited as Evidence that U.S. Troops in Europe should be substantially Reduced,* 28 Sept 1966 (Mansfield Collection)

25. 'Polled Senators Favour G.I. Cutback in Europe', *New York Herald Tribune,* 5 Sept 1966.
26. The text of the speech can be found in *Congressional Record,* 10 Oct 1966, pp. 25909–10.
27. These negotiations are discussed in G. Treverton, *The 'Dollar Drain' and American Forces in Germany* (Athens, Ohio: Ohio University Press, 1978).
28. *Congressional Record,* 6 Sept 1966, p. 21831.
29. *Congressional Record,* 18 Oct 1966, pp. 27330–1.
30. Raj, *American Military in Europe,* p. 127.
31. J. W. Finney, 'Mansfield Resumes Campaign For a Cut in Troops in Europe', *New York Times,* 20 Jan 1967.
32. M. Mansfield, letter to Senate colleagues dated 10 Jan 1967 (Mansfield Collection).
33. Letter from J. W. Fulbright to Senator Mansfield dated 12 Jan 1967 (Mansfield Collection).
34. Ibid.
35. Ibid.
36. For the texts of these resolutions see *United States Troops in Europe,* pp. 2–3.
37. Ibid., pp. 3–4.
38. J. W. Finney, 'GOP Seeks Shift on Europe Policy – Has White House Support in Effort to take Initiative in Senate from Democrats', *New York Times,* 13 Feb 1967.
39. D. S. Broder, ' "Great Debate" on NATO Due Today', *New York Herald Tribune,* 15 Feb 1967.
40. Quoted in 'Javits to ask Review before Europe Cutback' reproduced in *Congressional Record,* 16 Feb 1967, p. S2111.
41. Treverton, *The 'Dollar Drain',* p. 129.
42. L. B. Johnson, *The Vantage Point: Perspectives of the Presidency, 1963–1969* (New York: Polular Library, 1971) p. 309.
43. Ibid.
44. Treverton, *The 'Dollar Drain',* p. 129.
45. *United States Troops in Europe.*
46. See ibid., pp. 78–9.
47. Ibid., p. 57.
48. Ibid., p. 79.
49. Ibid., pp. 88–9.
50. Letter from Senator Joseph Clark to Mansfield dated 28 April 1967. Mansfield's reply on 3 May stated that he would appreciate Clark appearing before the committee at the appropriate time (Mansfield Collection).
51. Letter from Senator Miller to Mansfield dated 17 April 1967 (Mansfield Collection).
52. Memorandum to Senator Mansfield from Carl Marcy on Subject of

Joint Subcommittee to Study Troop Reductions dated 21 March 1967 (Mansfield Collection).

53. Ibid.
54. Treverton, *The 'Dollar Drain'*, p. 109.
55. Mansfield's comments from the *Congressional Record*, 13 July 1967 are reproduced in *Report of the Combined Subcommittee of Foreign Relations and Armed Services Committees on the Subject of United States Forces in Europe to the Committee on Foreign Relations and Committee on Armed Services, United States Senate*, 15 Oct 1968 (Washington: Government Printing Office, 1968) pp. 64–6, hereafter cited as Report.
56. On Bonn's backtracking see Raj *American Military in Europe*, pp. 186–7.
57. C. R. Gellner, *The Mansfield Proposals to Reduce United States Troops in Western Europe, 1967–1973*, Congressional Research Service, Library of Congress, 25 June 1980, p. 12.
58. S. Symington, *Congressional Record*, 27 Feb 1968, reprinted in *Report*, pp. 73–4.
59. *Congressional Quarterly Almanac 1968* (Washington: Congressional Quarterly, 1969) pp. 717–18.
60. F. Church 'Proposal to Europeanise NATO', *Congressional Record*, 7 March 1968, pp. S2387–S2388. Some of Pearson's comments are reprinted in *Report*, pp. 74–7.
61. *Congressional Record*, 19 April 1968, reprinted in *Report*, pp. 81–88.
62. J. W. Finney, 'Mansfield will Resume Effors to Cut U.S. Troops in Europe', *New York Times*, 11 Jan 1968.
63. See *Report*, p. 84.
64. See the piece by Chalmers Roberts in *Washington Post*, 18 June 1967, reprinted in ibid., p. 91.
65. For press coverage see ibid., pp. 89–91.
66. For Mansfield's response see ibid., pp. 88–9 and for Symington's see ibid., p. 91.
67. Memorandum to Senator Mansfield from Jim Lowenstein, Subject: Further Hearings on Senate Resolution 49, 8 May 1968 (Mansfield Collection).
68. See M. Mansfield, 'The Situation in Czechoslavakia and U.S. Forces in Europe', *Congressional Record*, 13 Sept 1918 reprinted in *Report*, pp. 97–100.
69. Ibid., p. 98.
70. *Postscript to Report on Czechoslovakia, NATO and the Paris Negotiations of September 1968: Report of Senator Mike Mansfield to the Committee on Foreign Relations, December 1968* (Washington: Government Printing Office, 1968) p. 7.
71. *Report*, p. 2.
72. W.C. Cromwell, *The Eurogroup and NATO*, Research Monograph Series No. 18 (Philadelphia: Foreign Policy Research Institute, 1974) p. 16.
73. Ibid., p. 9.
74. On Healey's role see ibid., p. 14.
75. M. Foley, *The New Senate: Liberal Influence on a Conservative Institution, 1959–1972* (New Haven & London: Yale University Press, 1980) p. 77.

76. Raj, *American Military in Europe*, p. 139.
77. Nixon's Remarks to the Royal Air Force Academy, quoted in R. Z. George, 'Contending Views of National Security 1969–1973', PhD diss (Boston: Fletcher School of Law and Diplomacy, May 1977) p. 250.
78. T. Lambert, 'Mansfield to Renew Proposal to Pull G.I.s out of Europe', *International Herald Tribune*, 11 July 1969.
79. For details see E. T. Lampson, *The United States and NATO: Commitments, Problems and Prospects*, Congressional Research Service, Library of Congress, 21 July 1972, pp. 96–7.
80. 'Mansfield to Press NATO Cuts', *New York Times*, 20 Oct 1969.
81. Ibid.
82. Lowenstein drafted the letter for Mansfield's signature. Note from Jim Lowenstein to Mansfield dated 12 Nov 1969 together with letter to Secretary of State Rogers also dated 12 Nov 1969 (Mansfield Collection).
83. *Congressional Record*, 1 Dec 1969, p. S15163.
84. Foley, *The New Senate*, p. 69.
85. See 'U.S. Troops Cut in Europe: Mansfield Again Urges', *New York Times*, 2 Dec 1969.
86. The text of Richardson's speech is reprinted in *Congressional Record*, 23 Jan 1970, pp. S430–S432.
87. The Senators were Norris Cotton of New Hampshire and Robert Packwood of Oregon, both Republicans. See 'U.S. Opposes a Cut of GIs in Europe as Threat to NATO', *New York Times*, 21 Jan 1970.
88. M. Mansfield, *Congressional Record*, 23 Jan 1970, p. S430.
89. D. W. Walker, *'Burden Sharing in NATO, 1966–1972: American Critics, the Administration and the European Response'*, dissertation presented for B A (Hons) in Modern History and Politics, Dept of Politics, University of Southampton June 1982, p. 28.
90. 'Nixon is Reported to Prefer NATO Troops to Subsidies', *International Herald Tribune*, 10 Oct 1970.
91. George, *Contending Views*, p. 280.
92. Ibid.
93. On this review see W. Beecher, 'U.S. Conducting Broad Review of NATO Strategy' *New York Times*, 9 Nov 1970; C. Roberts, 'Nixon Reportedly Rejects U.S. Troop Cuts in Europe', *International Herald Tribune*, 21 Nov 1970; and H. Brandon, 'Stand Fast for Nixon's Troops in Europe', *Sunday Times*, 22 Nov 1970.
94. J. M. Goshko, 'NATO Faces Problem That Will Not Die', *International Herald Tribune*, 5 Oct 1970.
95. See Lampson, *United States and NATO*, pp. 115–16 and Cromwell, *Eurogroup and NATO*, pp. 16–17.
96. Cromwell, *Eurogroup and NATO*, p. 16.
97. Ibid.
98. *Congressional Record*, 1 Dec 1970, pp. S19076–7.

CHAPTER 6

1. See *Congressional Record*, 1 December 1970, p. 19077.
2. H. B. Shill III, *'Senate Activism and Security Commitments: the Troops to Europe and National Commitments Resolutions'*, PhD diss (Chapel Hill: University of North Carolina, 1973) p. 330.
3. See, for example, R. L. Strout, 'Showdown–Senate Vs Nixon', *Christian Science Monitor*, 15 May 1971.
4. J. E. Schwarz, 'Senator Michael J. Mansfield and United States Military Disengagement: A Case Study in American Foreign Policy: The Majority Leader, his Amendment and his Influence upon the Senate' (University of North Carolina: PhD diss, 1977) p. 113.
5. The term 'educational exercise' is that of D. Abshire and is quoted in ibid., p. 124. Mansfield's remarks during the November debate give added support to this interpretation. (See *Congressional Record*, 23 Nov 1971, p. S19495) as did an interview with the author, Washington, 17 September 1975.
6. Quoted in ibid., p. 124.
7. In an interview with the author, Washington, 12 September 1975.
8. H. A. Kissinger, *The White House Years* (London: Weidenfeld & Nicolson, 1979) p. 938.
9. F. Emery, 'Senate Move to Recall Troops from Europe', *The Times*, 12 May 1971.
10. *Congressional Record*, 5 May 1971, pp. S6229–6230.
11. See 'Mansfield Renews Campaign to Cut US Forces in Europe', *International Herald Tribune*, 7 May 1971.
12. Guy de Jonquieres, 'Pressure for Troop Cuts grows in Congress', *Financial Times*, 11 May 1971.
13. Kissinger, *White House Years*, pp. 940–1.
14. See *Congressional Record*, 5 May 1971, p. S6229.
15. Remarks by Senator Symington, 'The Current Dollar Crisis and the Basic Injustice of our European Occupation', *Congressional Record*, 5 May 1971, pp. S6229–3430.
16. W. Millinship, 'Dollar Crisis Spawns "Bring the Troops Home" Move', *Observer Foreign News Service*, no. 28853, 14 May 1971.
17. D. Abshire, quoted in Schwarz, 'Senator Michael J. Mansfield', p. 120.
18, For a useful summary of these statements see 'US Troop Level Reduction in Europe Opposed', United States Information Service, 13 May 1971.
19. See ibid.
20. Ibid. See also J. W. Finney, 'Troop Cut Fought by White House', *New York Times*, 13 May 1971.
21. F. Farris, 'Senate Battle on Troops in Europe', *International Herald Tribune*, 13 May 1971.
22. Finney, 'Troop Cut Fought by White House'.
23. Kissinger, *White House Years*, p. 940.
24. Ibid., pp. 941–2.
25. J. W. Finney, 'Nixon Firm in Fight to Bar US Troop Cut in Europe',

New York Times, 14 May 1971.
26. F. Farris, 'Senate Battle on Troops in Europe', and Finney, 'Troop Cut Fought by White House'.
27. Kissinger, *White House Years*, p. 942. See also S. Rich, 'Nixon Veto Seen on Europe GI Cut', *International Herald Tribune*, 14 May 1971.
28. Kissinger, *White House Years*, p. 942.
29. Ibid., p. 941.
30. Ibid., p. 941.
31. Ibid., p. 942.
32. J. N. Yochelson, 'Mutual Force Reductions: West European and American Perspectives' in W. Hanrieder (ed), *The United States and Western Europe* (Cambridge, Mass.: Winthrop, 1974) pp. 251–81 at p. 255.
33. J. W. Finney, 'Nixon Firm in Fight to Bar US Troop Cut in Europe'.
34. Ibid.
35. S. Rich, 'Nixon Veto Seen on Europe GI Cut'.
36. *Congressional Record*, 11 May 1971, p. S6694.
37. Ibid., p. S6696.
38. J. W. Finney, 'Troop Cut Fought by White House'.
39. Kissinger, *White House Years*, pp. 941–2. Compare F. Emery, 'Nixon Prepared to Veto Cuts in NATO', *The Times*, 14 May 1971.
40. Schwarz, 'Senator Michael J. Mansfield', p. 121.
41. For details of the discussions held by Rogers with Mansfield and other senators see S. Barber, 'Nixon Wins Weeks' Grace in Plan to Axe NATO Troops', *Daily Telegraph*, 14 May 1971. Also useful is H. Brandon, 'Brezhnev May Get Nixon off the Hook', *Sunday Times*, 16 May 1971.
42. A. Raphael, 'Rogers says US Troop Cuts would Kill NATO', *Guardian*, 15 May 1971.
43. Kissinger, *White House Years*, p. 943.
44. Ibid., p. 943.
45. Ibid., p. 944.
46. Ibid., p. 944.
47. See ibid., pp. 944–5; *Congressional Quarterly Almanac 1971* (Washington: Congressional Quarterly, 1972); and J. W. Finney, 'Nixon Firm in Fight to Bar US Troop Cut in Europe'.
48. Kissinger, *White House Years*, p. 944.
49. Schwarz, 'Senator Michael J. Mansfield' p. 119.
50. Ibid.
51. S. Rich, 'Mansfield's Allies Preparing Compromise on NATO Cuts', *Washington Post*, 15 May 1971. Quoted in ibid, p.121.
52. Schwarz, 'Senator Michael J. Mansfield'.
53. 'Muskie having Second Thoughts on GI Withdrawal in Europe', *International Herald Tribune*, 19 January 1971. This point was confirmed in a personal interview with one of Muskie's staff.
54. Schwarz, 'Senator Michael J. Mansfield', p. 120.
55. This additional theme is discussed in R. B. Semple, 'Nixon Wins Wide Backing on Troop Total in Europe', *New York Times*, 16 May 1971.

56. See, for example, his 'Paying for NATO', *Washington Monthly* (July 1970).
57. *Congressional Record*, 18 May 1971, p. S7252
58. Ibid.
59. A. Raphael, 'Rogers says US Troop Cuts would Kill NATO'.
60. Kissinger, *White House Years*, p. 945.
61. This account is base on ibid., p. 945.
62. R. B. Semple, 'Nixon Wins Wide Backing on Troop Total in Europe'.
63. Ibid.
64. See 'NATO Troop Cut: Massive White House Lobby Effort', *Congressional Quarterly Almanac 1971*, p. 273.
65. Semple 'Nixon Wins Wide Backing on Troop Total in Europe'.
66. 'Truman Favours Stand on Troops', *International Herald Tribune*, 17 May 1971.
67. 'NATO Troop Cut: Massive White House Lobby Effort'.
68. A. Goldberg, 'A "Substantial" Troop Reduction is "Overdue"', *Washington Post*, 16 May 1971, reprinted in *Congressional Record*, 17 May 1971, p. S6992. The letter is available in the Mansfield Collection.
69. See *The Bulletin* (Bonn: Government Press and Information Office, 18 May 1971) p. 125. L. Fellows, 'Bonn Warns US on Troop Cutback', *New York Times*, 15 May 1971. Also useful is 'Troop Cut Move is Worrying NATO', *New York Times*, 16 May 1971.
70. *Kissinger, White House Years*, p. 945
71. For a discussion of this claim see *Congressional Record*, 17 May 1971, p. S7083.
72. For details of Brosio's statement see 'NATO Director Backs Nixon, Opposes US Troop Reduction', *International Herald Tribune*, 17 May 1971.
73. For example, 'The Mansfield Amendment: Why Not Vietnam', Washington Post editorial published in *International Herald Tribune*, 15 May 1971.
74. Interview with Senator Mansfield, 17 September 1975, Washington DC.
75. R. L. Strout, 'Showdown – Senate Vs Nixon'.
76. *Congressional Record*, 17 May 1971, p. S7116.
77. 'NATO Director Backs Nixon, Opposes US Troop Reduction'.
78. J. W. Finney, 'Mansfield Did Fine until Brezhnev Came Along', *New York Times*, 16 May 1971.
79. Useful background can be found in W. B. Prendergast, *Mutual and Balanced Force Reductions: Issues and Prospects* (Washington: American Enterprise Institute for Public Policy Research, 1978).
80. J. Record, *Force Reductions in Europe: Starting Over* (Cambridge, Mass.: Institute of Foreign Policy, 1980).
81. 'NATO Troop Cut: Massive White House Lobby Effort', p. 273.
82. Ibid.
83. Kissinger, *White House Years*, pp. 946–7. It is worth noting in passing that Kissinger is referring to 15 May whereas the speech was actually made on 14 May.

84. This, of course would be an example of each side engaging in worst case thinking.
85. F. Farris, 'Senate Battle on Troops in Europe'.
86. See A. Raphael, 'US Ready for Talks with Moscow on European Troop Cuts', *Guardian*, 17 May 1971. Also useful is 'Mr Nixon's Unlikely Ally', *The Boston Globe*, 18 May 1971.
87. F. Emery, 'Offer by Russians May Yet Rescue President Nixon from Senate Challenge on Military Cuts', *The Times*, 19 May 1971.
88. See A. Raphael, 'Rogers Says US Troop Cuts Would Kill NATO'.
89. *Congressional Record*, 18 May 1971, p. S7235.
90. *Congressional Record*, 17 May 1971, p. S7107.
91. Kissinger, *White House Years*, p. 946.
92. Ibid., p. 942.
93. T. Wicker, 'The Right Question', *New York Times*, 20 May 1971.
94. See S. Rich, 'Mansfield Vows to Maintain Pressure to Cut Europe GIs' *International Herald Tribune*, 19 May 1971, and J. W. Finney, 'Defeat Seen for Mansfield Troop Plan', *New York Times*, 19 May 1971.
95. Quoted in Finney, 'Defeat seen for Mansfield Troop Plan'.
96. Kissinger, *White House Years*, p. 947.
97. For an example see *Congressional Record*, 19 May 1971, p. S7410.
98. J. W. Finney, 'Defeat Seen for Mansfield Troop Plan'.
99. McClellan's comments on this can be found in *Congressional Record*, 19 May 1971, p. S7365.
100. For the various stages through which the Nelson Amendment passed see *Congressional Record*, 17 May 1971, p. S7106, *Congressional Record*, 18 May 1971, pp. S7227 and S7269, and *Congressional Record*, 19 May 1971, p. S7364.
101. Humphrey's comments can be found in *Congressional Record*, 19 May 1971, p. S7383, while that by Church is on pp. S7378–9.
102. *Congressional Record*, 19 May 1971, p. S7383. See also *Congressional Quarterly Almanac 1971*, p. 276.
103. See *Congressional Record*, 19 May 1971, pp. S7389–94.
104. Ibid., p. S7403.
105. For Javit's comment see ibid., p. S7416 and for the debate on this proposed particular amendment see pp. S7412–21.
106. Ibid., p. S7421 and *Congressional Quarterly Almanac 1971*, p. 276.
107. Kissinger, *White House Years*, p. 947 confuses this with the Fulbright Amendment when in fact it had been withdrawn. See ibid., p. S7422.
108. Ibid., pp. S7422–3.
109. Ibid., pp. S7423–5.
110. For the Mansfield statement see ibid., pp. S7426–8.
111. The roll-call is in ibid., p. S7439. See also *Congressional Quarterly Almanac 1971*, p. 115, vote 53.
112. 'Mr Nixon, the Senate and the World', *International Herald Tribune*, 22/23 May 1971.
113. Ibid. A useful appraisal can also be found in M. Frankel, 'After Troop-cut Battle', *New York Times*, 20 May 1971.
114. The following account of the discussion is based on 'US Senators Warn

NATO on Cost Load', *International Herald Tribune*, 4 June 1971.

115. 'Mansfield Plans New Bid to Cut Troops in Europe', *International Herald Tribune*, 8 July 1971.

116. The mail can be found in the Mansfield Collection.

117. J. S. Odell, 'The US and the Emergence of Flexible Exchange Rates: an Analysis of Foreign Policy change', *International Organization*, vol 33, no. 1 (Winter 1979) 57–81 at pp. 66–7.

118. Ibid., p. 58.

119. M. Mansfield, 'The New Economic Program and Western Europe' in *Congressional Record*, 14 September 1971, pp. S14245–9 at p. S14246. See also J. W. Finney, 'Mansfield Renews Troop Cut Effort', *New York Times*, 15 September 1971.

120. The report was issued 22 October 1971 as *Western Europe and the New Economic Policy. Report of Senator Mike Mansfield to the Committee on Foreign Relations, United States Senate* (Washington: Government Printing Office, 1971).

121. *Congressional Record*, 14 September 1971, pp. S14247–8.

122. B. Gwertzman, 'Troop Cutback in Europe is Voted by Senate Panel', *New York Times*, 19 November 1971.

123. F. Farris, 'Senate Gets Bill Cutting Troops in Europe by Twenty Per Cent', *International Herald Tribune*, 19 November 1971.

124. 'Text of Secretary Laird's Letter to Senate Unit on NATO Troops', *USIS Official Text*, 19 November 1971.

125. F. Farris, 'Senate Gets Bill Cutting Troops in Europe by Twenty Per Cent'.

126. F. Emery, 'Senators want 60,000 Troops to Quit Europe', *The Times*, 19 November 1971. See also A. Raphael, 'Call for Troop Cuts in Europe Angers President Nixon', *Guardian*, 19 November 1971.

127. For details of the system of *ex officio* membership of the Committee on Appropriations see S. Horn, *Un-used Power: The Work of the Senate Committee on Appropriations* (Washington: Brookings Institution, 1970) pp. 50–2.

128. Although this is not frequent, it does happen at times.

129. A. Raphael, 'Call for Troop Cuts in Europe Angers President Nixon'.

130. B. Gwertzman, 'Troop Cutback in Europe is Voted by Senate Panel'.

131. For the text see 'President Nixon's Letter to Stennis on US Troop Levels in Europe', *USIS Official Text*, 24 November 1971.

132. 'Moscow willing to talk to Signor Brosio', *The Times*, 24 November 1971.

133. *Congressional Record*, 23 November 1971, pp. S19501–4.

134. For details see ibid., p. S19516.

CHAPTER 7

1. For the text of Kissinger's speech see the *New York Times*, 24 April 1973. Emphasis has been added.

2. *Memorandum to Senator Mansfield from Charles D. Ferris, December 28, 1972*

regarding Trip to Europe, Fall 1972 (Majority Leader Files, Mansfield Collection, University of Montana, Missoula) p. 4.

3. Ibid., p. 4.
4. Ibid., p. 5.
5. Ibid., p. 6.
6. K. Kaiser, *Europe and the United States: The Future of the Relationship* (Washington: Columbia Books, 1973) p. 17.
7. *Congressional Quarterly Almanac*, vol. 29, *1973* (Washington: Congressional Quarterly, 1974) p. 3.
8. Extracts from the speech are reprinted in L. Baldwin, *Hon. Politician: Mike Mansfield of Montana* (Montana: Mountain Press, 1979) pp. 286–90.
9. See A. Schlesinger Jr, *The Imperial Presidency* (Boston: Houghton Mifflin, 1973) p. 235.
10. Quoted in ibid., p. 238.
11. The figures for the budget are drawn from *Congressional Quarterly Almanac 1973*, especially pp. 981–5.
12. Quoted in ibid., p. 980. For a stimulating analysis along the same lines as presented here and which interprets the battles over defence in the late 1960s and early 1970s as a struggle between those who emphasised 'national security' and those who emphasised 'national welfare' see R. Z. George, *'Contending Views of National Security'*, PhD diss (Boston: Fletcher School of Law and Diplomacy, 1977).
13. L. Gelb and A. Lake, 'Troop Levels in Europe and Budget Levels in the US', *Washington Post*, 29 March 1973.
14. Ibid.
15. G. F. Treverton, *The 'Dollar Drain' and American Forces in Germany* (Athens, Ohio: Ohio University Press, 1978) p. 109.
16. *Memorandum to Senator Mansfield from Charles D. Ferris, August 10, 1973 regarding Reduction of US Forces Abroad* (Majority Leader files, Mansfield Collection, University of Montana, Missoula).
17. For an account of the meeting see Gelb and Lake, 'Troop Levels in Europe', and S. Barber, 'Senators Demand Cut in US NATO Force as Costs Soar', *Daily Telegraph*, 16 March 1973.
18. See Gelb and Lake, 'Troop Levels in Europe'.
19. This is suggested in the Ferris Memorandum of 10 August.
20. Remarks by Senator Mansfield on Majority Conference Resolution on Reduction of Military Expenditure Overseas, *Congressional Record*, 15 March 1973, p. S4831.
21. *Meeting with Senators McClellan, Fulbright and Symington: Introductory Remarks on the Troop Reduction Resolution* (Majority Leader Files, Mansfield Collection).
22. Quoted in *Congressional Quarterly Almanac 1973*, p. 923.
23. Ferris Memorandum December 29, 1972, p. 1.
24. Quoted in *Congressional Quarterly Almanac 1973*, p. 924.
25. For details see ibid., pp. 891–3.
26. D. Binder, 'US Aide Firmly Opposes Cutting Troops in Europe', *New York Times*, 11 July 1973.

27. Senator Mansfield, *Statement in Hearings before the Subcommittee on Arms Control, International Law and Organisation of the Committee on Foreign Relations, United States Senate, Ninety-Third Congress, First Session on US Forces in Europe,* 25 July 1973 (Washington: Government Printing Office, 1973) p. 14.

28. See ibid., pp. 8–9.

29. Ibid., p. 12.

30. Ibid., p. 13. Mansfield reiterated the need for lean, mobile forces in an interview with the author in Tokyo on 10 December 1980.

31. See ibid., p. 15.

32. J. R. Schlesinger, in ibid., p. 60.

33. See ibid., p. 98.

34. The arguments about cost are taken from *ibid.* and from *Hearings before the Committee on Foreign Affairs and its Subcommittee on Europe, House of Representatives, Ninety Third Congress, First Session on US Forces in NATO,* 18, 19, 25, 26 June; 10, 11, 12, 17 July 1973 (Washington: Government Printing Office, 1973).

35. See *Hearings before the Subcommittee on Arms Control,* p. 61.

36. Ferris Memo, 10 August 1973.

37. Ibid.

38. For the final text of the Jackson–Nunn Amendment see Public Law 93–155 (Defence Procurement Bill) signed in law, 16 November 1973, Section 812.

39. The Administration's reaction is touched on in Treverton, *The 'Dollar Drain',* p. 47.

40. Personal interview with Senator Alan Cranston, 17 September 1975.

41. The letter dated 25 September 1973 can be found in Majority Leader Files.

42. Quoted in J. G. Phillips, 'Defense Report: Fiscal Conservatives join Pentagon Critics in Attempt to Reduce Military Spending', *National Journal Reports,* 6 Nov 1973, p. 1485.

43. See 'US Troop Cutback Defeated', *Washington Post,* 27 September 1973.

44. Ibid.

45. Quoted in Phillips, 'Defense Report', p. 1486.

46. Quoted in ibid., p. 1485.

47. Interview with Richard Perle, London, 12 February 1980.

48. Aiken's comments with his reservations about the amendment are in the *Congressional Record,* 26 September 1973 (daily edition) p. S17638.

49. G. D. Aiken, *Senate Diary* (Vermont: Stephen Greene Press, 1976) p. 223. See also Phillips, 'Defense Report', p. 1485.

50. Aiken, *Senate Diary.*

51. A. Sehlstedt, 'Senate Votes to Cut Troops by 40 per cent then Reverses Itself', *Baltimore Sun,* 27 September 1973.

52. The description of the actions of the Majority Leader's Office is based on notes found in the Majority Leader Files, Mansfield Collection.

53. See J. W. Finney, 'Troop Cuts: the Senate Guard is Changing', *New York Times,* 29 September 1973 on the resentment caused by the Administration's actions in switching votes. That Humphrey's involvement was the

decisive factor was suggested in interviews conducted by the author – during which, Humphrey was mentioned most frequently as one of the key figures on this issue.

54. P. Jenkins, 'Senate Orders 110,000 Troop Cut', *Guardian*, 29 September 1973.
55. Letter from Senator Stennis to Senator Mansfield, 24 October 1973. Majority Leader Files, Mansfield Collection.
56. See *Congressional Quarterly Weekly Report*, vol. 32, no. 5, 2 February 1974, p. 209.
57. See, for example, M. Foley, *The New Senate: Liberal Influence on a Conservative Institution, 1959–1972* (London: Yale University Press, 1980).
58. See *Congressional Quarterly Weekly Report*, pp. 198–201. The percentages used in the table are also drawn from this source.
59. H. B. Shill III, 'Senate Activism and Security Commitments: the Troops-to-Europe and National Commitments Resolutions', PhD diss (Chapel Hill: University of North Carolina, 1973) p. 478.
60. This was a term used frequently in Mansfield's speeches during the late 60s and early 70s. For a typical example see M. Mansfield, *Towards A Discerning Internationalism*, Remarks at the Eighteenth Semi-Annual Meeting of the Manufacturing Chemists' Association, New York Hilton, 26 November 1968.
61. Interview with Kennedy aide, 9 September 1975.
62. The analysis here is based in part on an interview with a former counsel to the Senate Armed Services Committee.
63. J. E. Schneider, *Ideological Coalitions in Congress* (London: Greenwood Press, 1979) p. 65.
64. The composition of each region is as follows:
    South: Alabama, Arkansas, Florida, Georgia, Louisiana, Mississippi, N. Carolina, S. Carolina, Tennessee, Texas, Virginia
    Border: Delaware, Kentucky, Maryland, Missouri, Oklahoma, W. Virginia
    Pacific: California, Oregon, Washington, Alaska, Hawaii
    Mountains: Wyoming, Arizona, Colorado, Idaho, Montana, Nevada, New Mexico, Utah
    Midwest: Illinois, Indiana, Iowa, Michigan, Minnesota, Ohio, Wisconsin
    Plains: Kansas, Nebraska, N. Dakota, S. Dakota
    Northeast: Connecticut, Maine, Massachusetts, New Hampshire, New Jersey, New York, Rhode Island, Pennsylvania, Vermont
65. C. O. Lerche, *The Uncertain South* (Chicago: Quadrangle, 1964) p. 266.
66. J. W. Finney, 'Troop Cuts'.
67. Ages are based on data from *Congressional Quarterly Almanac 1973*, pp. 36–8.
68. Quoted in Finney, 'Troop Cuts'.
69. For an excellent discussion of Senate norms and folkways see Foley, *The New Senate*.

CHAPTER 8

1. The term is used by G. Hodgson, *Congress and American Foreign Policy*, Chatham House Papers no. 2 (London: Royal Institute of International Affairs, 1979).

2. George Will, *Washington Post*, 19 February 1974, quoted in *Editorial Research Reports on America's Changing World Role* (Washington: Congressional Quarterly, 1974) p. 4.

3. On these agreements and their limitations see A. L. George, *Towards a Soviet–American Crisis Prevention Regime: History and Prospects*, ACIS Working Paper no. 28 (Centre for International and Strategic Affairs, UCLA, Nov 1980). For a balanced survey of Soviet behaviour during the war see H. Adomeit, 'Soviet Foreign Policy: Some Contradictory Trends' in P. Jones (ed), *International Yearbook of Foreign Policy Analysis*, vol. I (London: Croom Helm, 1974) pp. 42–7.

4. For a discussion of these messages within the overall framework of superpower crisis management see P. Williams, *Crisis Management* (London: Martin Robertson, 1976) pp. 171–82. See also C. Bell, *The Diplomacy of Detente: The Kissinger Era* (London: Martin Robertson, 1977) pp. 80–97.

5. The notion of political warning time was to be challenged most explicitly a few years later in S. Nunn and D. Bartlett, *NATO and the New Soviet Threat*, Report to the Committee on Armed Services, United States Senate, 24 Jan 1977 (Washington: GPO, 1977).

6. See R. Lieber, 'Britain Joins Europe' in A. M. Jones (ed), *United States Foreign Policy in a Changing World* (New York: McKay, 1973) especially pp. 164–75 for a fuller discussion of these competing conceptions of Europe.

7. *Transcript, Kissinger offers Clarification of Remarks on Europe, March 14, 1974* (official text issued by USIS, 15 March 1974) p. 2.

8. A useful summary of these developments can be found in E. T. Lampson, *Relations Between Western Europe and the United States* (Washington, DC: Congressional Research Service, 15 March 1974).

9. Kissinger's comment about European governments lacking legitimacy was particularly controversial. For his attempt to clarify and explain this statement see *Transcript, Kissinger offers Clarification*.

10. Secretary Kissinger Before Senate Finance Committee, 7 March 1974 (Official Text issued by USIS, 12 March 1974). See p. 16 for the comment about compatibility of foreign policies.

11. See *Transcript of President Nixon's Remarks and Question and Answer Session Executives Club of Chicago, March 15, 1974* (Official Text issued by United States Information Service, 18 March 1974). See p. 16.

12. *President Nixon's Houston Press Conference, 19 March 1974* (Official Text issued by USIS, 20 March 1974) p. 9.

13. See D. Binder, 'US and Bonn Set Basis of New Pact on Cost of Troops', *New York Times*, 20 March 1974 and D. Binder, 'US is Confident of Support on Cost of Troops in Europe', *International Herald Tribune*, 25 March 1974.

14. *Report by President Nixon to the Congress on the State of US Forces in Europe as Related to the Jackson–Nunn Amendment,* 22 February 1974 (Official Text issued by USIS, 25 Feb 1974) p. 2. See also H. Y. Schandler, *Jackson–Nunn Amendment* (Washington: Congressional Research Service, 6 May 1975).
15. R. Moose and J. Lowenstein, *U.S. Security Issues in Europe: Burden Sharing and Offset, MBFR and Nuclear Weapons,* September 1973 (A Staff Report for the use of the Subcommittee on US Security Agreements and Commitments Abroad of the Committee on Foreign Relations) (Washington: GPO, 2 Dec 1973).
16. See 'Paying For The U.S. Troops', *Financial Times,* 22 March 1974.
17. Quoted in 'U.S. and Bonn Sign Offset Fund Accord', *International Herald Tribune,* 26 April 1974.
18. See J. Muravchik, *The Senate and National Security: A New Mood,* Washington Papers 80 (London: Sage, 1980) pp. 49–50.
19. See S. Rosenfeld, 'Senator Nunn's NATO Manoeuvre', *Washington Post,* 21 June 1974 on the senator's preparation for the trip. The point about Brookings is based on conversations by the author with members of the Institute in 1974 and 1975.
20. S. Nunn, *Policy, Troops and the NATO Alliance,* Report to the Committee on Armed Services, United States Senate, 2 April 1974 (Washington: Government Printing Office, 1974) p. 4.
21. Ibid., p. 9.
22. Ibid., p. 10.
23. See 'Pentagon Considers Cutback in "Support" Troops in Europe', *International Herald Tribune,* 11 April 1974.
24. Ibid.
25. Rosenfeld, 'Nunn's NATO Manoeuvre'.
26. Resor's importance was mentioned on several occasions during interviews with Senate staff during September 1975.
27. The letter is reprinted in *Congressional Record,* 6 June 1974, p. S9950.
28. *Congressional Record,* 6 June 1974 (daily edition) p. S9916.
29. 'U.S. Troops in Europe', *New York Times,* 5 June 1974, reprinted in *Congressional Record,* 5 June 1974 (daily edition) p. S9730.
30. *Congressional Record,* 6 June 1974 (daily edition) p. S9924.
31. Ibid., p. S9924.
32. Ibid., p. S9923.
33. Rosenfeld, 'Nunn's NATO Manoeuvre'.
34. For details see Senate Vote 224 in *Congressional Quarterly Almanac 1974* (Washington: Congressional Quarterly, 1974) pp. 36–8.
35. *Congressional Record,* 6 June 1974 (daily edition) p. S9952.
36. Ibid.
37. See Senate Vote 225 in *Congressional Quarterly Almanac,* p. 36–8.
38. See *Congressional Quarterly Almanac 1974* (Washington: Congressional Quarterly, 1974) p. 45.
39. P. Lewis, 'U.S. Troops in Europe: Warning to Ford by Congress', *Financial Times,* 18 September 1974.
40. 'Report on Balance of Payments Deficit in Message from the President

Received During Adjournment' Reprinted in *Congressional Record*, 2 June 1975 (daily edition) pp. S9126–7.

41. Quoted in *Congressional Quarterly Weekly Report*, 7 June 1975 (Washington: Congressional Quarterly, 1975) p. 1162.
42. *Statement of Senator Mike Mansfield*. Filed and not used 16/17 May 1975. Majority Leader Section – Mansfield Collection, p. 1.
43. Ibid., p. 4.
44. Ibid., p. 2.
45. Note attached to ibid.
46. For Cranston's remarks see *Congressional Record*, 5 June 1975 (daily edition) p. S9767.
47. *Congressional Record*, 20 May 1975 (daily edition) p. H4422.
48. This paragraph is based on the *Congressional Record*, 5 June 1974 (daily edition) pp. S9767 to S9778.
49. *Congressional Record*, 6 June 1974 (daily edition) p. S9922.

CHAPTER 9

1. Stewart Alsop, *New York Herald Tribune*, 6 April 1951, quoted in W. Truitt, 'The Troops to Europe Decision: The Process, Politics and Diplomacy of a Strategic Commitment', PhD diss (New York: Columbia University, 1968) pp. 420–1.
2. H. B. Shill III, 'Senate Activism and Security Commitments: The Troops-to-Europe and National Commitments Resolutions', PhD diss (Chapel Hill: University of North Carolina, 1973) p. 495.
3. M. Oakeshott, 'On being Conservative' in *Rationalism in Politics* (London: Methuen, 1962) p. 169.
4. For a useful analysis of ways in which the President can exert influence in Congress, see G. C. Edwards III, *Presidential Influence in Congress* (San Francisco: W. H. Freeman, 1980).
5. A number of commentators have made this point. It also came out during a personal interview with Senator Mansfield on 17 September 1975.
6. A. Schlesinger Jr, 'Congress and the Making of American Foreign Policy', *Foreign Affairs*, vol. 51, no. 1 (October 1972) 78–113, especially p. 99.
7. See T. M. Franck and E. Weisband, *Foreign Policy By Congress* (New York: Oxford University Press, 1979).
8. See L. Radway, 'Towards the Europeanisation of NATO', *Atlantic Quarterly*, vol. 1, no. 2 (Summer 1983) 129–48. The implications of possible troop reductions are discussed in P. Williams (ed), *U.S. Troops in Europe: Issues and Choices*, Chatham House Paper (London: Routledge & Kegan Paul, 1984).

Index